The American Novel Now

The American Novel Now

Reading Contemporary American Fiction Since 1980

Patrick O'Donnell

A John Wiley & Sons, Ltd., Publication

This edition first published 2010

Blackwell Publishing was acquired by John Wiley & Sons in February 2007. Blackwell's publishing program has been merged with Wiley's global Scientific, Technical, and Medical business to form Wiley-Blackwell.

Registered Office
John Wiley & Sons Ltd, The Atrium, Southern Gate, Chichester, West Sussex, PO19 8SQ, United Kingdom

Editorial Offices
350 Main Street, Malden, MA 02148-5020, USA
9600 Garsington Road, Oxford, OX4 2DQ, UK
The Atrium, Southern Gate, Chichester, West Sussex, PO19 8SQ, UK

For details of our global editorial offices, for customer services, and for information about how to apply for permission to reuse the copyright material in this book please see our website at www.wiley.com/wiley-blackwell.

Library of Congress Cataloging-in-Publication Data

O'Donnell, Patrick, 1948–
The American novel now : contemporary American fiction since 1980 / Patrick O'Donnell.
p. cm.
Includes bibliographical references and index.
ISBN 978-1-4051-6757-4 (hardcover : alk. paper) – ISBN 978-1-4051-6755-0 (pbk. : alk. paper) 1. American fiction–20th century–History and criticism. 2. Literature and society–United States–History–20th century. 3. Literature and history–United States–History–20th century. I. Title. II. Title: Contemporary American fiction since 1980.

PS379.O35 2010
813′.5409–dc22

2009030168

A catalogue record for this book is available from the British Library.

Set in 10.5 on 13 pt Galliard by Toppan Best-set Premedia Limited
Printed and bound in Malaysia by Vivar Printing Sdn Bhd

1 2010

For Kaylee and Caiden, future readers

Contents

Preface

The narrative that follows, like any narrative, is full of gaps, elisions, inclusions and exclusions. I have been teaching contemporary American fiction to undergraduate and graduate students for over thirty years, and if there is an overriding lesson taught by the remarkable proliferation of styles, subjects, experiments in genre, innovations, and revisions of tradition that have taken place in the American novel since World War II, it is that any attempt to encompass the field of this work or to treat it as a totality is foolhardy. More to the point, such an effort would run counter to what the fiction itself teaches us: that we live in an increasingly complex world where language and the distortions of language, identity and its discontents, speech, object and affect are only apprehensible in their specificity and within the particular contexts they inhabit, and only then by means of the partial view that pertains to being human at a time when "the human" itself is under question. The best work of the imagination attends first to the particular, compelling the reader to enlarge her or his worldly perspective as the consequence of a local reading.

A narrative that attempts to draw out several of the significant filaments of the contemporary American novel since 1980 will, of necessity, shed light on the few rather than the many, but with the intention to focus on the few that offer exemplary instances of what will emerge in the long view of literary history over time as paradigmatic developments. The reader is cautioned that only a fraction of the contemporary American novelists since the late 1970s he or she may consider interesting or significant are discussed or cited in this volume: even just mentioning in a sentence or two all of the contemporary American novels published since 1980 that I consider to be of quality and importance would be merely to provide an annotated list of authors, titles, themes, and trends, so proliferate is the work. Many of the novels that I do select and discuss in detail will strike anyone who has read those lists of "the 100 bests" as unsurprising, though she will not find everything that is on those lists, and more than a little that is not. In providing a view of contemporary American fiction that shows how individual novels populating a highly variegated terrain bring into contact manifold questions of language, gender, nation, ethnicity, form, history, and identity, I have chosen to discuss, where appropriate, both widely read novels published by the mainstream commercial presses and less visible, often experimental work published by independent presses (see box). Since this body of work almost unfailingly presses the reader to consider his or her assumptions about the nature of world, writing, and reality – and often presses hard – any discussion of the contemporary novel must reflect on the choices made about which novels are considered. Such reflections are most effectively ingrained in the specific readings that follow and the contexts developed around those readings, but in general, the novels chosen for extended consideration are works of substance, and symptomatic – compelling embodiments of particularities that gesture toward the general – rather than (impossibly) representative. In other terms, each of the seventy-plus novels that I have selected for detailed discussion contribute significantly to the collective imaginative and artistic engagement with the contradictions and complexity of

Independent Presses

Small presses have played an essential role in making available experimental novels that otherwise initially might never have seen the light of day. Such presses as New Directions, Grove, Olympia, Black Sparrow, and City Lights have consistently published novels that constitute a significant portion of the modernist canon, including works by Joyce, Pound, West, Stein, Barnes, Nabokov, and Burroughs, to name but a handful. In the contemporary era (again, to name but a few), Sun & Moon, Arte Publico, Fiction Collective 2, and especially Dalkey Archives have introduced or kept alive the work of such writers as Rodolpho Anaya, Lynn Hejenian, Samuel R. Delaney, Raymond Federman, Rikki Ducornet, Stanley Elkin, Harry Mathews, Carole Maso, John Hawkes, Gilbert Sorrentino, Robert Coover, and Curtis White. Dalkey is also of special note because of its translations and reprints of twentieth century fiction. Combined with its sister literary magazine, the *Review of Contemporary Fiction*, Dalkey has been one of the prime movers behind the "making" of modern and contemporary fiction.

contemporary reality as it is mediated through the language of fiction and the form of the novel. Broadly speaking, the consideration of these novels allows me to address an old question within contemporary parameters: how has the novel, and the reading of novels, changed in the last three decades as the engagement between literature and reality has changed? How have we imagined this engagement?

Such questions have guided the decision to construct a narrative about the contemporary American novel since 1980. This book is intended for readers interested in gaining both an expansive perspective about what has happened in the world of contemporary American writing, and insight about an array of particular novels that – in addition to all the reasons previously cited – have been chosen because, in my view, they urge one to read more. While there have been compelling readings of contemporary American fiction writ large – most notably, the indispensable examples of Tony Tanner's *City of Words: American Fiction 1950–1970* (1971) and Marc Chénetier's *Beyond Suspicion: New American Fiction Since 1960* (1996), a translation of the 1989 French original, as well as important broader considerations such as Frederick Karl's *American Fictions 1940/1980* (1983) and Kathryn Hume's *American Dream, American Nightmare: Fiction Since 1960* (2000) – the aim of *The American Novel Now* is to provide a discussion of a range of American novels written from the Reagan era forward as we moved into a new millennium, the age of the Internet, the putative end of a Cold War that had dominated geopolitical conversations since the end of World War II, and the onset of new geopolitical realities in a post-Cold War setting. The period since the late 1970s has been a time of remarkable social and political change, and the novel, which has always been, historically, a genre that has reflected social change while striving to figure forth emerging worlds and transformational perspectives, has undergone considerable alteration as well, while retaining its dual status as linguistic mediation and mirror (however distorted) to reality. What many contemporary novels tell us is that "reality" has split, doubled, simulated, and multiplied, that the capacity to imagine "reality" has been put under severe pressure, and that identities – those of author, reader, fictional selves – have become increasingly entangled. While these tendencies can be traced back through the history of the novel, one of my goals in *The American Novel Now* is to examine how they continue to foliate in American writing since 1980 within the context of considerable social and historical change.

I have organized the discussion into five parts: the first provides an overview of developments in the contemporary American novel between the end of World War II and 1980; Part II considers the continuation of the novel's traditional bipolar investments in realism and linguistic experimentation as these play out in recent American fiction; in Part III, I take up the manifold ways in which contemporary fiction since 1980 has represented identity in terms of character, ethnicity, gender, and the "human"; Part IV considers the key question of history, and the relation between history and narrative, during a period that in some views comes at "the end of history"; in Part V, I discuss how recent American novels have portrayed the social collectives of the family, community, and nation, and the migration of identities across and beyond these. I conclude with a brief excursus that speculates on the future of the novel. The division of *The American Novel Now* into parts is not intended to be categorical, but evocative. While, for example, I focus on several novels that primarily engage questions of identity, gender, and sexuality in the third section of Part III, there are novels scattered throughout the book that are "about" gender (and equally "about" history, or ethnicity, etc.) in significant ways, and I encourage the reader to view individual novels within the multiple frameworks that evolve as the book proceeds. Indeed, one of the goals of this book is to invite the kinds of intertextual connections that only readers – close readers – can make, as they expand the horizon of their reading.

This is a book about reading contemporary fiction, for readers both familiar with the landscape and those for whom the terrain seems somewhat strange, unmapped. What I intend to provide here is not so much a map as a compass, one that allows the reader (to paraphrase a line from Theodore Roethke's "The Waking") to learn by going where she has to go. If the effect of reading *The American Novel Now* is to assist its readers, having seen what is here, to discover for themselves what lies beyond the limits of this book, then its best hopes will have been realized.

Acknowledgments

Thanks to my good friends Scott Juengel, David Madden, and Justus Nieland, who cheerfully read the manuscript and offered unfailingly helpful advice. I am appreciative of the support and advice of several of my friends and colleagues in East Lansing while completing this project: above all, Jen Fay and Steve Arch, as well as Clint Goodson, Sandra Logan, Robert Moses, Bill Penn, and Judith Stoddart. Conversations with them over the years about the matter at hand as well as literature and theory *tout court* have proven invaluable; the same goes for Hans Bak, in Nijmegen; Cedric Bryant, in Waterville; Marc Chénetier, in Paris; Jack Matthews, in Boston; Heide Ziegler, in Stuttgart; and Lynda Zwinger and Tenney Nathanson, in Tucson. Thanks to Tom Byers for invitations to serve as a faculty member over several summers at the University of Louisville summer institute on contemporary American fiction. This project was completed with the assistance of an Internal Research Program Grant from the Office of the Vice-President for Research and Grants at Michigan State University, and I am grateful for this timely support. In ways they could not know, my son, Sean, and my daughter, Sara, now well headed-out into their own contemporaneity, have helped me to write this and every book. My wife and partner of forty years, Diane O'Donnell, read the chapters and provided the clear eye of the best of readers to this book *for* readers of contemporary fiction. I am grateful to the editorial group at Wiley-Blackwell who have generously supported this project every step of the way, especially Emma Bennett, Isobel Bainton, and Caroline Clamp; my thanks to Juanita Bullough for an expert job of copy-editing. This book is dedicated to my grandchildren, who may travel down some of the roads mapped here, but will doubtless discover many others as yet unimagined.

Part I

Before 1980

In 1998, Norman Mailer's *The Naked and the Dead* was published in a fiftieth anniversary edition with a new introduction by the author. With its naturalistic perspective, psychological complexity, and jolting explorations of sexuality and violence, a novel that had marked the debut of a major writer working in the tradition of Theodore Dreiser, John Dos Passos, and Richard Wright, yet who possessed a distinctly contemporary political and aesthetic sensibility, had reached the half-century mark. For many, this big, brash, first novel of a draftee recounting the experience of the war in the South Pacific ushered in a new, energetic era of American fiction. As the critic for the *New York Times* put it, the publication of *The Naked and the Dead* was "a triumph of realism [that] … bears witness to a new and significant talent among American novelists" (Dempsey). The specific "triumph of realism" that the reviewer may have been referring to exists in such passages as these, describing the thoughts of a soldier on patrol:

> Croft watched them indifferently. He too had been bothered by Gallagher's speech. He had never forgotten the Japanese charge across the river, and occasionally he would dream of a great wave of water about to fall on him while he lay helpless beneath it. He never connected the dream to the night attack, he intuitively felt the dream signified some weakness in himself. Gallagher had disturbed him, and he thought consciously of his own death for a moment. That's a damn fool thing to kick around in your head, he said to himself. (444)

Croft goes on to remark that he "always saw order in death," and that he does not share "the particular blend of pessimism and fatalism" that affect some of the other men, but now, facing the fact that "the wheels might be grinding for him," he is uncertain about the logic of destiny (444–5). The combination of realized setting, colloquialism, philosophical speculation, dream-thought and conscious reflection marks a characteristic style and voice that would reach their acme in one of the premier works of the "new journalism," Mailer's *The Armies of the Night* (1968), which recounts the 1967 anti-Vietnam War march on the Pentagon and bears the subtitle of "History as a Novel/The Novel as History." Mailer would go on to establish a career known more for its performativity, macho egoism, and spectacular lapses in taste and judgment than for its literary successes. But his first big novel served as an announcement of the importance of understanding the rapidly changing relation between public and private life, and between the political and the personal under the shadow of a second world war whose aftermath would severely test liberal notions about human identity, the social order, and the power of language to represent or distort modern experience.

Only a matter of months later, quietly and without fanfare, a slim novel about wartime and postwar Germany was written by an American ambulance services volunteer that offered a different kind of announcement. In *The Cannibal* (1949), published by the avant-garde New Directions, John Hawkes provided a hellish view of violence and the disintegration of identity in a complex prose style vacillating between the stark clarity of the intrusive nightmare and the aesthetics of a displaced vision that can be regarded as an avatar of postmodern experimentalism (see box). In stark contrast to Mailer's existential realism, Hawkes's novel offered an intense,

Postmodernism

Having introduced the contested and ubiquitous term that is often used to characterize everything from contemporary literary works to architecture and gourmet food, I advise the reader that it is used here and throughout this discussion of contemporary American fiction in a very general sense, as indicative of fiction that foregrounds the significance-bearing qualities of language, the processes of construction or writing, the interplay of author, text, and reader, and intertextuality, or both the horizontal and vertical relation to other fictions and discourses. This sobering description does little to indicate the interest of postmodern fiction in parody and play, nor its historical reach, as Robert Alter has suggested, back to *Don Quixote*. Indeed, within postmodernism, what is not postmodern? This is a not an entirely trivial question that gives rise to postmodernism's relevance as a discursive or historical marker. But for much more, see Hassan, McHale, and Jameson, *Postmodernism*.

microscopic scrutiny of the war's excesses that limned the capacity of language to articulate the horrors of war and occupation. Reminiscent of Djuna Barnes's *Nightwood* (1936) and its surrealist exploration of the eccentric lives of Parisian wanderers, *The Cannibal* traces the progress of an assemblage of iconoclasts traversing the landscape of occupied Germany after World War II. The novel is organized as a series of allegorical tableaux populated by characters such as Madame Snow, the fallen aristocrat; the Census Taker; or Zizendorf, the "cannibal" of the novel's title who becomes the fascistic new leader of the locals amidst the chaos and unrelieved violence of the occupied zone. For Hawkes, who would later famously declare that he began writing with the "assumption that the true enemies of the novel were plot, character, setting and theme" (Enck, 149), the description of a house in *The Cannibal* becomes a metaphor of the postwar world, burdened by a brutal, repressive past that can only be escaped or erased via further acts of violence:

> The house where the two sisters lived was like an old trunk covered with cracked sharkskin, heavier on top than on the bottom, sealed with iron cornices and covered with shining fins. It was like the curving dolphin's back: fat, wrinkled, hung dry above small swells and waxed bottles; hanging from a thick spike, all foam and wind gone, over many brass catches and rusty studs out in the sunshine. As a figure that breathed immense quantities of air, that shook itself in the wind flinging water down into the streets, as a figure that cracked open and drank in all of a day's sunshine in one breath, it was more selfish than an old General, more secret than a nun, more monstrous than the fattest shark. (61)

Regarding this image of domestic space as nightmarish and cannibalistic, we can gauge the contrast between Mailer's journalistic realism combined with the probing of individual psychologies and Hawkes's linguistic experimentalism which dissolves the border between waking and dreaming. Two novels of war; two authors who can be seen to represent in split view but a few of the diverse possibilities of contemporary American writing from its onset: the discursive sweep of *The Naked and the Dead*, with its exposure of private life in the theater of war, compared to *The Cannibal*'s piercing explorations of the cultural unconscious in a language pastiche replete with irony and hyperbolic excess. From the beginning, contemporary American fiction as a body of work produced after World War II was remarkable for its heterogeneity, both its recapitulation of and its break from what had come before, its multifaceted negotiation of the relation between the social and imaginary orders.[1]

There were other vital, young writers whose energies bespoke the diversity and inventiveness of contemporary postwar writing emerging in the relatively brief period that followed World War II and preceded the Korean War which began in June, 1950 when the North Korean army crossed the 38th parallel, thus initiating the "Cold War" whose effects continue to be felt in contemporary American writing. During the months that extended between the publication of *The Naked and the Dead* and *The Cannibal*, a little-known young writer from Milledgeville, Georgia began publishing the chapters of a novel that would become *Wise Blood* (1952) in such venues as *Mademoiselle* and *Partisan Review*, respectively, amongst the premier "women's" and progressive literary magazines of the day. In what continues to be one of the best essays written on Flannery O'Connor, John Hawkes compares the work of his literary fellow-traveler to that of Nathanael West, whose iconoclastic *The Day of the Locust* (1939) offers an infamous satirical portrait of Hollywood greed and the cult of personality: "I would propose that West and Flannery O'Connor are very nearly alone today in their pure creation of 'aesthetic authority,' and … that they are very nearly alone in their employment of the devil's voice as vehicle for their satire or for what we may call their true (or accurate) vision of our godless actuality" ("Flannery O'Connor's Devil," 397). O'Connor, a devout, if somewhat unorthodox Catholic her entire, short life – she died at the age of 39 after a long struggle with lupus – would disagree with the notion that she employs "the devil's voice" in her fiction. Debating with Hawkes in their correspondence of several years' duration about matters of style, voice, and philosophy, O'Connor wrote that "[m]ore than in the Devil I am interested in the indication of Grace, the moment when Grace has been offered and accepted. … These moments are prepared for (by me anyway) by the intensity of the evil circumstances" (*Habit of Being*, 367–8).

In *Wise Blood*, the protagonist, Hazel Motes, an itinerant preacher and founder of the "church of truth without Jesus Christ Crucified" (55), deliberately blinds himself in an act of inverse revelation in a city where only false prophets walk the streets and false gods are worshiped as mundane signs and material objects are taken for wonders. Perhaps

Hazel Motes is a true prophet whose radical wake-up call can be delivered only through masochistic violence in a materialistic universe filled with the distractions and junk of contemporary culture that Haze encounters in the city: "When he got to Taulkinham, as soon as he stepped off the train, he began to see signs and lights. PEANUTS, WESTERN UNION, AJAX, TAXI, HOTEL, CANDY. Most of them were electric and moved up and down or blinked frantically" (29). Or, as his name might indicate, perhaps he is merely a random mote floating chaotically through the "haze" of time and space. The conclusion is indeterminate in a novel where we last view the protagonist through the shut eyes of his landlady who "felt as if she had finally got to the beginning of something she couldn't begin, and she saw him moving farther and farther away, farther and farther into the darkness, until he was [a] pin point of light" (232). As O'Connor consistently argued in her essays and letters, the manifestation of the sacred in the "Christ-haunted," unredeemed landscape of the contemporary South (rapidly becoming the high-tech "New South," even in O'Connor's lifetime) will inevitably appear to be ambiguously scandalous, but as several of her critics have suggested, what might seem the idiosyncratic fiction of a Catholic writer taking place in a regionalist setting clearly has broader implications for contemporary writing emerging in the midst of the Manichaean struggles of the Cold War and the encroachments of secularism and what social theorist Neil Postman terms "technocratic capitalism" (41).[2] Like speaking with the devil's voice, this is not a formulation that O'Connor would encourage, yet the strains of her writing as it envisions the spiritual progress of a radical anti-hero across a bifurcated landscape littered with the signs of materialist excess and the ruins of "nature" (both human and botanical) mark her own work as prophetic of much that is to come.

In the same year of *The Cannibal's* publication, James Baldwin, a Harlem-born expatriate who had just begun to garner attention for his commentaries on race and African American history in high-profile venues such as the *Nation*, the *New Leader*, and *Commentary*, published "Everybody's Protest Novel" in the Moroccan *Zero* and, in the United States, in the *Partisan Review*, the leading progressive journal of the day. In revolt against his literary mentor, Richard Wright, Baldwin critiques both *Uncle Tom's Cabin* (1852) and Wright's *Native Son* (1940) as works that – despite their liberal or revolutionary intentions – reinforce black stereotypes and remain trapped in the "sunlit prison of the American dream" (582) because they view race relations in terms of the "theological terror" (581) of the Manichaean battle between good and evil, oppressor and oppressed. In questioning this logic, Baldwin says of *Native Son*, which continues to be widely regarded as a novel that reveals and protests against the violence and brutality of black–white relations, that

> [b]elow the surface of this novel there lies ... a continuation, a complement of that monstrous legend it was written to destroy. Bigger [the protagonist of *Native Son* who accidentally murders a white woman and, thus, whose fate is sealed] is Uncle Tom's descendant, flesh of his flesh, so exactly opposite a portrait that, when the books are placed together, it seems that the contemporary Negro novelist and the dead New England woman are locked together in a deadly, timeless battle. (584)

At this moment, Baldwin is about to embark on his own career as a novelist with the publication of the autobiographical *Go Tell it on the Mountain* (1953), and the controversial *Giovanni's Room* (1956), with its portrayal of a protagonist exploring the alterities of his own sexual identity. In this essay, he enunciated many of the terms of the debate that will take place in the proliferation of multiethnic literatures in the United States following World War II about the nature of racial identity and ethnicity. From the beginning of his career, Baldwin thus served as a crucial, if controversial source for those writers invested in portraying the role of race in the formation of the social order, the status of race as "prison" or source of empowerment, and the complicated relationship between racial identity and sexuality.

The candor of Baldwin's critique of how race is portrayed, even in the fiction of those he admires, will be matched by the candor of his portrayals of protagonists struggling with identity in the novels to come. Indeed, the early post-war writing of Mailer, Hawkes, O'Connor, and Baldwin can be viewed as significantly building upon the "open" tradition of American literature – from Walt Whitman's homoerotic poetry of the open road and the underclass to Kathy Acker's blasphemous satires on Western religious values and sexual norms – which continues to challenge the decorousness of the literary and to open up new terrain for imaginative exploration. One charismatic exemplar of this tendency, supposedly written in three weeks in 1951 (apocryphally, on rolls of toilet paper, but actually on sheets of tracing paper taped together into a 120–foot roll) is Jack Kerouac's *On the Road*. The novel, not published until 1957, would quickly attain cult status as an avatar of "Beat" literature which celebrates openness, jazz-like improvisation, spontaneity, and alternative lifestyles. The story of the peripatetic journey of Sal Paradise and Dean Moriarity through an American landscape populated by the alienated and the dispossessed captures both Whitman's sense of the "open road" – the endless possibilities of American life – and that of "the other America" characterized by Michael Harrington in his 1962 book of that title about the lives of impoverished citizens and migrant workers. Kerouac's celebration of jazz in the novel through the cadences of a distinctive prose style that would become the hallmark of "Beat" literature is evident in Sal's description of a group of young musicians:

> The leader was a slender, drooping, curly-haired, pursy-mouthed tenorman, thin of shoulder, draped loose in a sport shirt, cool in the warm night, self-indulgence written in his eyes ... Then there was Prez, a husky, handsome blond like a freckled boxer, meticulously wrapped inside his sharkskin plaid suit with the long drape and the collar falling back and the tie undone for exact sharpness and casualness, sweating and hitching up his horn and writhing into it, and a tone just like Lester Young himself. ... The third sax was an alto, eighteen-year-old cool, contemplative Charlie-Parker-type Negro ... He raised his horn and blew into it quietly and thoughtfully and elicited birdlike phrases and architectural Miles Davis logics. These were the children of the great bop innovators. (239)

The legend of Kerouac's writing the novel "on the roll," while untrue, serves as an apt metaphor for both the style and subject of *On the Road*, where drifting and wandering, "phrasing" and style are elevated into an ethos for navigating life's perils and contingencies.

In the same year that Kerouac was writing *On the Road*, another novel that extended the open tradition, J. D. Salinger's *The Catcher in the Rye*, garnered immediate attention upon its publication and has remained, along with Nabokov's *Lolita* (1955), a source of continuous controversy. Like *On the Road*, *Catcher* is comparable to those American novels, particularly its nineteenth-century predecessor, *Huckleberry Finn*, that promote forms of vernacular candor and challenge middle-class pieties and decorum. Indeed, so controversial is the speech of the novel's 17-year-old narrator, Holden Caulfield, that it became "the most frequently banned book in schools between 1966 and 1975" (Sova, 70). Holden's remarkable opening lines set the tone for his diatribe against education, adulthood, and American success:

> If you really want to hear about it, the first thing you'll probably want to know is where I was born, and what my lousy childhood was like, and how my parents were occupied and all before they had me, and all that David Copperfield kind of crap, but I don't feel like going into it, if you want to know the truth. (1)

In telling his tale of rebellion, Holden's liberal use of words such as "phony," "lousy," "crap," "goddam," and, famously, "fug" for the four-letter word which could not be printed at the time, offers only the most superficial explanation for the novel's banning from provincial high-school classrooms (while, contradictorily, being embraced as a "classic" taught to generations of American high-school students). Instead, it is Holden's charismatic and unrelenting attack on authority, rules of all kinds, and adult hypocrisy that doubtless landed the novel in hot water with local school boards. Authored by the most reclusive writer in the annals of contemporary American literature, Salinger's novel effectively gave voice to the emerging youth culture of the postwar generation – perhaps, according to the retrospective view of *Washington Post* book critic Jonathan Yardley, in ways not always for the best:

> a case can be made that "The Catcher in the Rye" created adolescence as we now know it ... [Salinger] established whining rebellion as essential to adolescence and it has remained such ever since. It was a short leap indeed from "The Catcher in the Rye" to "The Blackboard Jungle" to "Rebel Without a Cause" to Valley Girls to the multibillion-dollar industry that adolescent angst is today.

Whether one regards *Catcher* as the contemporary equivalent to *Huckleberry Finn* or as a galling foreshadowing of Generation X, the influence of Salinger's sole novel on the readership of contemporary American fiction is undeniable.

If Kerouac and Salinger defined a new generation of readers of contemporary American fiction, with the publication of *Invisible Man* in 1952, Ralph Ellison, along with Baldwin, set forth many of the terms of writing about race and identity for the generations of writers to come who are part of the explosion of ethnic literatures in the

United States from the 1960s to the present. *Invisible Man* is many things. It is a *Bildungsroman* set along classical lines that traces the progress of its protagonist from his childhood and education in the rural South to city-life in Harlem. Equally, it is an anti-*Bildungsroman* that traces this same progress as a movement toward invisibility and a return to the womb/underground of an urban basement. In the novel's ambiguous conclusion, the novel's unnamed central figure can be viewed as a social lackey-cum-violent revolutionary awaiting rebirth; or, as a subversive con man who resists the dominance of white, capitalist society by maintaining his invisibility while, literally, stealing power from "the man"; or, as a messianic visionary who will usher in a new era of racial relations amidst the social strife depicted in the race riot that leads to the protagonist's flight underground. *Invisible Man* is, also, an encyclopedic narrative that, in part, stages the narrator's quest for place and identity as pastiche that conjoins ancestral literary works and genres, from the Bible and African American folklore to *Moby-Dick*, the social protest novel, and the symbolic narratives of Proust or Mann.

The question of what constitutes race and racial identity central to *Invisible Man* – Ellison's only published novel, despite the fact that he continued writing until his death in 1994 – is raised through a series of transformative episodes described in metaphorical detail by the novel's unnamed narrator, the "invisible man" of the title. These include a "battle royal" where, seeking a college scholarship, he speaks before a group of white businessmen, but only after having endured a humiliating boxing match with other black aspirants for the prize of a scholarship; a dreamlike journey in which he visits the symbolically named Trueblood, a black man who has committed incest with his daughter and who is viewed by a racist white community as the embodiment of black degradation; his employment in a paint factory making a white paint that attains its "purity" via the admixture of a drop of black color; his involvement with "the Brotherhood," a political organization that resembles the Black Muslim movement of the 1930s and 1940s in Harlem and Detroit; and his subsequent flight into the dark basement of a building during a race riot where he remains, a dark figure rendered invisible by the blinding white light he steals from the power company. Ellison's rich, analogical novel, with its reflexive portrayal of the relation between black and white on multiple levels, from the linguistic to the political, represents a defining moment in the progression of a racial discourse. Toni Morrison describes the history of this discourse in American writing as moving "from its simplistic, though menacing, purposes of establishing hierarchic difference, to its surrogate properties as self-reflexive meditations on the loss of difference, to its lush and fully blossomed existence in the rhetoric of dread and desire" (*Playing in the Dark*, 64). Ellison's novel, in effect, touches upon all of the stages of this discursive progression in the narrative of a man who is invisible because he is a black man whose "color" and identity are both defined by and vanish before the white light of the dominant culture of postwar America.

Mailer, Hawkes, O'Connor, Baldwin, Kerouac, Salinger, Ellison: all surfaced as distinctive new voices in the period between the conclusion of World War II and the commencement of a ceasefire on the Korean Peninsula in July, 1953. Along with the likes of Mary McCarthy, Chester Himes, and Eudora Welty, who began publishing by the mid-1940s and whose status as major authors began to be established in the postwar decades, and others such as Vladimir Nabokov, Saul Bellow, and William Burroughs, who gained visibility as major new "American" writers during the 1950s (Bellow was born and raised in Canada, and Nabokov is a Russian who had begun his career with the publication of *Mashen'ka* [*Mary*] in 1926), these authors charted the course for the proliferate American fiction of the last half of the century. The small number of women in this list is notable: one literary historian has remarked that "according to Elaine Showalter, [the decade of the 1950s] was literally the low point for American women writers in this century. For these were the years when medical and media Freudians emphasized 'the tragedy of American women' and 'domestic experts' urged their 'return to the kitchens and the nurseries.' In college texts and anthologies of American literature, Showalter adds, 'women averaged only about 3 per cent of the writers represented' " (Siegel, 37). Equally notable is the fact that both Grace Paley and Tillie Olson, who both started publishing their writing only after many years of raising children and laboring in the workforce, and who would become catalysts for the explosion of women's writing and the feminist movement in the 1960s, were establishing the foundations for their powerful renditions of women's lives and speech during this decade. Jean Stafford, one of the writers of the 1940s and 1950s who Showalter effectively recovers in *A Jury of Her Peers*, an essential history of women's writing in America, published an important novel,

The Catherine Wheel, in 1952, and her *Collected Stories* in 1969. Working across the 1950s and into the 1960s on the novel she began in 1945 – perhaps the most undeservedly ignored major work in the annals of modern and contemporary American fiction – there is Marguerite Young, whose poetic and labyrinthine *Miss MacIntosh, My Darling* (1965) meticulously records the dreams, perceptions, relationships, and affective engagements of its remarkable title character as an intersubjective agent in a cast of dozens. The emerging work in progress of these frequently overlooked writers is essential to the founding of contemporary American writing.

An "era" does not have an actual beginning or end: it is an heuristic convenience we use to indicate paradigmatic shifts that overlap and proceed at variable rates. In the same decade that the writers I have discussed were establishing the ground for contemporary American fiction, modernist writers more often associated with the period between the two world wars were producing significant work. In the 1950s, William Faulkner, who won the Nobel Prize for Literature in 1949 and who continues to serve as the major influence for a host of contemporary writers and movements, published *Requiem for a Nun* (1951), *A Fable* (1954, which won the National Book Award in that year), and the final two volumes of "the Hamlet" trilogy (*The Town*, 1957; and *The Mansion*, 1959). Faulkner's fellow Southerner, Katherine Anne Porter, was in the process of completing her last novel, *Ship of Fools* (1962). John Dos Passos published six new books, including a novel, a memoir, and a biography of Thomas Jefferson, and Edna Ferber published the penultimate novels of her career in *Giant* (1952) and *Ice Palace* (1958). Scribner's brought out Ernest Hemingway's *The Old Man and the Sea* (1952), the last major work of his fiction to appear during his lifetime; and in the same year, John Steinbeck published his last major novel, *East of Eden* (1952). Yet if we consider the work of new and emergent writers of the American 1950s, or the work of a slightly older generation of writers that will come to full prominence in the years between 1950 and 1980, there is an observable sea-change following World War II. A new sexual candor and exploration of the role of gender and sexuality in the representation of life in fiction; a growing sense of the importance of race in America and the possibilities to be explored in the tracing of ethnic identities; a fascination with linguistic play, encyclopedic scope, and the parody of form that has its roots in Joycean modernism and that will gain in intensity as the writing of contemporary American fiction proceeds under the rubric of postmodernism; innovations in realist narrative strategies that enabled explorations of subjects taking place against the backdrop of the Cold War and the proliferation of the suburban middle class in America; a continuous reflection on existentialist notions of self and agency that can be traced to Sartre, Camus, Kierkegaard, and Nietzsche, especially as these are related to violence and the limits of the human; the rise of new technologies and mass media that fuel a recognition of the degree to which cultural discourses are becoming increasingly intermedial such that the act of reading is as much a matter of viewing and performing as it is of literacy and interpretation – all of these intensities can be said to characterize the uniqueness of contemporary writing in terms of both continuity and innovation. In the chapters to follow, I will be discussing how the post-1980s novel develops according to these and related tendencies. Having elicited some of these strains in contemporary writing following closely upon World War II, I will suggest in the remainder of this chapter how they are reflected in a number of notable instances, across the range of the contemporary American novel before 1980, that navigate between the status of fiction as a production of language and fiction as a mirror of reality.

* * *

"Oh, my Lolita, I only have words to play with" (32). Thus laments Humbert Humbert, the narrator and protagonist of Vladimir Nabokov's *Lolita*, ostensibly the "Confession of a White Widowed Male" (3) relating in meticulous detail his obsession with a 12-year-old "nymphet" and the tragicomic circumstances of their relationship. A Russian-born exile, Nabokov had produced nine major novels in Russian before turning to English and composing what many consider to be amongst the most linguistically dexterous novels ever written in that language. *Lolita* was published in 1955 with the alternative Olympia Press in Paris because no American publisher at that time would touch a novel portraying sexual intimacies between a child and an adult, though this is to take at face value a kaleidoscopic narrative that is both the diary of a self-described "monster" and a love story, both an elaborate verbal artifice (just "words … to play with") and a trenchant depiction of the burgeoning mid-century American road culture and the infelicities of domesticity. As related in *Reading Lolita in Tehran*, Azar Nafisi's poignant account of her attempt to read and discuss the novel with a small group of women in Iran, the novel has continued to generate controversy, admiration, and censure world-wide. Perhaps this is because of the double nature of a narrative that is replete with phantoms, doubles, and mirrors; *Lolita* can be read simultaneously as an elaborate language game and a tragic account of an irretrievably lost childhood. In *Lolita*, the elasticity of the English language is explored both texturally and thematically, and the reader is encouraged to become an active participant in the novel's many word games, far-flung verbal coincidences, and evolving patterns of significance. Does the appearance of such names as "Aubrey McFate," "Grace Angel," "Ted Falter," and "Anthony Miranda" in the list of students in Lolita's eighth-grade class (which the paranoid Humbert keeps as "evidence" that his elaborate pursuit of Lolita both at home and on the road is all part of a larger plot manufactured by his dark alter ego, Clare Quilty) indicate the work of chance or design? And if the latter, imposed by whom – Humbert? The author? Providence? Is Humbert's "nymphet" a "real girl" (but only to the extent that any character in a fiction can be "real") or the fantastic creation of desire run amok? Is *Lolita* mere "play" or the work of a serious moral imagination plumbing the ugly depths of an obsession, or indeed, both at once? Nabokov's fascination with what John Shade, the poet of Nabokov's *Pale Fire* (1962), refers to as the "combinatorial delight" (69) of language calls upon us to actively interpret, evaluate, and judge what the author has left behind as a record of the human imagination's astonishing capacity to alternate freely between beauty and monstrosity, and to find one in the other.

Nabokov is one of many modern and contemporary writers for whom linguistic play, narrative complexity, saturated intertextual reference and encyclopedic range mark the primacy of language as the constitutive element of all fiction: internationally, Samuel Beckett, Jorge Luis Borges, Georges Perec, and Italo Calvino are part of this company. Literary movements in France such as OULIPO (the acronym for the Ouvroir de Littérature Potentielle, or Workshop for Potential Literature, which included Calvino and Perec) and that of the "new novel" evidenced in the work of Alain Robbe-Grillet, Nathalie Sarraute, and Marguerite Duras, as well as philosophical and theoretical movements such as the "Tel Quel" school which included such figures as Julia Kristeva, Philippe Sollers, and Roland Barthes, and the arrival of "deconstruction" in America in the work of Jacques Derrida at "The Stucturalist Controversy Symposium" of 1966, help to inform intensifying focus on the "work" of language in contemporary American fiction from *Lolita*'s publication in the United States in 1958 to the current moment.

In considering novels that foreground language as a transformative force, whether redemptive or destructive, one can follow a number of trajectories from mid-century American fiction to the 1980s. One extends from Nabokov to a novelist as different from him as Kathy Acker, whose novels began appearing in the 1970s with titles like *Childlike Life of the Black Tarantula by the Black Tarantula* (1973), *I Dreamt I was a Maniac: Imagining* (1974), and *Adult Life of Toulouse Lautrec* (1978). Acker was clearly influenced by William S. Burroughs, whose *Naked Lunch* (1959), published by the same French press that had first published *Lolita*, has been an icon of "underground" writing in America since its publication. While the novels of Burroughs and Acker, which have often been viewed as "obscene" and "pornographic" in their scathing critiques of American capitalism and patriarchy, may seem a far cry from Nabokov's aestheticism and his well-known rejection of politics ("I am neither a didacticist nor an allegoriser. Politics and economics, atomic bombs, primitive and abstract art forms, the entire Orient, symptoms of 'thaw' in Soviet Russia, the Future of Mankind, and so on, leave me supremely indifferent," he once wrote [cited in de la Durantaye, 308]), all three authors share an interest in showing the degree to which figurative language can control, distort, or change reality. Burroughs, indebted to the Beat tradition, attacks 1950s middle-class values in scenes of sexual degradation, drug-induced hallucinations, and scandalous, parodic renditions of the politician's speech and the salesman's pitch in a world where heroin ("junk") is the only real commodity. In later work, he would develop the "cut-up" technique to rearrange fragments of received or traditional linear discourse into new patterns that would subvert dominant modes of thought. For Burroughs, "America" is a disorderly system of conflicting discourses that contend for empowerment. Similarly, for Acker, "the West" is represented in collage-like narratives as an assemblage of speech acts that vocalize territorial disputes, impositions of authority, and jarring attempts to reconstruct the male-dominated social order by shouting in a different tongue. I will return to Acker's fiction of the 1980s in a later chapter, but it is interesting to note in what ways the early novels of a writer identified with the French "Theater of the Absurd" typified in the plays of Antonin Artaud, postmodern "punk" and performance art are comparable to those of a Russian exile whose novels are often viewed as exemplars of modernist elitism and aestheticism. For both Nabokov and Acker, "Language! It's a virus!," to cite the work of one of Acker's colleagues, performance artist Laurie Anderson, who is "borrowing" from Burroughs in the same way that Burroughs (and Acker) challenge authorial control by "borrowing" (plagiarizing) the work of previous writers (*Home of the Brave*). Nabokov is primarily interested in the perceptual deceits and linguistic fabrications of the individual madman, author, or magician, while Burroughs and Acker characteristically portray identity as a Frankensteinian sociolinguistic construct. But for all three writers, at the level of grammar and syntax, by means of its figures and affect, language has the power to construct reality as well as to contaminate thought, to gain a purchase on the ideal through perverse means or to destroy the idealizations of the status quo through parody and theft.

The linguistic turn in contemporary American fiction can be seen in dozens of significant writers and works published between World War II and 1980, and as we shall see, it continues to be a major element of the writing since the mid-1980s.[3] To name a few examples: there is Richard Brautigan, now nearly forgotten but once attaining counter-cultural status in the 1960s and 1970s as a "hippie" successor to the Beats. Brautigan offered strange, translucent figures of speech and the laid-back patois of characters drifting through a twilight of drugs and mysticism in such novels as *Trout Fishing in America* (1967) and *In Watermelon Sugar* (1968), works that helped to chart the alienations of a generation. While she wrote no novels, in the assemblage of her short stories Grace Paley structured the relation between talking, loss, and the passing of time amongst the working-class denizens of her native Brooklyn. In language experiments that stretch the boundaries of fiction, Raymond Federman (*Double or Nothing*, 1971), Walter Abish (*Alphabetical Africa*, 1974), and Donald Barthelme (*The Dead Father*, 1975) seized upon language itself as the object of fiction's study. Like Brautigan and Paley, Stanley Elkin, certainly amongst the most undervalued of major contemporary American writers, is interested in speech, patois, the power of the turn of phrase, and the vocabulary of vocation. In *The Dick Gibson Show* (1971) and *The Franchiser* (1976), Elkin portrays characters who, like Ben Flesh of the latter novel, live by their wits and their speech, and evidence the degree to which identity is a matter of linguistic expression. Ben Flesh is a traveling salesman and franchise king; as he travels, he talks incessantly on every topic under the sun, becoming one of the most remarkable "voices" in contemporary American writing:

> I drive the road. I go up and down it. I stay in motels and watch the local eyewitness news at ten. Murders are done, town councils don't know what to do about porno flicks, everywhere cops have blue flu, farmers nose-dive from threshers, supply and demand don't work the way they used to ... The left hand don't know what the right is doing and only the weather report touches us all. The time and the temperature. What we have for community. ... We should take over the stations and put out the real news. For everyone murdered a million unscathed, for every fallen farmer so many upright. We would put it out. Bulletin: Prisoners use sugar in their coffee! Do you see the sweet significance? We argue the death penalty and even convicts eat dessert. The cooks do the best they can. The have their eyes out for the good fruit and the green vegetables. Oh the astonishing manifestations of love! ... The state's bark always worse than its bite, brothers, and goodness living in the pores of the System, and Convenience, thank you, God, the measure of mankind. Nobody, nobody, nobody ever had it so good. Take heed. A franchiser tells you. (64)

This is but a fragment of the running conversation Elkin's protagonist conducts with the reader, who is engaged as a rhetorical interlocutor in "making up" Flesh's character as a highly idiosyncratic embodiment of collective elocutions and desires.

If the fiction of Stanley Elkin represents the multiple ways in which the self can be externalized through language, then that of his long-time friend and colleague at Washington University in St. Louis, the philosopher/novelist/essayist William H. Gass, portrays selves and worlds formally contained within the language of their own making, believing that, in the words of one critic, "the work is a closed spatial construction with, at best, an indirect relationship to the world" (Caramello, 99). The title of Gass's monumental work of over two decades, *The Tunnel* (1995) – to be discussed in a later chapter – indicates the constructivist turn of his formalist narratives. His earlier novels, including the *Omensetter's Luck* (1962) and *Willie Master's Lonesome Wife* (1968), and the short-story collection, *In the Heart of the Heart of the Country* (1968), all exhibit the principle enunciated in his essay, "Philosophy and the Form of Fiction": "the worlds which the writer creates … are only imaginatively possible ones; they need not be at all like any real one, and the metaphysics which any fiction implies is likely to be meaningless or false if taken as nature's own" (*Figures*, 9–10). In direct contrast to the realist traditions of the novel, Gass advocates in his fiction and several volumes of essays, including *Fiction and the Figures of Life* (1970), *The World Within the Word* (1978), and *Finding a Form* (1996), that novels and stories be self-contained, formally consistent imaginative entities that offer "additions to reality" rather than being regarded merely as "ways of viewing reality" which results in a "refusing [of] experience" (*Figures*, 25).

Gass coined the term "metafiction" for the kind of writing that embodies "only imaginative possible" worlds, or writing "in which the forms of fiction serve as the material upon which further forms can be imposed" (*Figures*, 25).[4] Often conflated with the conceptualizations of postmodern fiction characterized (reductively, in his view) by John Barth as "merely emphas[izing] the 'performing' self-consciousness and self-reflexiveness of modernism, in a spirit of cultural subversiveness and anarchy … a fiction that is more and more about its processes, less and less about objective reality and life in the world" (*Friday Book*, 200), "metafiction" has been broadly used to describe the novels of Robert Coover, Joseph McElroy, John Hawkes, Max Apple, and Donald Bartheleme, in addition to those of Elkin, Gass, and Barth.[5] The fact that every writer thus mentioned is white and male, and that most have ties to the academy, has led to the perception that metafiction is elitist and abstract, taking place in a rarified domain severed from the harsh realities of life on the planet during a time of violent social change and conflict. A work that is often considered to be an exemplary metafiction, Barth's *Lost in the Funhouse: Fiction for Print, Tape, Live Voice*, was published in 1968, the year of the Tet offensive at the height of the Vietnam War. Barth's assemblage (neither, simply, a collection of short stories, nor a novel in any traditional sense) is remarkable both for its prophetic intermediality as well as its metafictional inventions of a sperm describing its ascent up the uterus and depictions of the act of writing fiction itself in terms of blockage, exhaustion, and renewal.[6] The signal interests of *Lost in the Funhouse* – identity struggling to be born, the writer agonizing over the title of a book he has not yet begun, the contest between the projections of voice (Echo) and the involutions of the self (Narcissus) – superficially at least, suggest the degree to which metafiction is chiefly concerned with its own making.

Literary war broke out between advocates of the metafictional ethos such as Gass and Barth, and surprisingly, John Gardner, the author of a retelling of the Beowulf legend in *Grendel* (1971) and the fantastical *The Sunlight Dialogues* (1972) shortly after the publication of Gardner's *On Moral Fiction* (1978). The notorious "Gardner–Gass debates" of the late 1970s occurred when the two novelists faced off in print on matters of aesthetics, the ethics of fiction, realism, and the work of the imagination. The debates between a writer who staunchly defended his view that fiction must be regarded as a linguistic object and one who felt that "ethical" fiction must compel the reader to make moral choices amidst competing realities took place against the backdrop of the ongoing Cold War, the rising and falling chances for peace in the Middle East during the Carter administration, and continued social upheaval in the struggle for civil rights. Although the debates offer a set of complex agreements and disagreements over the social purpose of art, they have been received in a rather reductive mode as a contestation between postmodernism's investments in parody, play, construction, and self-reflexivity and more traditional concerns with mirroring reality or the modernist interest in constructing a purchase on reality through acts of perception. Reduced even further, this becomes a familiar argument in American literature writ large, between freedom of the imagination to invent "possible worlds" and the constraint of literature's responsibility to reflect and judge the social contract.

To be sure, as Barth himself argues, to regard metafiction or postmodern fiction as solely or primarily about itself is to ignore its capacity for achieving "the synthesis or transcension of … antithesis": "My ideal postmodernist author," Barth writes, "neither merely repudiates nor merely imitates either his twentieth-century modernist parents or his nineteenth-century premodernist grandparents." "The ideal postmodern novel," he continues, "will somehow rise above the quarrel between realism and irrealism, formalism and 'contentism,' pure and committed literature, coterie fiction and junk fiction" (*Friday Book*, 203).[7] And as Gayle Greene, among others, has demonstrated, postmodern "metafiction" is in fact hardly the purview of white, male intellectuals. Many contemporary novels by women, she suggests, have strong metafictional tendencies, including Sylvia Plath's *The Bell Jar* (1963), Erica Jong's *Fear of Flying* (1973), and Gayle Godwin's *The*

Odd Woman (1974); from Britain, Margaret Drabble's *The Waterfall* (1969); from Canada, Margaret Lawrence's *The Diviners* (1974) and Margaret Atwood's *Lady Oracle* (1976); and from South Africa, Doris Lessing's *The Golden Notebook* (1962). The list of metafictionists also includes British writer Angela Carter, the author of postmodern fantasies in such assemblages as *Fireworks* (1974), *The Blood Chamber* (1979), and *Nights at the Circus* (1984), and Clarence Major, an African American writer whose *All-Night Visitors* (1969), *Reflex and Bone Structure* (1976) and *Emergency Exit* (1979) placed him at the forefront of the Black Arts Movement of the 1960s and 1970s.

The novel has always been a genre doubly engaged in reflexive questions about form, language, and narrative strategy as well as about its role as a medium for reflecting reality and an agent for social change. The writing of the contemporary American novel reflects this duality both within the novels and careers of individual authors and in the larger trajectories across writers and subjects that I will be considering in this volume. Appositely significant novels written within the vein of traditional realism continued to appear amidst evolving postmodern and metafictional experiments. Harper Lee's *To Kill a Mockingbird* (1960), Hubert Selby, Jr.'s *Last Exit to Brooklyn* (1964), Dow Mossman's *The Stones of Summer* (1972), or John Cheever's *Bullet Park* (1969) offer prominent examples of realism's continuance, and in a subsequent chapter, I will consider a group of post-1980 novels that extend and revise traditional realism. At the same time, a number of postmodern narrative strategies can be observed in contemporary American novels before 1980 whose distancing from or proximity to social and historical reality are as variable as that of Toni Morrison's *Song of Solomon* (1977), which both represents growing up black in a Midwestern city and portrays a mythological return to origins; Thomas Pynchon's *Gravity's Rainbow* (1973), a phantasmagoric exploration of the postwar landscape and the apocalyptic "Zone" of contemporary existence; Susan Sontag's *Death Kit* (1967), which combines documentary, fantasy, and monologue in the story of a suicide; William Gaddis's *The Recognitions* (1955), perhaps the last great modernist American novel in its encyclopedic, labyrinthine portrayal of an art forger making his way through a world of simulacra; or Joan Didion's *A Book of Common Prayer* (1977), a novel portraying the lives of two women who become involved in the radical politics of an imaginary Central American republic.

The "story" of contemporary American writing in this regard is one of aggregations and parallels, and one where no matter how "realistic" or "metafictional" the work may be, on some level, it is attentive to and reflective about its status as a construction of language. The linguistic turn I have described is thoroughly consonant with novels invested in representing contemporary society such as *Herzog* (1964), Saul Bellow's semi-epistolary novel about midlife crisis; John Updike's *Rabbit, Run* (1960), the first of the decadal "Rabbit" tetralogy portraying the alienated life and relationships of its middle-class protagonist, Harry Angstrom; Joyce Carol Oates's *them* (1969), which explores the plight of working-class characters in Detroit from the 1930s to the mid-1960s; Walker Percy's *The Moviegoer* (1961), whose central figure, Binx Bolling, might be said to be suffering from posttraumatic stress disorder after his return home from the Korean War in search of a calling; *The Confessions of Nat Turner* (1967), William Styron's divisive novel of the legendary leader of a slave revolt told in the voice of Nat Turner (Styron was criticized on all sides for presuming, as a white Southerner, to ventriloquize the voice of a black slave at a point in time when the Black Power and Black Arts Movements were coming into their own); Mary McCarthy's *The Group* (1962), a satirical portrait of a group of New England women coming to adulthood in the 1930s which, like the more popular, but less substantial *Peyton Place* (Grace Metalious, 1956) generated controversy as it touched on "taboo" subjects such as homosexuality, unwed mothers, and abortion; John Rechy's *City of Night* (1963), a landmark gay novel whose protagonist is a hustler who moves from one urban dystopia to another in search of identity; or N. Sott Momaday's *House Made of Dawn* (1968), the Pulitzer Prize-winning first novel by the leading contemporary Native American writer that relates the story of the protagonist's escape from and return to family and community on the reservation.

If we turn to the proliferation of contemporary ethnic literatures in the United States before 1980 (a proliferation that has continued to accelerate since the mid-1908s), we find here as well a double engagement with the kinds of linguistic and generic experimentation often identified with postmodernism combined with representations of the social order, not as viewed through the reflections of a mirror, but rendered with an awareness that language is at the foundation of that order. From the Berkeley free-speech movements of the mid-1960s to the militant revolutionary movements of the 1960s and 1970s, from the inheritance of existentialism to deconstruction, the recognitions of the multiple connections between language, power, and cultural identity have continued to inform the construction of ethnicity in contemporary American fiction. The novels of Philip Roth in the 1960s and 1970s, from early, more realist novels such as *Letting Go* (1962) and *When She Was Good* (1967), to the notorious novel about growing up Jewish, *Portnoy's Complaint* (1969), to metafictional works such as *My Life as Man* (1974) and the first "Zuckerman" novel, *The Ghost Writer* (1979), depict Jewish American identity in crisis as the result of tumultuous cultural changes in family, community, and sexuality. Rudolpho Anaya's landmark *Bless Me, Ultima* (1972) makes use of myth, symbol, and folklore in relating the story of a young man's worldly and spiritual education at the hands of a healer. For many years, Anaya's novel was published by a small press and, until the mid-1990s, was far less visible than the now-faded *The Teachings of Don Juan: The Yacqui Way of Knowledge* (1968), Carlos Castaneda's novel/autobiography/anthropological tract; in contrast, *Bless Me, Ultima* now claims a wide following as one of the first significant Chicano/Latino novels in the United States. Toni Morrison's early novels – *The Bluest Eye* (1970), *Sula* (1972), and *Song of Solomon* – all have affiliations with the magical realism of Gabriel García Márquez or Alejo Carpentier in their portrayals of the violent and alienating social conditions that afflict the lives of her characters. In *The Woman Warrior: Memories of a Girlhood among Ghosts* (1976), Maxine Hong Kingston creates a pastiche of autobiography, ghost tale, myth, and social commentary to tell interlacing stories of growing up as a second-generation Chinese American girl growing up in Stockton, California. Similarly, Ishmael Reed's early fiction, particularly *Mumbo Jumbo* (1972), employs a variety of literary forms and linguistic styles to touch upon a multitude of contemporary issues from conspiracy theory to Black militancy. Leslie Marmon Silko's *Ceremony* (1977) blends storytelling, poetry, and journalism in the narrative of a young man returning from the trauma of war to a new life on the Laguna reservation. In *The Chosen Place, the Timeless People* (1969), Paule Marshall, another second-generation American born to parents from Barbados, portrays complex relationships between the land, language, politics, identity, and the distribution of power on a fictional island located in the Caribbean; her work is part of a wave of important novels to come written by American writers with

Caribbean origins who are part of the postcolonial diaspora, including Jamaica Kincaid, Edwidge Danticat, and Michelle Cliff.

In the narrative of the contemporary American novel, literary theory and developments in the writing of fiction seem to run on parallel tracks. There is a vital connection between Derridean deconstruction, which fundamentally questions how language signifies, and some of the most important novelists of the 1960s and 1970s – Barthelme, Hawkes, Acker, Gass, and Nabokov among them – who investigate the multiple ways in which language constructs reality, rather than the other way around.[8] I have already touched upon metafiction's theoretical leanings: the theory/fiction connection is equally manifest if we compare the language and gender theories of the key French feminists, Hélène Cixous, Luce Irigaray, and Julia Kristeva, which arrived in the United States as part of the "explosion of theory" of the 1970s, and the consonant fiction of several novelists concerned with the role of gender in the construction of identity. Collectively, the French feminists demonstrated the extent to which language is gendered and serves as a medium of patriarchal transmissions of power; at the same time, they argued, language contains within itself the capacity to mock and disrupt patriarchy. From early to late, as I've indicated, Kathy Acker's novels contribute to the project of mockery and disruption in fictional pastiches that combine the surrealistic and satiric in their attacks upon capitalism and power. Interestingly, fantasy and science fiction have offered contemporary writers of the 1960s and 1970s generic modes that allowed them to explore the lineaments of gender and the gendering of language. Joanna Russ's *The Female Man* (1975) depicts the relationships between four women from different worlds, one of them from a planet where a plague has killed off all of the men, and women must reproduce using technology. The novel allows Russ to explore through the conversations of her characters a host of stereotypes and alternative lifestyles and sexualities – from that of the "woman warrior" to the female submissive. In *The Left Hand of Darkness* (1969), Ursula K. LeGuin offers a political fable in which the representative of a federation of planets attempts to establish diplomatic relations with the world of Gethen, inhabited by a hermaphroditic people who are, for the major part of a lunar month, gender-neutral, but for two days of each month, become male or female depending upon the sexual interests of their partner. This device allows LeGuin to explore the relationship between gender and language as highly mutable and, yet, constrained by time and culture. Samuel R. Delaney's massive *Dhalgren* (1975), an apocalyptic novel set in a Midwestern city that has been totally isolated owing to some unknown global catastrophe, depicts the adventures of a bisexual protagonist whose speech and perceptions change radically as he performs varying sexual and gender roles. And while not technically science fiction, Marge Piercy's *Woman on the Edge of Time* (1976) is the story of a woman supposedly suffering from schizophrenia who encounters a woman from a future civilization where the progressive feminist agendas of the 1960s and 1970s have been realized, yet where class hierarchies and repressive regimes remain in place. Together, these novels provide imaginative bases for continued examinations of the multiform connections between language, gender, and sexuality occurring in post-1980 American fiction, especially as it intersects with new work in gender theory by the philosopher, Judith Butler, whose *Gender Trouble* (1990) serves as a watershed in viewing gender and sexuality as culturally constructed, ritualistic, and performative.

Much of what constitutes gender theory rests upon the assumption that both the grammar and history of language have social consequences. Behind this assumption lie the larger contextual questions, "What is history?" as a form of narrative discourse, and "Whose history"? as a narrative inflected by ideological pursuits.[9] These questions are of particular relevance to an era in which the first "television war," Vietnam, was portrayed as a nightly event on the living-room TV screen, when the illusion of historical progress continued to be battered by everything from apocalyptic fears about a third world war to a string of political assassinations in the 1960s that significantly changed the course of American history, and when new histories of women, working-class people, and ethnic minorities, formerly suppressed, began to be unearthed, formulated, and taught. These developments and others led to increasing reflection in the contemporary novel on the relation between narrative and history. Linda Hutcheon has coined the term "historiographic metafiction" to characterize contemporary fictions that both instantiate one or multiple narrative histories and simultaneously question the terms of their own making.

So intensely felt is the importance of the relationship between fiction and history by contemporary writers that the list of works published before 1980 that could fall under the rubric of "historiographic metafiction" is enormous. The list becomes even larger when one considers works that fall into the more traditional category of the historical novel such as Gore Vidal's *Julien* (1964), about the Roman emperor, Flavius Claudius Julianos, or *Burr* (1973), about the man who was Vice-President of the United States during Thomas Jefferson's first term; James Welch's *Winter in the Blood* (1974), which depicts the relation between the present and the past on the Blackfoot Indian Reservation; Gayl Jones's *Corregidora* (1975), a narrative of a great-granddaughter's search for the truth of her ancestral past as a descendant of slaves; and Wallace Stegner's *Angle of Repose* (1971), based on the letters of the pioneer storyteller and poet, Mary Hallock Foote. There are, as well, any number of "hybrid" works combining historical and essayistic writing, reportage, and storytelling consonant with the emergence of "the new journalism" typified in Mailer's *The Armies of the Night* with such works as Truman Capote's *In Cold Blood* (1965), about murderers of a Kansas farm family in 1959; Joan Didion's *Slouching Toward Bethlehem* (1968), a collection of essays and fictional riffs about counter-culture, eccentricity, and the cult of personality in the California of the 1960s; Annie Dillard's *Pilgrim at Tinker Creek* (1974), a series of reflections on nature from a self-conscious narrative perspective; and Tom Wolfe's *The Right Stuff* (1979), a fictionalized documentary about the Mercury 7 astronauts. In the past two decades, "creative non-fiction" has emerged as a rubric for the hybrid writing visible in these works that blend autobiography, documentary, history, and fiction.

One of the hallmarks of historiographic metafiction, E. L. Doctorow's *Ragtime*, when published in 1975, leapt to the forefront as a narrative about the making of history in its rendition of American history and family life in the era of its title (between the turn of the century and World War I) with its insertions of such historical figures as Harry Houdini, J. P. Morgan, Henry Ford and Sigmund Freud into the life of its fictional characters. Adapted into a film directed by Miloš Forman in 1981, *Ragtime* was hugely popular, much more so than John Barth's earlier *The Sot-Weed Factor* (1960), an assemblage of interlinked historical and fictional tales of pre-revolutionary Maryland and Virginia, including a hilarious retelling of the Captain John Smith–Pocahontas legend. Robert Coover's *The Public Burning* (1977) offers an hallucinatory rendition of Cold War politics and history during the McCarthy era in recounting events that lead up to the execution of

Julius and Ethel Rosenberg, accused of being spies, Communists, and selling atomic weapons secrets to the Soviet Union (Doctorow also had portrayed some of these events in *The Book of Daniel* [1971], told from the perspective of one of the Rosenbergs' surviving sons). *The Public Burning* is notable for its skewering of the then Vice-President of the United States, Richard M. Nixon. Kurt Vonnegut's *Slaughterhouse-Five* (1969) uses the science-fiction device of time travel to portray the protagonist, Billy Pilgrim, witnessing the firebombing of Dresden and its aftermath in one of the most harrowing scenes of contemporary American fiction. Two novels of the Vietnam War, Michael Herr's *Dispatches* (1977) and Tim O'Brien's *Going After Cacciato* (1978), combine autobiography, reportage, and historical accounts to portray the war in ways that challenge the received mediation of the conflict via television and the press. Finally, there is the much-overlooked *Rabbit Boss* (1973), Thomas Sanchez's multi-generation novel of a Washo Indian family that recounts over a century of Native American history from a pastiche-like perspective comprising poetry, myth, historical rendition, and personal experience both hallucinatory and painfully realistic.

The intensities of contemporary American fiction before 1980 proliferate in the writing that comes after: the constructive power of language, the relation between fiction and history, the complex intertwining of affect and social experience in the production of narrative – all give rise to filiations that will be of interest to us in the remainder of this volume. In concluding this brief overview of contemporary American fiction before 1980, I will provide preliminary readings of three major novels – Bellow's *Herzog*, Pynchon's *Gravity's Rainbow*, and Morrison's *Song of Solomon* – that incorporate many of these intensities as a means of introducing the symptomatic method of reading post-1980 fiction in the chapters to follow. In so doing, I intend to discuss within each chapter a selective group of novels not as merely representative of some tendency or significant development in recent fiction, but as indicative of the "condition" of contemporary writing, manifesting its most deeply felt quandaries, fraught excursions into the territory beyond its own imagined limits, and complex recognitions of the wavering interface between the real and the imaginary.

* * *

When Saul Bellow published *Herzog* in 1964, it came as clear signal that he had changed directions. The well-known author of the vigorous, picaresque journeys of Augie March (*The Adventures of Augie March*, 1953) and Eugene Henderson (*Henderson the Rain King*, 1959) had published an inward-looking, meditative novel about a middle-aged man writing hundreds of letters never sent, agonizing over his failed marriages and his alienated children, his stalled career, and the small matters of an aging body and mortality. It would be the first of a succession of Bellow's novels portraying the agonies of consciousness, including *Mr. Sammler's Planet* (1970), *Humboldt's Gift* (1975), and *Ravelstein* (2000). *Herzog* may not necessarily be the source for the term "midlife crisis," but it certainly is one of the most penetrating portrayals of the fabled condition that seems to afflict American males between the ages of 45 and 55. The onset of the crisis comes for Moses Herzog, alone in his abandoned summer home in the Berkshires, as he begins to obsess about his second wife's affair with another man – an obsession dispelled when he transforms the murderous intention to kill his wife's lover into an acceptance of existence and his own flawed nature in all of their contrariety. Unlike Augie and Henderson, the odyssey of the erudite and sophisticated Moses Herzog is primarily a mental one structured not by road or sea-lane but by the fragments of the undelivered letters that he writes to his ex-wives, friends and enemies, political leaders and functionaries of every stripe, real and fictional correspondents from the philosophers Martin Heidegger and Teilhard de Chardin to his second wife's psychiatrist and the Monsignor of his girlfriend's parish.

A rambling letter to "General Eisenhower," who at the time of the letter's writing had been succeeded by John F. Kennedy as President of the United States, offers a singular example of Herzog's missives:

> Dear General Eisenhower. In private life perhaps you have the leisure and inclination to reflect on matters for which, as Chief Executive, you obviously had not time. The pressures of the Cold War ... which now so many people agree was a phase of political hysteria, and the journeys and speeches of Mr. Dulles rapidly changing in this age of shifting perspectives of statesmanship to one of American wastefulness. ... Perhaps you will be asking yourself who your present correspondent is, wither a liberal, an egghead, a bleeding heart, a nut of some kind. So let us say he is a thoughtful person who believes in civil usefulness. Intelligent people without influence feel a certain self-contempt,

> reflecting the contempt of those who hold real political or social power, or think they do. … The old proposition of Pascal (1623–1662) that man is a reed, but a thinking reed, might be taken with a different emphasis, by the modern citizen of democracy. He thinks, but he feels like a reed bending before centrally generated winds. Ike would certainly pay no attention to this. Herzog tried another approach. (199–201)

Herzog's letter written to a public figure who has retired into private life touches directly on a concern pursued throughout the novel: the relation between public and private identity; the gap extending between politics in the hands of the powerful blowing "centrally generated winds" and the reed of the individual, liberal self, who has the choice to engage (and perhaps change) his own powerlessness, or retreat into a reclusive mode of being that includes writing unsent letters in an empty house. To extend the metaphor of the "thinking reed," this self is the "hollow man" of T. S. Eliot's poem, existentially aware of an emptiness at the core that, paradoxically, drives thought and begets agency. In other terms, Herzog is an embodiment of the self before death. Herzog's letters are replete with reflections on mortality, yet he cogitates and writes endlessly, almost as if mere thinking and talking were a defense against the onset of change and death. The novel concludes with Herzog lapsing into silence, now that the "spell" of his fixation on his wife's adultery is over, and one might read the novel as redemptive, yet Bellow is careful to dramatize in *Herzog* the dilemma of consciousness, which is only "conscious" to the degree that it is aware of its own means and ends.

Herzog assumes central importance in the narrative of the American novel before 1980, and not just only because its author won the Nobel Prize for Literature in 1976. What is, arguably, Bellow's finest novel offers one of the most compelling portraits available of what it means to be "a thinking reed" in the latter half of twentieth-century America, where identity, divided between privacy in the faltering domestic realm and the inadequacies of public life, verges on a form of schizophrenia typified in Herzog's temporary madness and letter-writing mania. Phillip Roth, who regards Bellow as something of a mentor, once wrote that:

> the American writer in the middle of the 20th century has his hands full in trying to understand, describe, and then make *credible* much of American reality. It stupefies, it sickens, it infuriates, and finally it is even

> a kind of embarrassment to one's own meager imagination. The actuality is continually outdoing our own talents, and the culture tosses up figures almost daily that are the envy of any novelist. (*Reading Myself*, 120)

Roth could have been describing Moses Herzog in this passage as well as Saul Bellow: the subtle conflation of author and protagonist, consciousness and self-consciousness that *Herzog* stages provides one of the most powerful fictional renditions we have of living in a condition where reality outstrips the imagination. This will become of increasing concern in contemporary American writing where reality, as perceived, continues to overtake our capacity to represent it.

No two novels are more different from each other than *Herzog* and *Gravity's Rainbow*, the third novel by Thomas Pynchon, a writer whom Rick Moody praised in glowing terms in his 1997 review of Pynchon's *Mason & Dixon*:

> The novelist Robert Coover, speaking of influences in American fiction, once remarked that apprentices of his generation found themselves (in the 1950s) grappling with two very different models of what the novel might be. One, Coover said, was Saul Bellow's realistic if picaresque *Adventures of Augie March*; the other was William Gaddis's encyclopedic *Recognitions.* Writers my age (mid-thirties), however, don't have the luxury of a choice. Our problem is how to confront the influence of a single novelist: Thomas Pynchon.

The most influential writer of a generation is notorious for the labyrinthine complexity of his fictions, even that of the relatively short and approachable (thus, often-taught) *The Crying of Lot 49* (1966), a novel of cults, conspiracies, and satirical attacks on 1960s California white suburban culture. Set in wartime Britain, Germany, and a postwar "Zone" of indeterminate geography, *Gravity's Rainbow* bears reference to such predecessors as Joseph Heller's satiric *Catch-22* (1961), a send-up of the bureaucracy and brutality of war set in the Mediterranean during World War II, and Jerzy Koskinski's surrealistic *The Painted Bird* (1965), which describes the nightmarish journey of a child through the theater of World War II Europe. Both of these novels are often viewed as sharing similarities with fiction of the absurd and black humor such as Ken Kesey's *One Flew Over the Cuckoo's Nest* (1962), set in an insane asylum, Terry Southern's screenplay for

Dr. Strangelove, a comic/satiric envisioning of nuclear holocaust, and Kurt Vonnegut's *Cat's Cradle* (1963), which satirizes a Cold War that produced such "policies" as MAD ("mutually assured destruction") that, in effect, globalized the mind game of the prisoner's dilemma.

Yet *Gravity's Rainbow* is not exactly a novel of World War II (or Vietnam, the "closer" war to the novel's writing), nor is it exactly an absurdist rendering of Cold War and apocalypse (though it ends with a vision of nuclear bombs hitting an American movie theater), nor can it be wholly encapsulated by Scott Simmon's prescient characterization of the novel as our most comprehensive contemporary "historical and cultural synthesis of Western actions and fantasies" (55). From its infamous opening line – "A screaming comes across the sky" (3), announcing the arrival of a V-2 rocket striking the City of London – to its closing, apocalyptic strains penned by William Slothrop, the Colonial ancestor of the novel's titular protagonist, Tyrone Slothrop, proclaiming that "There is a hand to turn the time / Though thy Glass today be run, / Till the Light that hath brought the Towers low / Find the last poor Pret'rite one ... " (760), *Gravity's Rainbow* charts the fluctuations of force, capital, and desire that circulate through the postwar era. Scanning that final hymn, it is impossible to overlook the novel's eerily prophetic cast: no post-9/11 reader could avoid interpolating current history into the stunningly clairvoyant line, "Till the Light hath brought the Towers low."

Perhaps the most elaborate example of encyclopedic narrative in contemporary American literature and a rival to *Moby-Dick* in that regard, *Gravity's Rainbow* references the history of rocket science, ballistics, theology, astronomy, the occult, thermodynamics, the mechanics of plumbing, German Expressionist film, and sexology, to name but a few of the disciplinary trajectories pursued in the novel. Moreover, it invents new subdisciplines of its own in its intricate catalogues of exotic candies, urban detritus, obscure sexual practices, or modes of extrasensory perception. Appositely, the first English translations of the work of social theorist Michel Foucault were making their way to American shores near the time of the publication of *Gravity's Rainbow*: *Madness and Civilization* (1965), *The Archaeology of Knowledge* (1972), *The Order of Things* (1973), and *The Birth of the Clinic* (1973) established Foucault in the United States, along with Derrida, as the leading presence in poststructuralist thought. Both Foucault and Pynchon share a fascination with the ways in which knowledge is organized, and how the organization of knowledge underlies politics, war, crime, and madness; both are fascinated with a singular "idea of order" as a principle that informs seeming opposites – as Foucault shows in *Madness and Civilization*, reason and madness, as social, political, and juridical categories, share the same logic. As one of Pynchon's recurrent characters, Pig Bodine, opines, " '*Everything* is some kind of plot' " (603), and certainly Pynchon is concerned throughout his work to disclose multiple and intersecting plots, partial or paranoid, as the connective tissue of the social order.

Accordingly, *Gravity's Rainbow* is about plots of all kinds, from political conspiracies to those of our dreams, and about what lies outside of plots in what one character describes as " 'an Ellipse of Uncertainty' " (427) bordering the area where the disciplining and categorization of knowledge cannot go. There are characters in *Gravity's Rainbow* – dozens of them – and there is a protagonist who disappears and whose identity is scattered across a postwar "Zone" populated by nomads and outcasts, historical accidents and conspiracies gone awry. But the novel skews such elements as chronology, character development, and narrative progress in order to reveal the ways in which "self" and "world" are fabricated out of our need for order and our fear of entropy. Indeed, *Gravity's Rainbow* defies any attempts to organize its multiple logics, or to explain all of the connections between its manifold narratives, while pressing questions about the plots of history, knowledge, and the social order, and the extent to which they implicate "us," only definable in relation to "them." In its sheer anatomization of contemporary reality, *Gravity's Rainbow* remains the signal occurrence of the late twentieth-century American novel.

Set in an unnamed Midwestern metropolis (one that resembles the environs of Detroit or Cleveland, the latter close to her native Loraine, Ohio), Toni Morrison's *Song of Solomon* follows the logic of the classic *Bildungsroman* – the novel of a young man moving through childhood and adolescence to adulthood – save that its central figure, Macon "Milkman" Dead III, is a case of arrested development who is compelled by the violence around him and the consequences of his own selfishness to journey to the site of his ancestral origins in order to discover "himself." The symbolically named protagonist of the novel acquires his nickname when he is observed still feeding from his mother's breast well beyond an age that might be considered normal;

his legal name has been bestowed upon him as an inheritance from his grandfather whose original family name has been skewed by the drunken scrawl of a white Yankee soldier on an identity card. A descendant of slaves who have been forcibly transported from their homeland and who have migrated to Northern cities following the Civil War, Milkman bears names that are both patriarchal and matriarchal, but none the true ancestral name which, as for many African Americans, was destroyed by the slave system when African names were replaced by those derived from plantation owners, the Bible, localities, or distorted pronunciations and records. Literally and symbolically dead at the beginning of the novel where he is lost in a solipsistic maze of self-gratification, misogyny, and failed ambition, Milkman begins a quest for identity that is inextricably linked to a recovery of the past and his own family history. To do so, he must engage in a series of historical reversals, including a return to the South and the scene of his ancestry.

Unlike *Roots* (1976), Alex Haley's immensely popular tracking of an African American family genealogy back to its African origins (a novel published just one year earlier and subsequently exposed to claims of plagiarism), *Song of Solomon* is not an historical fiction but, rather, a blending of myth, folklore, symbolism, realism, and the history of slavery in a novel intensively focused on questions of identity:[10] what kind of identity does Milkman have without a proper name? To what degree is his identity a simulacrum of cultural desires that arise out of loss and alienation? To what extent is his selfhood a matter of his race, ancestry, and historical experience, and how have these both shaped and, to some degree, imprisoned him? In its portrayal of the quest for identity of its black, male protagonist, Morrison's novel is responsive to the specific context of the continuing impact of the Black Power movement born in the 1960s and Afrocentric movements that have their origins in nineteenth-century America; at the same time, it references the stories of Oedipus and Icarus, and the African folkloric traditions of the flying ancestor, in the narration of Milkman's journey from city to country, North to South, present to past. The capaciousness of Morrison's narrative resides in its capacity to unearth connections between Western mythologies and African folkloric traditions, and between the specificities of regional or national social circumstances and the deeper historical strains to be traced across time and location.

Through much of the first half of the novel, Milkman is one of the most unlikable characters in contemporary fiction: he treats his mother, sisters, and lover as disposable objects; save for one transformative instant, he cowers before his domineering father, accepting his arbitrary beneficence without question while secretly hating him; most of his time is spent finding ways to enhance his vanity or fulfill his personal desires while, all around him, racism, violence, and degradation abound. And even as he commences a ritualistic journey that will – at least symbolically – reunite him with the legacy of his ancestors, his betrayed aunt Pilate, and his closest friend, Guitar, who, as a violent revolutionary, has rejected Milkman for his narcissism and apoliticism, it is unclear at the novel's end to what degree Milkman gains new life or cancels himself out. Is his jump across the chasm of Solomon's Leap and into the arms of Guitar, who has shot and killed Pilate in an attempt to take revenge upon Milkman for, supposedly, cheating him out of a nonexistent hoard of gold, an act of suicide, revenge, or self-sacrifice?:

> Without wiping away the tears, taking a deep breath, or even bending his knees – he leaped. As fleet and bright as a lodestar he wheeled toward Guitar and it did not matter which one of them would give up his ghost in the killing arms of his brother. For now he knew what Shalimar knew: If you surrendered to the air, you could *ride* it. (337)

The ambivalent cast of *Song of Solomon* is an aspect of its power, for in this novel of coming-to-identity, Morrison forthrightly addresses the paradoxical aspects of what it means to be black in contemporary America and an environment where the impulse to escape historical reality is as strong as the impulse toward self-transformation within history. She will continue to do so in the triad of novels that trace the lives of African American women from slavery to modern times (*Beloved*, 1987; *Jazz*, 1992; *Paradise*, 1999) through a centrality of vision that led to her winning the Nobel Prize in 1993.

The arc that extends from *Invisible Man* to *Song of Solomon*, and from Ellison's unnamed protagonist surviving in an urban basement on stolen light and power to Macon Dead III flying, like his African ancestors, across a chasm in an act which may be one of self-sacrifice or murder figures a critical trajectory in contemporary American fiction that negotiates the relation between race, body, history, identity, and language. As we have seen, in different ways, *Herzog*, *Gravity's Rainbow*, and *Song of Solomon* equally consider how contemporary identity comprises "only words," but the gravity of this equation is to be found in the relation between language and reality, and how the former reflects, distorts, or transforms the latter. In Part II, I will consider how post-1980 American fiction regards this relation in a diverse array of novels that run the gamut from embodiments of new realism to postmodern experiments.

Part II

From New Realisms to Postmodernism

The sheer array of styles observable in contemporary American writing rivals the diversity of the writers themselves. From the transparency of apparently conventional forms of realism to the hyperbolic linguistic play of postmodernism experiments, the heterogeneity of contemporary American writing foregrounds the notion that "anything can happen," as Tom Le Clair and Larry McCaffrey titled their 1983 collection of interviews with contemporary American novelists. The contestation between the imagination and reality that undergirds the proliferation of styles in contemporary American writing brings to mind again Philip Roth's statement of 50 years' vintage that contemporary writers have their "hands full in trying to understand, and then describe, and then make *credible*, much of the American reality. It stupefies, it sickens, it infuriates, and finally it is even an embarrassment to one's own meager imagination" (*Reading Myself*, 120). The observation conceives of the human imagination and contemporary reality engaged in a battle to outstrip each other, leading to a profusion of stylistic and aesthetic strategies that variously reflect, refract, distort, derail, exoticize, or offer radical departures from "the real." The range of labels to describe trends in contemporary American writing is telling: "new realism," "dirty realism," "minimalism," "maximalism," "surfiction," "avant-pop" – these, along with dozens of others, including the more familiar tags of "postmodernism," "metafiction," and "avant-garde," are indicative of a literature in search of a language to contend with reality, or more accurately, a literature recognizing that the infinitely complicated relation between reality and the imagination can only be viewed partially, through the finely ground lens of a specific aesthetic and style. In this section, we will observe ways in which post-1980 contemporary writing continues to address the quandary that Roth presciently posed at a moment when contemporary American fiction was about to explode into a profusion of styles and particularities: how can we imaginatively portray reality, when reality – in its excess and absurdity – threatens to overtake our capacity to frame it, to see what lies within and beyond it?

"This American Life"

For a number of significant post-World War II American writers, meeting Roth's triad of challenges – to understand, to describe, and to make credible the sheer outrageousness and contrasting ordinariness of contemporary American life – has led to a succession of novels and stories that continue to expand the reach of literary realism. Chief among these are John Updike's "Rabbit" novels (*Rabbit Run*, 1960; *Rabbit Redux*, 1971; *Rabbit is Rich*, 1981; and *Rabbit at Rest*, 1990) which chart, decade by decade, the (only superficially) mundane adventures of its middle-class protagonist, Harry Angstrom, as these register the social, political, and cultural changes in America over the 40 years of his fictional life. While metafictional experimentation was enjoying its heyday in the work of Donald Bartheleme, John Barth, and Robert Coover, other writers such as Raymond Carver, Anne Beattie, Lorrie Moore and Grace Paley were reinventing the short story as they charted minute, evocative variations in the lives of "ordinary" subjects speaking the local patois and inhabiting domestic environments in fictions that subtly register "enormous changes at the last minute," to employ the phrase that serves as the title of Paley's 1974 collection. Across the span that extends from the 1960s to the present, Tom Wolfe, often credited as one of the founders of the "new journalism" which mixed external fact and description with sociological observation and projections of collective fantasy, brought his journalist's sense of realism's heterogeneity – with decidedly mixed success – to the social satires of *The Bonfire of the Vanities* (1987) and *A Man in Full* (1998). Writers as different as Richard Ford, Mary Gordon, William Kennedy, Anne Tyler, Richard Russo, and Alison Lurie continue to share the common project of representing American life within the rich context of local circumstances, probing beneath the surface of the quotidian for the complexities of the "real." Others, including John Irving, Tom Robbins, James Welch, and Toni Morrison (whose *Beloved* I discuss in Part IV) engage in realism of a particular kind – "magical realism" – which combines local detail and historical representation with the mythical, supernatural, and absurd in the tradition established by Latin American writers such as Gabriel García Márquez and Carlos Fuentes.

The list of those important post-World War II writers whose work lays some claim to extending and expanding the traditions of novelistic realism is long and venerable. Literary realism – to be sure, an amorphous designation, given the manifold ways in which these writers portray the undercurrents and excesses of contemporary American life – is alive and well in the turn from the late twentieth century into the twenty-first. In considering novels that use and transform the strategies of realism to portray American lives during a time when the challenge to imagine a reality that defies imagining increases daily, we can dwell on only a few revealing examples. Prominent among these is Steven Millhauser's imitation of the classic American rags-to-riches story in *Martin Dressler: The Tale of An American Dreamer* (1996). Millhauser is the author of five novels and six story collections bearing titles such as *From the Realm of Morpheus* (1986), *The Barnum Museum* (1990), and *Dangerous Laughter* (2008) that characteristically discern the fabulous in the ordinary; in *Martin Dressler*, he portrays the degree to which America as imagined and advertised has replaced – indeed, is the double of – the "real" America. The son of a cigar-shop owner, the ambitious and shrewd protagonist of the novel builds an empire in Gilded-Age America by constructing increasingly elaborate enterprises (a refurbished cigar stand, a lunchroom that turns into a McDonald's-like franchise, a tourist hotel and shopping mall) until at the ripe age of 27 he completes the "Grand Cosmo" – as its name indicates, "a complete, self-sufficient world, in comparison with which the actual city was not simply inferior, but superfluous" (265). The Grand Cosmo is a fantastic simulation of the cosmos as realized and imagined, comprising alternative realities and cultural inventories "that rendered the city unnecessary" (265):

> the Grand Cosmo offered a variety of what is called "living areas" in carefully designed settings. Thus on the eighteenth floor you stepped from the elevator into a densely wooded countryside with a scattering

> of rustic cottages, each with a small garden. The twenty-fourth floor contained walls of rugged rock pierced with caves ... Those with a hankering after an old-fashioned hotel could find on the fourth and fifth subterranean levels ... an entire Victorian resort hotel with turrets and flying flags ... Still other floors and levels offered ... perspective views (room-like enclosures with windows that provided a three-dimensional view of a detailed scene resembling a museum diorama and supplied with live actors: a jungle stuffed with lions, a New England village with a blacksmith and a spreading oak tree, an urban avenue). (266)

It turns out, however, that the Grand Cosmo is too ambitious, too complex and labyrinthine: it attracts few customers, and represents the decline and fall of Martin's empire as he sinks into its interior, the arc of his career complete at an early age, a plight that afflicts several of Millhauser's protagonists.

The realism of *Martin Dressler* lies in its embodiment of what the French social theorist, Jean Baudrillard, terms the "simulacrum" of contemporary reality, or the imitation and replacement of reality with a system of signs and images that renders reality, in its messiness and partiality, inferior and irrelevant. For Baudrillard, Disneyland (or the Grand Cosmo of a future era) is an imaginary place that "is there to conceal the fact that it is the 'real' country, all of 'real' America ... [it] is presented as imaginary in order to make us believe that the rest is real, when in fact all of Los Angeles and the American surrounding it are no longer real, but of the order of the hyperreal and of simulation" (Baudrillard, 175). The sense of contemporary reality as a vast imitation comprising spaces and images that are, themselves, imitations is captured in a comment made to Martin by his advertising agent, Harwinton: "'The world sits there. It may have a meaning. As a private citizen, I am entitled to believe that it does. But as an advertiser, I train myself to experience the world as an immense blankness. It's my job to provide that blankness with meaning'" (205). Interestingly, Millhauser sets this "tale of an American dreamer" who builds a simulacrum that imitates/replaces the real world in late nineteenth-century America, suggesting that contemporary "hyperreality" in Baudrillard's terms has its origins in the rise of industrial capitalism; conversely, *Martin Dressler* can be viewed as the simulation of a "past" – and an imitation of such nineteenth-century novels as William Dean Howells's *The Rise of Silas Lapham* (1885) – to which we have a nostalgic relation as a lost time that never really existed in the first place. Above all,

Martin Dressler simulates the American Dream of material success that inevitably collapses of its own weight because it requires, as it expands, resources that cannot compete with its imaginary requirements. In this tale of a dreamer, Millhauser portrays how the constructed worlds of contemporary reality stop short of reality itself, which always lies beyond as already having passed away.

With over thirty-five novels to her credit, as well as three dozen short story collections, eight novellas, eleven additional novels under other names ("Rosmand Smith" and "Lauren Kelly"), seven volumes of young adult and children's fictions, and dozens of volumes of essays, drama, and poetry, Joyce Carol Oates may well be the most prolific writer in American literary history. She is also a consummate contemporary realist who portrays the irrationality and violence waiting to erupt through the thin crust of "normal" existence. In *them* (1969), Oates's subjects are working-class people living on the margins of society; *Wonderland* (1971) traces the life of its protagonist from impoverished childhood in the Great Depression to professional success and family turmoil in the 1960s; *You Must Remember This* (1987) and *We Were the Mulvaneys* (1996) are tumultuous family histories set against the social backdrop of, respectively, Cold War 1950s America and the post-Vietnam era; in *The Falls* (2004), what begins as stereotypical honeymoon ends in tragedy as a newlywed's husband disappears over a guardrail into Niagara Falls – the novel chronicles the rippling historical effect of this accident/suicide and the "family curse" it initiates.

One of Oates's most satirically barbed portraits of American life is to be found in *American Appetites* (1989), in which a small community of intellectuals and professionals is destroyed by an accident that reveals the frailty and superficiality of their assumed normalcy. In what some have viewed as a *roman à clef* starring thinly disguised Princeton friends and colleagues (Oates began teaching at Princeton University in 1978), Oates tells the story of a successful professional couple, Ian and Glynnis McCullough – he, an academic, historian and demographer, she, a writer of cookbooks – known and loved for their elaborate dinner parties populated by well-fed and well-educated friends, whose lives come to a halt when Ian accidentally pushes Glynnis through a plate-glass window during a drunken argument. The argument has transpired over Glynnis's mistaken assumption that Ian is having an affair, but what transforms a familiar scene into an extraordinary episode is the sudden, totally unexpected upwelling of emotion and violence that leads to a series of tragicomic consequences: Ian is charged with murdering Glynnis; other couples separate, divorce, and openly cheat on each other, as if the discharge of violence in the McCullough household were a catalyst that releases everyone from the bonds of a fictive happy and normal domesticity; following a trial in which he is acquitted, but only after "betraying" his dead wife by speaking openly for the first time about her initiating the violence that led to her death, Ian marries the woman his wife erroneously identified as his lover and begins life anew.

The novel illustrates the total collapse of the American bourgeois nuclear family: Glynnis dead; Ian disgraced, despite the overturning of his murder conviction; their college-age daughter, Bianca, estranged and fled to foreign climes to escape her father. But in this depiction of normalcy gone amok, Oates mixes comedy and horror in such a way that one can only regard Ian's thoughts at the end of the novel as strong evidence of satirical intent: "[h]e did not regret, in that instant, that Glynnis was dead. For Sigrid Hunt would not have been possible for him, had Glynnis not died" (331), even as in utter contradiction he contemplates that he "will blow [his] brains out when the season turns" (332). The targets of Oates's satire are the "American appetites" that provide the title of the novel (as well as that of Glynnis's last cookbook) which are excessive and overindulgent on every level. Food, sex, alcohol, even philosophy become the addictive means used by the well-off circle of friends in Hazleton-on-Hudson to distract themselves from the paucity of what Ian, as a statistician, terms "the individual's very essence – the statistic 'self.' That such a self existed nowhere but in demographic charts did not render it any less real" (5). The novel mocks the insularity and insecurity of this world of hyper-civilized American adults, who appear under a slightly different lens or in altered circumstances to be cannibals, addicts, and children wholly given over to an appetite for "the good life," their atavistic dark sides metaphorically sublimated in the "rationalizations" of menu and recipe, dinner seating and marriage. Ian gives the game away in a meditation on his favorite sport, squash:

> He ... liked the game because it was a game, and not life: it had a beginning, and an end; it was played in a specific place ... it had its rules, regulations, and customs ... [i]ts dimensions were so scaled down

> ... one could not speak of it as a metaphor for life [...] unless everything in which human beings involve themselves with an unreasoned intensity is a metaphor for life. (172)

American Appetites reveals that Ian's "unless" is not a qualification but a fact of life for the inhabitants of Oates's novel: "unreasoned intensity" is the undercurrent that runs through all of their stories, a paradoxically instinctual and socialized greed for experiential satiety only half-met through the excesses of American materialism. For Oates in *American Appetites*, the game of life, as fragile as the reflective pane of glass through which Glynnis McCullough falls, progresses by virtue of intensities that defy any logics we may devise to control, explain, or legitimate the appetite for experience in contemporary American culture.

The catastrophic intrusion of the accidental into the ordinary is also the energizing plot element of Russell Banks's *The Sweet Hereafter* (1991), but cast in a tragic mode, and occurring in the lives of the rural working class. Banks's novels and stories are known for their realistic portrayals of disenfranchised, marginalized subjects, living on the fringes of history and along the back roads of American society: *Trailerpark* (1981) is a collection of stories about the assorted inhabitants of a mobile-home park in New England; *Continental Drift* (1985) is a novel that features a working-class protagonist pursuing the American dream of class mobility in Florida who has a fatal encounter with a group of Haitian refugees; *Rule of the Bone* (1995) portrays the maturation of a 14-year-old high school dropout who forms a life-changing relationship with an "illegal alien" from Jamaica; *Cloudsplitter* (1998), is a richly detailed historical novel about the radical Abolitionist, John Brown. In *The Sweet Hereafter*, set in the rural small town of Sam Dent in upstate New York, a school bus accident has led to the death of 14 children. In one sense, the "hereafter" is the novel itself, or the aftermath of accident and its effect on the town as told through the perspective of Dolores Driscoll, the school-bus driver, Billy Ansel, the father of twins who have died in the crash, Mitchell Stephens, a lawyer who has arrived in Sam Dent in order represent some of the parents of the dead children in a lawsuit, and Nichole Burnell, a 14-year-old survivor of the crash confined for life to a wheelchair. Each of these characters is a direct or indirect witness to the accident who relates how its occurrence divides the history of Sam

Dent, as well as his or her own life, into the "before" and "after" of the traumatic event. These multiple perspectives give rise to any number of uncertainties about something that has clear, mortal consequences: was Dolores driving the bus over the speed limit on a snowy day? Did an animal run across her field of vision, causing her to swerve into a guardrail and over an embankment down into a water-filled sandpit? Is Mitchell Stephens merely a mercenary attorney looking for a profit in human tragedy? Is he really concerned to represent "the little guy" against more powerful interests that may be in some way responsible for the accident, or he is paying an installment against the guilt he has accrued in his destroyed relationship with his own daughter? Where, in fact, does the responsibility for the accident, and the dead and maimed children, lie?

Collectively, the diverse chorus of voices that make up the novel intimate a larger question that informs much of Banks's work: who is responsible for all of the lost children of 1980s and 1990s America, the runaways and the impoverished, those addicted to drugs (as is Mitchell Stephens's daughter) or dead from lack of adequate care? The corollary question – what has losing them done to us? – is answered by Billy Ansel as he reflects on the tragedy:

> People who have lost their children – and I'm talking here about the people of Sam Dent and I am including myself – twist themselves into all kinds of weird shapes in order to deny what happened. Not just because of the pain of losing a person they have loved … but because what has happened is so wickedly unnatural, so profoundly against the natural order of things, that we cannot accept it. It's almost beyond belief or comprehension that the children should die before the adults. It flies in the face of biology, it contradicts history, it denies cause and effect, it violates basic physics, even. It's the final contrary. A town that loses its children loses its meaning. (78)

The intrusion of the "unnatural" into the "natural" highlights the degree to which the presence of and responsibility for children – and by extension, a meaningful continuance, a "sweet hereafter" – is taken for granted by the adults of Sam Dent, who are busy pursuing their own pleasures and escapes from small town boredom in drugs, alcohol, and adultery. As the novel's plot unfolds, the blame comes to rest on Dolores, who Nichole falsely claims was driving too fast; like all of the characters in the novel, Nichole's motives are mixed: by lying, she takes revenge on her father for years of sexual abuse in denying Mitchell Stephens sufficient grounds to sue the bus manufacturer, and she prevents the descent of the town into endless litigation over the accident. The novel concludes with a scene set at a destruction derby – that peculiarly American event in which junk automobiles are intentionally driven into each other until only one remains running. Everyone in the community of Sam Dent is present at this staged crash site where a ritual of scapegoating and expiation is enacted as "accidents" take place under artificial control. *The Sweet Hereafter* suggests that it is only through such mechanisms that the town can cope with its loss, but the inevitable placing of responsibility upon a single individual, based upon a lie, is a disavowal of the collective guilt recorded by the voices of the novel. As Mitchell Stephens asserts in thoughts that echo those of Billy Ansel,

> the people of Sam Dent are not unique. We've all lost our children. It's like all the children of America are dead to us. ... In my lifetime something terrible happened that took our children away from us. I don't know if it was the Vietnam War, or the sexual colonization of kids by industry, or drugs, or TV, or divorce, or what the hell it was ... but the children are gone, that I know. (99)

For Banks, the responsibility for this loss, these deaths, belong to all; in the social allegory offered by *The Sweet Hereafter*, the reasons are to be found in the culpabilities of an avaricious contemporaneity in post-1980s America and the spawning of a new lost generation.

Francine Prose is the author of a dozen novels that explore in precise detail the commonplaces, absurdities, and tragedies of American life. Often peering through a lightly satirical eye, Prose writes of family and community in New York's Little Italy during the 1950s in *Household Saints* (1981), of the excesses and limitations of "New Age" cosmopolitanism in *Hunters and* Gatherers (1995), of the incongruities of academia in *The Blue Angel* (2001), and of personal transformation and American liberalism in *A Changed Man* (2005). One of her most pointed portrayals of class and cultural differences occurs in *Primitive People* (1992), modeled on Henry James's *The Turn of the Screw* as a tale of a young woman arriving at a strange household in order to care for two strange children. While James's novella is an eerie tale of ghostly possession that studies the transmissibility of "evil" as a form of adult knowledge, Prose's novel is a comic, satiric skewering of elitist assumptions about racial others and the "primitive" cultures from which they originate. As *Primitive People* richly suggests, the "barbarians" are the white inhabitants of the large houses and manors located in a wealthy enclave of the Hudson River Valley, not the inhabitants of the island (Haiti) from which the novel's protagonist comes in order to start a new life in America.

Having been betrayed by her lover and no longer able to continue living in a country immersed in civil strife, Simone has entered the United States from Port-au-Prince illegally and secured employment as a governess and housekeeper at the home of Rosemary Porter, who is separated from her husband and only distantly connected with her two children, 10-year-old George and 6-year-old Maisie (an echo of the heroine of James's *What Maisie Knew*, another tale of a child's exposure to adult knowledge). While Rosemary sculpts inane versions of earth-mother figures in one part of the house, Simone cares for the two odd children in another: Maisie seems obsessed with death and detritus ("a morbid child … [s]he took Simone on her own house tour, a tour of the old and discarded. … She showed Simone a plot in the yard where their former pets were buried"[19]), while George obsessively watches reruns of a *National Geographic* special about Eskimos that portrays the slaughter of seals in vivid detail. As in the two stories by James, the children in *Primitive People* are in need of salvation from the narcissistic adult world that surrounds them, and Simone makes it her job to engage them in more normal activities, but their immersion into the static, emotionally violent world of their parents, already commenced in childhood, is predetermined. Near the end of the novel, during a disastrous Christmas dinner in which it is revealed to everyone, children included, that Rosemary's best friend, Shelly, is having an affair with her husband, and that the couple are planning to wed and take possession of the house and children come next Christmas, Simone perceives that the children "had reverted completely to what they were when [she] arrived. There was no sign of her having been there, of having helped the children" (224).

Prose uses the Jamesian framework to limn the inverted, mocking comparison of the "advanced" civilization that Simone enters and the "primitive" world from which she has come: just as the children are already adults when Simone arrives (in a society where adults behave like children), so the civilized adults of Hudson Landing are barbaric in their attitudes and actions. Kenny, the family's hairstylist and

Shelly's live-in boyfriend (such are the incestuous tribal arrangements amongst the adults in Hudson's Landing) tells Simone that

> "Rosemary jokes about inbreeding, but it's hardly a joke. They naturally select for elegant heads and tiny little brains, the lowest possible cranial capacity without actually being a pinhead... The whole family is like a pack of extremely high-functioning Afghan hounds. Well, really, the whole neighborhood – it's a longitudinal thing. They're like a bunch of babies, instant erase, no guilt." (23)

Not only is the "neighborhood" notable for its shrunkenheadedness and collective amnesia, it is also remarkable for its latent or manifest violence: a couple artificially induces an argument with a waitress so that the ensuing adrenaline rush will allow them to metabolize calories more quickly; Rosemary compares Southern women to "female penguins fighting over the biggest rock" (75); Simone and the children are nearly shot by an insane next-door neighbor who regards the environs as his personal hunting preserve. For Simone, observing from the outside the effects of the domestic wars surrounding her, the Porter children "remind her of Haitian children as they took on the look of civilian non-combatants in a war that has dragged on so long that nothing more can shock them" (165). Prose's novel proposes that affluent, white, suburban America is a thinly domesticated form of the "primitive" third world that Americans imagine or that they enter only voyeuristically as tourists "in package tours of Port-au-Prince ... nervously patting their wallets in time to the frenzied drums while sinewy dancers leaped about and a poor chicken lost its life," wanting "their hands plunged in animal blood – or at least the thrill of watching someone do the plunging for them" (110). In *Primitive People*, what constitutes the constant of American life is the capacity to relocate the barbarity that underlies the normative and the ordinary "over" or "down" there, in some other culture or body far from us.

Realism's ability to capture reality is questioned in John Edgar Wideman's *Philadelphia Fire* (1990). The query is implicitly posed in the mentality of a homeless man, J. B., who wanders through the deteriorating metropolis of mid-1990s Philadelphia:

> What we need is realism, the naturalistic panorama of a cityscape unfolding. Demographics, statistics, objectivity. Perhaps a view of the city from on high, the fish-eye lens capturing everything within its distortion ...

> If we could arrange the building blocks, the rivers, boulevards, bridges, harbor, etc. etc. into some semblance of order, of reality, then we could begin disentangling ourselves from this miasma, this fever of shakes and jitters, of self-defeating selfishness called urbanization. In time a separation (spelled in case you ever forgot, with a *rat*) between your own sorry self and the sorrows of the city could be effected. ... Realism: the solid arbitrariness of the paltry wares set out each morning in the market square to make a living. (157–8)

This advocacy for realism as a means to address the inversions and imbalances of the contemporary city comes from one of the leading African American novelists of his generation, who portrays the other Pennsylvania metropolis, Pittsburgh, and its black, working-class Homewood neighborhood in *Hiding Place* (1981), *Damballah* (1981), and *Sent for You Yesterday* (1983). Wideman is also the author of *The Cattle Killing* (1996), where he depicts Philadelphia in stories of its growth set in the eighteenth century; *Brothers and Keepers* (1984) and *Hoop Roots* (2001), multi-genre memoirs of growing up and basketball; and *Fanon* (2008), a fragmented biography of the famous French political theorist whose work has been the source of inspiration for Black revolutionary movements in four continents.

Wideman's writing is characteristically experimental, tracking the movement between speech and thought, hallucinatory vision and sudden, stark recognition. In *Philadelphia Fire*, as the passage above suggests in positing realism as the cure for selfishness and isolation, he tests the capacity of representational realism to portray a horrific historical event. The novel depicts the aftermath of the 1985 bombing by the Philadelphia police of a row house in West Philadelphia inhabited by MOVE, an African American political group several of whose members were prosecuted in 1978 for the death of a police officer in a raid on the group's headquarters. In 1985, in an attempt to evict MOVE members from their home on Osage Avenue, the police made the disastrous decision to bomb the roof of the house by helicopter; the ensuing fire destroyed not just the MOVE house but an entire city block, and caused the death of six adults (including John Africa, the founder of MOVE) and five children. Haunted by the event, the protagonist of *Philadelphia Fire*, Cudjoe, returns to Osage Avenue and the neighborhood where he grew up after ten years of self-imposed exile in order to see if he can find the unknown child who purportedly ran from the fire and disappeared into the maze of city streets.

Cudjoe's quest (never completed in a novel of incomplete quests and journeys) takes up the first of *Philadelphia Fire*'s three parts, each offering an attempt to comprehend what has been lost in the fire – literally and symbolically, the future of the city itself, the novel's real protagonist.

Cudjoe, who is both a "mirror" of city's loss and the "black hole" into which all of the chaos and grief arising from that loss disappears (122), attempts to uncover/recover the reality of the city through oral history as he interviews those who remember the bombing. J. B. roams the neighborhoods in an hallucinatory, alcohol-induced state exposed to its underside while the novel's narrator – who elsewhere provides alternating descriptions of the city as a Rabelaisian body and a magical labyrinth – tracks his movements and commends "realism" as the means to redeem the city's past. In the free indirect discourse of the novel's second part which portrays his years as a teacher before the bombing, Cudjoe recounts his failed attempts to stage Shakespeare's *The Tempest* with schoolchildren as a way to imagine the potential for liberation of a future generation from poverty and racism. Yet each of the strategies employed to understand what has happened to the city in the wake of the fire – realistic description, eyewitness account, literary invention, visionary journey – finally serve only to expose the black hole of what the city lacks and has lost in history. The realism of *Philadelphia Fire* lies not in what it exposes, but what remains concealed beneath the ashes and detritus of the city's self-destruction; echoing Roth's plaint that the meagerness of the imagination cannot cope with the outrageousness of contemporary reality, Wideman portrays the American metropolis as a place that defies any narrative gesture to encapsulate it. *Philadelphia Fire* thus comprises one of contemporary American fiction's frankest acknowledgments of the failure of realism to encompass the reality of an urban catastrophe and the violence of American life, which in turn is a manifestation of the capacity of the imagination to know its own limits.

"Dirty Realisms"

In July 1983 the eighth issue of the British magazine of new writing, *Granta*, was devoted to what editor Bill Buford termed "dirty realism." The issue, comprising works by then young American writers Richard

Ford, Raymond Carver, Tobias Wolff, and Jayne Anne Phillips, among others, is an eclectic assemblage devoted to the idea that a new kind of realism was emerging in the wake of the postmodern experiments of the 1960s and 1970s – a form of naturalistic writing that would expose the underside of American domesticity, regionalism, class, popular culture, and media. While the term was loosely articulated by Buford primarily as a "marketing strategy," according to Robert Rebein, it has served since *Granta 8*'s inception (followed up by *Granta 19: More Dirt*) to indicate contemporary American writing that renders an "effect in both subject matter and technique that is somewhere between the hard-boiled and the darkly comic," and that follows the "impulse … to explore dark truths" located in narratives of family, class, addiction, and escape (Rebein, 43). Taking on the challenge to graph the margins and extremes of contemporary American existence in naturalistic terms, "dirty realism" has continued to investigate the terrain that encompasses our resistance to imagining it.

Certainly amongst the most notorious of contemporary American writers (and joining the notorious company of Brett Easton Ellis, Kathy Acker, James Ellroy, and Dennis Cooper in this regard), Chuck Palahniuk has written a series of novels that explore the ritual violence of sports in *Fight Club* (1996), religious cults in *Survivor* (1999), serial murder in *Lullaby* (2002), reality TV in *Haunted* (2005), and the pornography industry in *Snuff* (2008). In *Choke* (2001), Palahniuk depicts the adventures of a 24-year-old medical student, diarist, and sex addict, Vincent Mancini, who pays for his education and his mother's full-time medical care (she suffers from dementia) as a con artist with a strange game: he causes himself to choke on food at expensive restaurants, thus generating a bond for life with the patrons who save him, and who often send him cash gifts on his birthday to commemorate their redemptive acts.

Like many of Palahniuk's protagonists, Vincent is a compulsive, nihilistic personality who looks for meaning in habitual acts of variegated repetition and finds none. Indeed, the entire novel comprises Vincent's movements through a series of situated environments where he acts out his impulses, each one embodying a "theme": the sexual therapy center that Vincent visits in order to surreptitiously engage in sex with other addicts ("Wednesday nights mean Nico. Friday nights mean Tanya. Sundays mean Leeza" [16]; his mother's room in the hospital where she often mistakes him for the court-appointed lawyer who has defended her on various charges during her nomadic career as a prostitute and swindler; the colonial American living-history museum where he works with his friend Denny, a compulsive collector of rocks, as an "Irish indentured servant" – "For six dollars an hour, it's incredibly realistic" (30). Seinfeld-like, Vincent navigates these "sitcom" scenarios where, with mundane regularity, sexual compulsion, historical simulation, and memory loss are on display in a world "about nothing." Haunting these environments is the ever-present visage of death – in the sex acts, described in pornographic detail, where Vincent has to imagine roadkill in order to avoid ejaculating too quickly; in the hospital where his mother lies dying with "[h]er thin puppet arms" and "[h]er shrunken head" (21); at "Colonial Dunsboro," where Vincent perversely tells schoolchildren about the grisly diseases that swept Europe and America during the eighteenth century to counter the sugar-coated view of colonial times purveyed elsewhere in the living museum.

Ida Mancini, the woman who Vincent believes is his mother, tells him that addiction " 'is a cure for knowledge,' " a means to " 'escape what we know' " (149; 150), and it is clear in a novel that contains a catalog of mnemonic acronyms for the symptoms of deadly diseases, a list of historical plagues, and scattered descriptions of intrusive medical procedures that what we know and wish to escape most is the fact of mortality. *Choke* suggests on multiple levels that life itself is a kind of addiction, and contemporary culture a form of unreality that "is more powerful than the real" (160), as Ida tells Vincent, " 'the world of intangibles.' ... By intangibles she meant the Internet, movies, music, stories, art, rumors, computer programs, anything that isn't real. Virtual realities. Make-believe stuff. The culture" (159–60). In its grisly, often gross detail, the novel suggests that unreality and "the real," addiction and mortality are the obverse of the same coin: what appears to be an escape is just the flip side of entrapment in a carceral, mortal reality (Ida has read Foucault), the "safe organized place" of the quotidian, "speed-limited and zoned and taxed and regulated, with everyone registered and addressed and recorded" (159). As the resident philosopher of *Choke*, Ida, who confesses moments before her death that she has kidnapped Vincent as an infant from "a stroller in Waterloo, Iowa" (269), argues that the flight into the virtual – the living museum that simulates history, the images of pornography imitated in the acts of sexual addicts, the rationalized passages of life and narrative to be found in all the world's 12-step plans – fall well short of an ideal that resonates at the end of the novel. This ideal will affect many of Palahniuk's readers as a postmodern throwaway, a flailing gesture in the face of the violent death-filled reality that he portrays in his novels: "'I want you to invent it. ... To create your own reality. Your own set of laws'" (284), Ida exclaims to Vincent as a child. Having traversed several models of identity in the course of the novel ("stupid runt," stud, grifter, indentured Irish servant, Christ), Vincent the adult follows Ida's advice in concluding his diary with the statement that he, Denny, and friends are the new "Pilgrims, the crackpots of our time, trying to establish our own alternate reality. To build a world out of rocks and chaos" (292). Ironically, the fiction in which this situationist future is posited is itself a product of a contemporary culture that is all too real to us, Palahniuk suggests, in its virtuality, yet perhaps still capable of producing signs of life.

When Dorothy Allison's *Bastard Out of Carolina* was published in 1993, it caused a notable stir for its open-eyed portrayal of child abuse, poverty, and family dysfunction in the South. Set in and near Greenville, South Carolina in the 1950s, the novel is narrated by Ruth Anne "Bone" Boatwright, born to a teenage mother out of wedlock and subjected to years of physical and sexual abuse at the hands of her stepfather. The novel is narrated from the perspective of Bone as an adult tracking her memories of growth into adolescence and premature womanhood from the ages of 5 to 12: the chronology roughly corresponds to the onset of her mother's marriage to Glen Waddell and her departure with him for territories unknown after he has raped and beaten Bone. While focused on the wrenching relationship existing between an abused child and a mother tortured by her child's suffering but incapable of separating herself from her abusive husband, *Bastard Out of Carolina* is also an assemblage of stories about the complex relationships of the extended Boatwright family – all of Bone's aunts and uncles – and more broadly about the class, culture, and region they inhabit. In a lineage that derives from Erskine Caldwell, Harper Lee, Flannery O'Connor, and – further back – William Faulkner and Mark Twain, Allison portrays characters culturally stereotyped as "rednecks" and "poor white trash," but like these authors, she writes against stereotype in probing these characters' histories, minds, and emotions; moreover, she writes about the "tabooed" and inextricably linked topics of child molestation, rape, and sexuality with a candor and realism one rarely finds in the literary annals of any region. To some extent, *Bastard Out of Carolina* is a *Bildungsroman*, its narrator telling the story of progression from innocence to experience, and from childhood to adulthood compressed within a cruelly brief span of years: in the final scene of the novel, Bone relates that at the age of 12 "I was who I was going to be, someone like her, like Mama, a Boatwright woman" (309). Yet Bone's story is also distinctive, not only for the relative brevity of the passage to adulthood, but also the ways in which it is a story of gender, class identification, and familial bonds between women. *Bastard Out of Carolina* is above all a survivor's story that does not flinch from delineating the conditions for survival when the quanta of love and trust have been severely depleted.

One of the most incisive aspects of the novel inheres in its reflection on ugliness and rage. Implicitly, Allison suggests that the assumed cultural aesthetic for women is that they be attractive (to men), passive, long-suffering in the face of male anger and aggression, and nurturing even when threatened with violence. But Bone is filled with rage at her victimization, and often gives expression to it verbally, causing even more abuse to descend upon her. Her stories and dreams often contain violent images; her thoughts of sex are often connected with fire and anger. When she is not expressing rage, Bone is frequently in a state of irritation, her thick skin serving as a form of protection from the devastation of her childhood. Conflating her physicality with her nickname, Bone reflects that "[i]t was often the bones in my head I thought about, the hard porous edge of my skull cradling my brain, reassuring me that no matter what happened I could heal up from it eventually. ... The sturdy stock we were boasted to be came down in me to stubbornness and bone" (111).

Bone frequently notices "ugliness" in herself and others. She describes her grandmother as "ugly herself, she said so often enough, though she didn't seem to care" (21); she sees her own body as "obstinate ... [g]awky, strong, ugly ... I was stubborn-faced, unremarkable, straight up and down, and as dark as walnut brown. This body, like my aunts' bodies, was born to be worked to death, used up, and thrown away" (206). Bone befriends a girl whose features are marked as ugly and "albino" by other children, and defends her against slurs until the two friends have a falling-out, at which point Bone says to her: "'You're ugly. ... You're God's own ugly child and you're gonna be an ugly woman. A lonely, ugly old woman'" (171). This is certainly one of the worst things that can be said to a woman in the culture of *Bastard Out of Carolina*: it is said here by Bone to Shannon Pearl, who shortly thereafter suffers a horrible death; it is said by one of Bone's uncles to his wife, sending her into a state of severe depression; after the death of Bone's namesake, Aunt Ruth, Bone's mother remarks that her deceased sister "was never pretty. ... When we were little I think Ruth would have given just about anything to be pretty. ... When she got pregnant, she was so happy. ... I asked her why she acted so happy, and she stared at me like I was just plain crazy. Told me it was proof. Being pregnant was proof that some man thought you were pretty sometime, and the more babies she got, the more she knew she was worth something." (230–1)

This interlinked discourse of rage and "ugliness" is clearly associated with cultural dominants that have enabled the abuse Bone suffers and set limits for the women of the novel: her mother's passivity, her own "unwomanly" affect and demeanor, the view of women as valuable only for sexual gratification and reproduction – all are elements of a heteronormativity where rhetorical and physical violence against women is symptomatic, not aberrant. *Bastard Out of Carolina* is set in the South of the 1950s, but the startling clarity and realism of Allison's writing in a novel published in the 1990s that continues to shock and illuminate its readers suggests that there is little real historical difference between "then" and "now" in these matters, and that the issues the novel addresses extend well beyond the region in which it is located. The political ramifications of the novel extend as well beyond the question of gender identity, which is central to it: many of the characters in the novel are poor and white, some are poor and black; all are living in a country at a time of relative prosperity and experiencing the dislocations of family and community that come with the ever-widening gap between the rural poor and the increasingly affluent middle class in post-World War II America. *Bastard Out of Carolina* is hence the compelling story of one of William Carlos Williams's "pure products of America" who does not "go crazy" as do many around her, but who survives everything to become, in the contradictory combination of fatalism, threat, and promise that the phrase contains, "already who I was going to be."

One of the writers included in *Granta 8*, Jayne Anne Phillips, writes also about family relations and family dysfunction in contemporary America. Comprising stories that explore the interiorities of runaways, teenagers, drifters, and criminals, *Black Tickets* (1979) established her presence as an important new writer whose realism was to be found in the alignment of mentality and event. Her first novel, *Machine Dreams* (1984), is a family chronicle that explores the inner lives of its characters as the nation moves through the Great Depression to the Vietnam War; in *MotherKind* (2000), Phillips portrays the emotional and psychological complexities of motherhood in a daughter's relationship with her dying mother as she faces the challenges of her own newborn child. *Shelter* (1994), as its title suggests, is a novel about protection. Set in a summer camp for "Girl Guides" in West Virginia at the height of the Cold War, the novel depicts the inner lives and fateful interactions of several youthful and adult characters in the sequestered space of Camp Shelter and the forest that surrounds it. The main characters of the novel are five children and one adult: 15-year-old Lenny and her 12-year-old sister, Alma; Lenny's friend Catharine, nicknamed Cap; Alma's friend, Delia; Billy, the school-age son of the camp cook; and Parson, a delusional escaped convict who has come to the area in pursuit of a former cellmate (Billy's stepfather, Carmody), and who has occupied an abandoned shack near the camp. *Shelter* portrays all five characters coming together in a climactic, violent episode that forges a bond between them, but the bulk of the novel is devoted to exploring the interaction between character and environment, both the domestic hells from which the children have temporarily escaped in coming to Camp Shelter, and the reversed Eden of the camp itself.

In several respects, *Shelter* is an example of the subgenre of novelistic allegories such as William Golding's *Lord of the Flies* (1954) or Stephen King's *The Body* (1982, the basis for the film *Stand by Me*) that portray an ad hoc community of children being initiated into adulthood – an initiation that inevitably involves a confrontation with mortality and sexuality. But the allegorical dimension of Phillips's novel is its least compelling aspect: Parson tramps through the woods with a phallic blacksnake wrapped around his neck which he shows to Lenny, who is equally attracted to and repulsed by it, an encounter that too obviously symbolizes the teenager's dawning sexual knowledge. Set in July 1963, the true force of *Shelter* lies in the way that Phillips portrays the individual psychologies of the novel's four speakers – Lenny, Alma, Buddy, and Parsons – within both the local context of a youth camp designed to provide a protective home away from home and a socialized encounter with the natural world, and the global context of a world that had reached the brink of a nuclear confrontation between superpowers only nine months earlier. We hear of the ongoing Cold War primarily through the hysterical right-wing political views of the camp director, Mrs. Thompson-Warner, who gives lectures to the girls on the perils of Communism. While no explicit comparison is ever made between this "evil" and those related to home life (a partial list includes the fact that Buddy is sexually abused by Carmody; Cap's parents are in the midst of a corrosive divorce; Delia's father has recently committed suicide), or to what treachery and violence may lie in wait outside the camp ("*[t]he forest is all around us and we're like a country inside it*" [149], writes Alma in her diary), it is clear that Phillips wishes her readers to see the nation and camp, domesticity and interiority as connected by virtue of their failure to protect us from knowledge or harm.

The epiphanic event of the novel occurs when the four girls decide to go skinny-dipping in a secluded pond, one of many seemingly protected spaces in the novel where body, sexuality, and nature are brought into contact. But others are there, lurking in the shadows: Buddy and his stepfather, who is drunk to the point of insanity; and Parsons, who has been following Carmody with the intent to confront and, perhaps, kill him. In a rush of events, Carmody jumps into the pond and attempts to rape Lenny; Parsons follows and tries to wrestle Carmody away from Lenny, but is knocked momentarily unconscious; finally, Billy strikes his stepfather with a rock, and the rest join in with stones and boulders, effectively committing group homicide. The group decides to place the body in a hidden cave (another shelter); the novel concludes with an epilogue narrated through Billy's consciousness four months after these events in which he surveys his "kingdom," now that the camp has closed – possibly for good – and his abusive stepfather has been removed from the scene. Clearly, Phillips is not interested in resolutions in *Shelter*, either allegorical or realistic; instead, the novel can be seen as a series of contact points between intersecting planes of reality, such as when Buddy, seeing his stepfather lying unconscious and drunk in a truck by the roadside, recalls the

> cars and trucks with faces in the Golden Books Mam used to buy … She'd get him one every time from the notions rack, since they'd always just cashed their assistance check. … He didn't like those snaggle-faced

> fire trucks and buses with eyes. A car was not supposed to sing and wink; a car should be a machine and fly by on the two-lane, either side of those double lines. (204)

Within a few strokes, the need for order in the face of the world's irrationality – personified in his stepfather – is rendered in the associative memory of a child; moreover, this need is put in terms of a realism that contends with a cartoonish conception of a vehicle that has become dangerous in Billy's experience. *Shelter*'s realism lies in its recognition that reality is a set of perceptions, contingencies, and associations that form into the content of experience, which is always intimate yet bears the traces of contact with a world in which knowledge of all kinds portends the erasure of innocence.

The death of innocence is moot in the urban novels of Richard Price, where everyone is complicit in the travails of a world ever on the verge of social chaos. In his eight novels, screenplays, and TV scripts (Price is the co-writer for the HBO series, *The Wire*), Price has surveyed the urban neighborhoods and portrayed streetwise denizens of New York City, the housing projects of New Jersey and ghettos and working-class neighborhoods of Baltimore. In *The Wanderers* (1974), Price portrays a street gang in the Bronx projects during the 1960s; *Bloodbrothers* (1976) is an ensemble narrative about an urban working class-family; *Clockers* (1992) depicts the drug gangs operating in the New Jersey projects; and *Freedomland* (1998), also set in the projects, is a mystery about a kidnapping that reveals – as does much of Price's fiction – the connection between the police, the legal system, the gangs, petty criminals, and law-abiding citizens living locally in the neighborhoods. The Lower East Side of Manhattan is the setting for *Lush Life* (2008), a police procedural about a homicide that taps into the intimate lives of all those who come into contact with the crime – victims, perpetrators, witnesses, police, lawyers, the press – as well as providing a topography and linguistic map of the neighborhood in which the crime takes place. The crime itself is the shooting of one of three white men drunkenly walking together after the bars have closed on a side street near Delancey in lower Manhattan. As the chief officer assigned to the case, Matty Clark, and his detective partner, Yolanda Bello begin to interview witnesses, canvass the neighborhood, and find motives, multiple stories emerge and interconnect: the stillborn acting career of Eric Cash, one of the three men in the group who is initially the primary suspect in the shooting; the wanderings of 17-year-old Tristan, living in the Lemlich housing projects and seeking initiation into the gangster life; the story of Matty's failed marriage and his troubled relationship with his two sons. In *Lush Life*, the crime itself is but the germinating seed for entanglement of desires, lies, motives, stories, and disavowals that brings together dozens of characters into an ad hoc community of those caught up in the crime's wake.

Characteristically, much of *Lush Life* is given over to talk: conversations, interrogations, testimonies, asides, anecdotes, and jokes fill the novel, and there is no contemporary American writer who is Price's equal in capturing the multicultural, neighborhood vocabularies of the American urban environment. Nor is any contemporary writer more adept at giving the reader a tangible feel for the urban locale, as the following itinerary of the Lower East Side seen during the patrol of a drug task force in search of "perps" suggests:

> Restless, they finally pull out to honeycomb the narrow streets for an hour of endless right turns: falafel joint, jazz joint, gyro joint, corner. Schoolyard, crêperie, realtor, corner. Tenement, tenement, tenement, museum, corner. Pink Pony, Blind Tiger, muffin boutique, corner. Sex shop, tea shop, synagogue, corner. Boulangerie, bar, hat boutique, corner. Iglesia, gelatería, matzo shop, corner. Bollywood, Buddha, botánica, corner. Leather outlet, leather outlet, leather outlet, corner. Bar, school, bar, school, People's Park, corner. Tyson mural, Celia Cruz mural, Lady Di mural, corner. Bling shop, barbershop, car service, corner. And then finally, on a sooty stretch of Eldridge, something with potential: a weary-faced Fujianese in a thin Members Only windbreaker, cigarette hanging, plastic bags dangling from crooked fingers like full waterbuckets, trudging up the dark narrow street followed by a limping black kid half a block behind. (3–4)

The sheer heterogeneity of the scene is notable: the hybrid labyrinth of the streets serves both to camouflage and reveal the identities and motivations of those who roam them as the police conduct a profiling exercise. Ever-changing owing to the bifurcating forces of gentrification and ghettoization, the Lower East Side is the true protagonist of *Lush Life*, the plot of this procedural taking a back seat to the description of the city's streets, smells, sounds, and languages. While the perpetrator is eventually caught as the result of a series of contingencies that render procedural aspects of the novel somewhat moot, as its title suggests, the solving of the crime is not the real story here; rather, it is the story of the city itself awash in its own rich, lush life – a city that is also "a lush" in the sense of being drunk, addicted, operating irrationally, pursuing the ends of amalgamated desires. The citizens of the city, Price suggests, are caught up in attempting to match the reality they encounter on the streets with inner needs that can often find their articulation in the aggressions of speech and act. Price's realism demands the profiling of human desire in a city that serves as the site for desire's proliferation and mystery.

Only Wor(l)ds

Humbert Humbert's plaint – " 'Oh, my Lolita, I only have words to play with' " (32) – is one of the mantras of contemporary fiction often tagged as "postmodern." An ancestor of the fictions of American "high postmodernists" such as Bartheleme, Barth, Sontag, Pynchon, or Gass, *Lolita* is an intensive reflection on the making of a world out of words, a linguistic construct that – depending on the writer – alters, replaces, distorts, fragments, mimics, or mocks "reality." For Humbert, the world he makes out of words *is* his reality, just as the novel we read – an object made out of words and spaces, type and paper – is a piece of reality as real as any other object in the world. The questions that many contemporary writers pose in fictions that reflect on the power and frailty of the imagination as something that produces fiction is: to what degree is the world as we know it a product of our ability to linguistically capture it? How does the reach and limitations of language affect our capacity to construct identities operating within other constructs that we term "world," "reality"? Nabokov provided one answer to these questions in his memory of a newspaper story about "an ape in the Jardin des Plantes who, after months of coaxing by a scientist, produced the first drawing ever charcoaled by an animal: this sketch showed bars of the poor creature's cage" (qtd. in Boyd, 512). However fanciful an account of "the prison-house of language," to use Fredric Jameson's key term and title in his reflection on the linguistic interpenetration of historical world orders, Nabokov's anecdote underscores what we find in his fiction: an ironic, deeply reflexive unfolding of artificial worlds that mirror the ways in which we imagine the world to "really" be. In 1970, near the height of the first wave of postmodern language experiments, literary critic Tony Tanner would trace the thread of American writing that runs from Emerson to Barth that, optimistically, renders language capable of shaping systematically coherent worlds. Amongst the language experiments of the 1960s and 1970s, this would become a point of debate: is contemporary reality so fragmented that the imagination cannot anneal it? Can Humpty-Dumpty never be put back together again? Or, in creating competing language-worlds – worlds often with their own rules, codes, and geometric contours – are we, in fact, reshaping reality?

These questions continue to haunt the making of contemporary American fiction. Since 1980, the questions have taken on enhanced complexity with the advent of multiculturalism, the explosion of the canon, and the rich interpolation of experimental and traditional narrative strategies – the admixture of linguistic reflexivity and various realisms – often to be seen in the same novel, chapter, even sentences of recent writers. Doubtless it was always this way: one can find in *Lolita* satirically realistic depictions of American road culture set alongside Humbert's evocations of an imaginary child, as if a hallucinatory drawing had been superimposed upon a photograph of a desert highway; Donald Bartheleme's fictional architectures are verbal collages that contain pieces of actuality (other text-objects) conjoined with typographic renderings of babel. What is notable, however, about the profusion of post-1980 novels that contain a high degree of linguistic reflexivity and meditate in diverse ways on the constructedness of language and the multiple realities

Three from FC2

One of the most adventurous publishers of language experiments since the mid-1970s is FC2. FC2 began as the Fiction Collective in 1974, an independent, cooperative publishing venture amongst avant-garde writers such as Ronald Sukenick, Jonathan Baumbach, and Mark Mirsky. The Collective published dozens of important innovative writers in its early years, including Clarence Major, Fanny Howe, Raymond Federman, Chris Mazza, and Mark Leyner. Three examples of recent novels published by FC2 include Steve Tomasula's *The Book of Portraiture* (2006), a scrapbook of texts and images that traces the human need to make representations across a millennium, Kate Bernheimer's *The Complete Tales of Ketzia Gold* (2002), an assemblage of fairytale-like narratives that comprise a novel of growing up in the ironic fantasyland of contemporary reality, and Toby Olson's *The Blond Box* (2003), a meditation on the relationship between art and desire as well as a suspenseful mystery. *The Blond Box* reflects Olson's development over 30 years of a unique fictional aesthetic that combines eroticism, the uncanny, and stark detail.

it (mis)represents, is that they reflect a consciousness of their place in an ongoing literary history in which the entanglements of language with history, identity, and culture continue to foliate. How words can "world" within the specific chronologies of language and history continues to be a question aggressively addressed by contemporary American writers.

Donald Antrim's novels are conceptual architectures containing hyperbolic, hilarious meditations on contemporary identity and its capacity for relationship. *Elect Mr. Robinson for A Better World* (1993) is an example of black humor that satirizes small-town politics in its grotesque rendering of the freakish inhabitants of a beachside community; in *The Hundred Brothers* (1998), a reunion of 99 of 100 brothers in the ancestral home, turns into a carnivalesque display of fraternal relations, rivalries, and fantasies; in *The Afterlife: A Memoir* (2006), Antrim brings his wit and sense of the absurd to an otherwise harrowing account of his relationship with an alcoholic mother. As its title may suggest, *The Verificationist* (2000) is a novel about the overlapping of fantasy and contemporary reality and the difficulty of verifying which is "more real." Like *The Hundred Brothers*, *The Verificationist* begins with a hypothetical question: in the case of the former, "what would happen if there were a hundred brothers and ninety-nine of them met in the family mansion?"; in the case of the latter, "what would happen if a group of psychologists from a research institute met at a pancake house for dinner and professional conversation?" The mismatch of the situation (elitist professionals meeting for dinner in order to eat breakfast at a local IHOP) fuels Antrim's send-up of disciplinary inbreeding and infighting as the pancake dinner descends into chaos amidst arguments over therapeutic methods, flirtatious conversations, and startling personal revelations. The novel is literally a "send-up" as Tom, *The Verificationist*'s central consciousness, who is on the verge of initiating a food fight with his colleagues, begins to hover in the air above the crowd and is prevented from floating away only through the fierce embrace of Bernhardt, his arch-rival. Through the cartoonish portrayal of Tom's out-of-body experience, Antrim provides a helicopter view of a contemporary identity assemblage and the bubble world it inhabits.

Floating above his colleagues, Tom, a youth program coordinator for "Young Women of Strength," fumblingly pursues his own fantasies while observing those of others. A one point, a young waitress whom he clearly desires floats up toward him, and he grasps her legs in order to keep her from floating away, then engages in contorted attempts to maneuver her body so that she can be face-to-face with him; meanwhile, he begins to feel Bernhard's erection against his back as his colleague struggles to hang onto him. This slapstick theatricalization of floating anxiety and desire is repeated at several points in the novel where, figuratively, human need is "spatialized," as if the world comprised three-dimensional encapsulations of want, lack, and affect through which one glides. Speculating on his troubled marriage and his lack of progeny, Tom asks himself:

> what are the possible uses, in a childless house, of an empty room? Let's assume, for discussion purposes, that the room remains unused, its doors unopened, its broken walls unpainted and the unclean windows securely locked. Nothing gets put in the room, and nothing can come out. The room functions symbolically as a container for anything that is imagined, hoped for, dreamed about. If the room is a baby's room, then it is a room missing a baby, and this is of course another way of saying the room contains loss. The room is not empty, exactly; something unseen lives inside. (55)

The externalizing of "something unseen" that "lives inside" characterizes much of what comprises *The Verificationist*; Tom, the roaming perspectival authority of the novel, assumes the role of viewing the bodies of his colleagues from unusual angles as a means of verifying their identities through a visual inspection of physical lack or excess. Thus, just as envisioning the empty room of a childless household figures forth loss, so Tom's view from above of two male colleagues' bald spots manifests their variant passive-aggressive personalities, "particularly considering the different techniques each man adopted in relation to his bald spot, and what these techniques revealed about the men in relation to one another" (103). *The Verificationist* is organized as a push-me-pull-you, seriocomic journey through a series of perceptual spaces that structure and externalize desire and its lack, intimating a world that is composed of a series of adjacencies – "a random assortment of substantive realities" (158), as Tom puts it, which are haunted by the visible traces of affect, relation, identity. In short, the novel comprises worlds within worlds, each exposing its surface as the content of its inwardness.

The inextricability of inwardness and relation is the subject of *Indivisible* (2000), Fanny Howe's fragmentary, semi-autobiographical exploration of maternalism in the life of an experimental filmmaker and foster-mother who struggles with her religious beliefs, politics, and memories of troubled relationships as she comes to terms with middle age. Howe is the prolific author of over forty volumes of poetry, fiction, and essays, and she is widely regarded as one of the chief avant-garde writers of the contemporary era. Her novels are typically a fusion of philosophy, political theory, diary, poetic aside, dream, and dialogue that record the inner lives of her protagonists; in the case of *Indivisible,* the narrator, Henrietta ("Hen" or "Henny"), juxtaposes the account of her life to Schoenberg's theory of musical composition: "There are sequences of sounds that musicians arrange by twelves, repeating the same twelve notes but in alternating and random sequences. They themselves don't know which three or four notes will come out close, in relation to each other" (15). The atonal structure of the 12-tone composition is applicable to the verbal structure of *Indivisible*, where Henny's writing/composing gradually reveals the tones and themes of her life, emerging randomly yet bearing a patterned relation to each other.

To extend the musical analogy, as Henny recounts her complicated longstanding relationships to her friends, Lewis, Libby, and Tom, her husband, McCool, and her foster children, the fragmentary pieces of narrative that constitute the novel, like those compositions that "break off from the goal-oriented strands of traditional music," generate a "sound pattern made out of parameters and crossings, rather than predictable sequences" (65). *Indivisible* is a narrative aspiring to the condition of music, so that along with more conventional passages in which Henny describes her work as a filmmaker, her attendance at Libby's bedside when she is dying of cancer, or her conversations with Tom, an aspiring monk with whom she discusses the maternal desire of an adoptive mother as well as philosophy and religion, we encounter frequent discursive offshoots, such as the following:

> To tell someone that a person contains the blueprint of the cosmos can be misleading because the person can't just lean over and read it. The blueprint doesn't exist without someone beaming the light on it and I hate to say it, but this operation takes a lifetime of excruciating searching. I can't say that this blueprint forms "another" level of reality because I would automatically be separating them with the word "another." (205–6)

This seeming aside goes to the heart of the novel in the idea that reality is heterogeneous yet inseparable, indivisible: in its diversity, it does not operate on a series of levels or hierarchical planes, but as a totality in which glimmers of its design are randomly discernible.

As an autobiographical fiction, *Indivisible* is a discursive "graph" that gives shape to the representation of a life, but also a kind of writing, we are reminded in Henny's frequent references to the material composition of music, films, and buildings, that aspires to be indivisible from sound, image, or architecture. The form of the novel as well as its subject suggests that everything is connected, but not in the familiar register of contemporary paranoia; rather, Henny is always reflecting on her double role as foster mother to several children (both a "real" mother in a substantive sense, while a "fake" mother in a literal sense), even when she is ostensibly thinking about something entirely different, and especially when she explicitly informs us that this "is not directly a story about maternalism, about the hours and years of caretaking, rushing to and fro from pick-ups and drop-offs, the homework, the dressing … chasing, fearing, reading, rocking, singing, raging, trudging, lugging … comforting and punishing, allowing and bitching, the meals after meals and washings-up and washings-down … " (179). The catalogue goes on, and in its excess and specificity, indicates that, indeed, this *is* a story about maternity in which everything is metonymically connected to everything else as a matter of the sheer ongoingness of existence. Henny is everywhere concerned "indirectly" about her relation to her children as essential to her concept of self: natured, nurtured, subjects of state control, born of divine plan – how do her children embody the linkage to her? More largely, Henny frequently refers to her sense of being "invisible," a word which is clearly likened to "indivisible" as expressions for her sense of the relation of self to world; appositely, Howe's writing consists of an attempt to make identity visible as an entity indivisible from a manifold reality – for her, not only is the "personal" the "political," it is also inseparably linguistic, objectified, agential, maternal, communal, isolated, spiritual, biological. As a mathematical concept, indivisible refers to that which is incapable of undergoing division without a remainder; so, for Henny in *Indivisible*, which might be conceived as an attempt at non-repressed writing, there is no remainder to the process of differentiating life in writing, nothing extraneous to that which is remarked or illuminated, nor anything, for that matter, written beforehand.

In the "Afterword" to *The Jade Cabinet* (1993), Rikki Ducornet writes that this final novel in her "Tetralogy of the Elements," like the three preceding it (*The Stain*, 1984; *Entering Fire*, 1986; and *The Fountains of Neptune*, 1989), "investigates the process of fabulating, creating and remembering" (157). Ducornet's fiction, extending to seven novels and two short story collections, often fabulates on the origins and power of language, and the conflation of its metaphoric and metamorphic capacities: "If fiction can be said to have a function, it is to release that primary fury of which language, even now, is miraculously capable – from the dry mud of daily use. So that furred, spotted, and striped, it may – as it did in Eden – scrawl under every tree as revelation" (157). This Adamic notion of language informs the volumes of the tetralogy, each named for one of the four elements; in the case of *The Jade Cabinet*, the element is air, and the novel is a figuratively rich reflection on the relationship between writing and voice, the airy conversion of language into speech.

The labyrinthine plot of this novel set in a simulation of late Victorian England relates the stories of Etheria, raised mute by her father, Angus Sphery, who experiments on his daughter with his theories of a primal language. Memory, Etheria's sister, who serves as the novel's narrator and historian; Radulph Tubbs, an industrialist who gains Etheria's hand in marriage in exchange for a dowry of jade figures; Baconfield, an architect who becomes Tubbs's partner in the pursuit of increasingly bizarre business schemes and building plans; and the *Hungerkünstler*, a version of Kafka's "hunger artist" who is seized upon by Angus Sphery as a creature possessing the primal language he has spent a lifetime seeking out. As the names of its characters suggest, *The Jade Cabinet* is a postmodern allegory where embodiments of voice (ironically, Etheria, who cannot speak), memory and history (Memory), rapacious, chaotic desire (the *Hungerkünstler*), the counter-desire for monumental human order set over against nature (Tubbs), and the quest for a language in which sign and signified are perfectly conjoined (Sphery), are brought into contact.

Underlying all is the element of air, the perfect blank of the "aether" that is penetrated by voices which employ the same element to produce sound. Air or aether signify the void that humans fill with architecture and demarcate with invisible boundaries; the blank page upon which the mute Etheria inscribes her ideogrammatic language, or Memory the family history, is a similar void intimating the analogy to be drawn between writing and speech. The evanescence of human traces is manifested in the plot of the novel (Etheria disappears after her marriage to Tubbs; all of Tubbs's plans for permanent monuments to empire and ego come to nought) which posits as a counterforce the quest for permanence and origins: thus, Sphery exclaims that

> "If I could discover the origins of language ... I would know the origins of mankind. Mankind and ... his myths! Simultaneously! The roots of the imagination and ... *all its fruits*! The sciences, yes, and the arts. Because ... Language is Imagination! Language is Memory! And the brain ..." he pondered, "the brain is like a gigantic sphere. It *hums*! It hums the music of the spheres!" (69; all ellipses in original)

The primary reason that Sphery becomes enamored with the *Hungerkünstler*, a sideshow fraud who latches onto anyone that will feed her vanity and desire, is because she incorporates, in his view, "*all possible primitive phonemes; she whistles, whickers, nickers, snorts; she moos, twitters, honks and hoots; she growls, buzzes and snarls. She is simultaneously harmonious and cacophonous. Language exists here at its purest, primal roots*" (76; original emphasis). Yet this quest for purity and primacy occurs in the world of objects and languages "after Babel," after the fall into language and the age of dissimulation – a world so changeable that memory becomes, as Memory suggests, a mapping of mutability rather than a preservation of the past: "Let's suppose that memory is like a jade cabinet, but a cabinet belonging to an infinitely resolute collector. Each time we look inside, the jade appears to be the same, yet the mind is forever replacing one chimera for another that resembles it. Let's suppose the memory is a cabinet of chameleons and the mind as unstable as the moon" (92). Though *The Jade Cabinet* is set in late Victorian England and portrays historical figures such as Charles Dodson (Lewis Carroll, the progenitors of literary nonsense, a genre premised upon the instabilities of mind and meaning), it is really an exploration of a contemporary reality where the illusion of permanence and stability has been sundered. Yet, for Ducornet, this condition unleashes the possibility for coming to terms with the primacy of the embodied imagination which, like Memory's memory, works most to register how everything changes and, thus, how everything is always unworldly, different.

The link between memory and mutability is also central to David Markson's remarkable *Wittgenstein's Mistress* (1988). Although he began his career writing genre novels (his semi-parodic western, *The Ballad of Dingus McGee* [1966], was subsequently adapted into the film *Dirty Dingus McGee*, starring Frank Sinatra), Markson's significance amongst the most innovative contemporary American writers is established by *Wittgenstein's Mistress* and the novels that followed – *Reader's Block* (1996), *This is Not a Novel* (2001), *Vanishing Point* (2004), and *The Last Novel* (2007). Each of these works is an intertextual palimpsest that regards reality as a multi-discursive flow of language, voice and text, and consciousness as a means of channeling this global flux. In *Wittgenstein's Mistress*, the consciousness is that of Kate, who imagines herself to be the last, or only person in the world, and who issues from her house on a beach, in Markson's eerie premonition of Twitter, thousands of "messages" – primarily brief, one-sentence paragraphs – that make up the novel. These messages are often connected through Kate's capacious associational logic, but just as often she leaps disjunctively from one topic to another, leaving it to the reader to make connections or discern echoes across widely separated entries in the novel. Kate's messages – an outpouring of memories and erroneous recollections, reflections on art and culture, representations and misrepresentations of biographical and historical facts – entail a hodgepodge of obsessions and interests: painters from Michelangelo and Rembrandt to Van Gogh, de Kooning and Rauschenberg; literary figures from Homer and Euripides to the Brontës, Rupert Brooke, and William Gaddis; Heidegger and Nietzsche; Brahms; the opera star, Maria Callas; the naming of cats (including Rembrandt's cat); ancient Athens and Troy; underwear; car accidents; wristwatches; masturbation. As Stephen Moore suggests in an "Afterword," Western Culture writ large is the subject of *Wittgenstein's Mistress*, but "culture" as "unstable and subjective, a fading memory of 'baggage' that teases Kate with false connections, 'inconsequential perplexities,' and meaningless coincidences. It is a disorderly jumble where Euripides seems to have been influenced by Shakespeare, where Anna Akhmatova is a character in *Anna Karenina*, where William de Kooning wears a soccer jersey in Giotto's Renaissance studio" (245–6).

Yet in this madness there is method; in this jumble there is design – not so much that of the shape of individual subjectivity in the conventional sense, but more of a nominalistic cultural memory, as if the last woman on earth bore the impossible burden of being the singular repository of everything that could be recovered from the traces of human transience across the earth. What is recovered and remembered is entirely dependent on Kate's tics and obsessions, which suggests that the only guarantor to cultural history and authenticity is the individual receptor, analogous to the readers of the novel, who are compelled to trace out its indeterminate, dispersed patterns and connections in myriad ways largely dependent upon the specificities of each reader's intertextual memory, projections, associational logic, cultural repertoire. This version of the language philosopher Ludwig Wittgenstein's infamous first proposition in the *Tractatus Logico-Philosophicus* that "the world is all that is the case" – that reality as perceived and experienced is a subset of reality as it exists – is confirmed by Kate in such messages as: "Perhaps all such thoughts might very well fall into the same category as the thought that there is somebody at a window in a painting when there is nobody at the window in the painting, since I would appear to have verified that paintings are never basically what one thinks of them being either" (92). Kate, a painter herself, is intensely self-conscious about her capacity to remember facts, conversations, works of art, and encounters with other artists, to the degree that she constantly questions whether she actually did read this book, or meet that cultural celebrity, or is simply inserting figures who aren't really there into her "painting" of the cultural landscape. The elision between "the case" of reality and reality as composed by Kate is notable and often has humorous consequences; yet, the paradox the novel proposes is that Kate's message-assemblage is all that we have of the textual world entitled *Wittgenstein's Mistress*, and that we must make of it what we will, even though both the madness and method of reading it (and the analogous activity of accessing "culture," in general) necessarily involves misreading, misremembering, and fantasizing. Indeed, Markson suggests, this may be the motive for reading, and its burden – as if we were the last readers on earth.

Ben Marcus is the author of witty, surrealistic set-pieces that test the relation between form and meaning, language, and psychology. The imaginative reach that he exhibited in *The Age of Wire and String* (1996), where topics such as the weather, food, sleep, and society are rendered as sites or schemas in a language that moves erratically from the hallucinatory to the mathematical is extended in his first novel, *Notable American Women* (2002), which establishes him as one of the most compelling experimentalists of his generation. Framed by communications from a father, Michael Marcus, who identifies himself as not the "local father" of Ben Marcus but the embodiment of fatherhood as cannibalistic principle, and a mother, Jane Marcus, embodying maternality as a form of discipline, *Notable American Women* is a *Bildungsroman* and a parodic instruction manual that traces the life and death of language in an absurdly formalistic universe. For Ben Marcus, the author and protagonist, has been systematically raised in a gendered language regime where breath, wind, voice, and movement, associated with patriarchy, are "shushed" by ninja-like women who establish a new dominant order of stillness and silence.

Much of the humor of *Notable American Women*, which traces the history of this linguistic social revolution, arises from the assemblage of tests, systems, and inventions that have been developed by various factions to measure the formation of identity and the flux of language; one such device is the "home weather kit," developed by "Quiet Boy Bob Riddle," which is designed "to definitively prove that speech and possibly all mouth sounds disturb the atmosphere by introducing pockets of turbulence, eventually causing storms. By speaking into the tube that feeds the translucent-walled weather simulator … Riddle demonstrates the agitation of a calm air system" (87). This Rube Goldberg invention is a valuable item in a world that is politically divided between the party of speech and the party of silence, as is the "Speech Jacket," a "mouth harness" designed by Riddle "that limits its wearer to a daily quota of spoken language, beyond which he or she must remain silent until the next day, or else trigger a mild explosive that will destroy the mouth" (88). The materiality of voice and affect is registered in this bizarre conception as having effects on everything from the weather to the physical composition of the human body, which is "trained" under the elitist, matriarchal order of "the Silentists," led by the charismatic Jane Dark, to repress speech and emotion. We can regard this as a comic inversion of conventional psychological theory, which conceives the body as symptomatically registering repressions that are both revealed and displaced in language.

In part, *Notable American Women* is a satire on the notion of gendered language, at least as conceived in binary and parental terms: the fictional Jane Marcus who directs the fictional Michael Marcus on how to raise an increasingly unproductive fictional son, Ben Marcus, has the same name as the real Jane Marcus, a renowned feminist literary critic, who has a real son named Ben Marcus, the writer. But rather than being an absurdist autobiographical protest penned by the real Ben Marcus about how he was raised according to certain theories of mind and language (although it well could be this), *Notable American Women* might be viewed as a send-up of systematicity and control *tout court*, as well as hilarious extrapolation of categorical thinking when it is pushed beyond the borders of its conceptual limits. What would a world look like that is built upon the assumption that language and emotion are physical substances that can be manipulated and controlled through the imbibing of certain tonics or the use of strange implements? It would look like this:

> A female head liberation system (FLUSH) follows the theory that experiences, which may or may not cause an emotional response in women (we may never know), filter first through her head.
>
> If the head's hollow space (chub) is filled with materials like cloth, an ice Thompson, wood, or behavior putty (also known as action butter), then less life can enter, and perhaps fewer emotions will result. (116)

The novel depicts myriad similar materializations of the attempt to socially control thought, speech, reading, behavior, and emotion in a narrative of gender domination and child-rearing, and while the concretizations of these mechanisms are absurdist, they are also eerily familiar. *Notable American Women* thus offers a parodic, funhouse mirror reflection of a social order, like ours, founded upon binary assumptions about the mind, body, speech, and gender that appear to be bizarre and irrelevant, when viewed as instructed.

Magnifying Reality, Multiplying Genre

One of the most influential twentieth-century narrative theorists, the Russian formalist Mikhail Bakhtin, conceptualized the novel from its beginnings in the sixteenth century as a "bastard" genre that ceaselessly delegitimates other genres into its own heteroglot assemblage: "[t]he novel parodies other genres (precisely in their role as genres); it exposes the conventionality of their forms and language; it squeezes out some genres and incorporates others into its own peculiar structure, reformulating and re-accentuating them" (*Dialogic Imagination*, 5).

This historical notion of the novel as a cannibalistic genre finds expression in a number of contemporary novels whose "postmodernism" is marked by rapid movements through discursive levels and amongst multiple genres and subgenres. We encounter, for example, in Gilbert Sorrentino's encyclopedic *Mulligan Stew* (1979), parodic versions of almost every received form of narrative; as its title would indicate, the novel is a heterogeneous mixture of detective fiction, poetry, parodic takes on high modernist classics (in particular, Joyce's *Ulysses*), pulp fiction, cartoonish lampoons of postmodernist reflexivity (including scenes where Sorrentino's characters complain about being trapped in a novel by Gilbert Sorrentino), riddles and rebuses, diaries, letters, and satires upon authorial anxiety. The sheer heterogeneity and excess of works like *Mulligan Stew* has been described by critic Tom LeClair as evidence of the capacity of such novels to address "the size and scale of contemporary existence, how multiplicity and magnitude create new relations and new proportions among people and entities" (*Art of Excess*, 6). Though his discussion is limited to a handful of novels that have, in his view, achieved "mastery" by matching worldly with novelistic complexity, LeClair suggests more generally that the heterogeneity of contemporary fiction in novels that multiply genre and magnify reality is a strong imaginative means for coping with a reality that

Three Contemporary Encyclopedias

The confabulations that constitute the contemporary encyclopedic is most notably represented by Pynchon's *Gravity's Rainbow* and Gaddis's *The Recognitions*, as well as novels to be discussed by DeLillo (*Underworld*), Silko (*Almanac of the Dead*), and Gass (*The Tunnel*). Behind this impulse is the desire to incorporate the world's knowledge into a capacious narrative system. Three exceptional examples of post-1980 encyclopedic narratives include Alexander Theroux's *Darconville's Cat* (1981) and Joseph McElroy's *Women and Men* (1987) – both largely ignored masterpieces – and David Foster Wallace's *Infinite Jest* (1996), the crowning achievement of an exceptionally talented writer who died at age 46. *Darconville's Cat* is a dark-humor romance set in academia; a novel of obsessive desire and erudition, it is an anatomy of literary genres. *Women and Men* traverses an array of "disciplines," and interweaves dozens of stories that intersect in the lives of two Manhattan apartment-house neighbors who never meet. *Infinite Jest* takes place in a near-future North America where Canada, the United States, and Mexico have been fused into one nation and where the calendar has been reorganized to accord with the ascendancy of popular commodities. A Dickensian cast of characters cross paths and lines of communication in Wallace's parody of popular culture, local knowledge, and advertising.

seems ever-expanding in terms of encyclopedic "size and scale" (for more examples, see box on preceding page). In the works discussed in this section, I will observe how a number of post-1980 American novelists, microscopically or encyclopedically, weigh the scales of contemporary existence.

Nicholson Baker might argue that size and scale matter, but inversely from those novelists whom LeClair defines as achieving mastery through excess, for Baker, contemporary complexity and heterogeneity lie in the miniscule. Just as a microscope magnifies what cannot be seen with the naked eye, so Baker writes novels in which the overlooked objects elements of daily life, when brought into focus through an expansion of time, acquire an unforeseen significance. *Room Temperature* (1990) occurs over the time it takes a narrator to feed his infant daughter her bottle; *Vox* (1992) recounts a single phone-sex conversation between two strangers; *Checkpoint* (2004) takes up a single afternoon as it records a conversation between two friends, one of whom is planning to assassinate President George W. Bush. In each of these novels, common objects and commonplaces lead to surprising illuminations.

Baker's first novel, *The Mezzanine* (1988), remains one of his most compelling depictions of how the quotidian, when scrutinized, reveals a reflective complexity. Told in the first person, the novel occurs during the few minutes it takes for an office worker to ride up an escalator as he returns to work after his lunch hour and a brief excursion to buy shoelaces. The meticulous mnemonic logic of *The Mezzanine*'s narrator is on full display during his ride up the escalator. Scattered moments from childhood ("kid-memories"), conversations with fellow workers, his visit to the restroom and his shoelace-buying adventure, snapshots of brief moments in his relationship with a significant other identified as "L." – all evolve as the narrator reflects on the objects and histories that occupy his mind during the preceding lunch hour: the cultural history of straws from paper to plastic, shoelaces and the tying of shoes, paper cups, milk and the delivery of milk in childhood, vending machines, staplers, popcorn, earplugs, paper towels. Carrying his Penguin edition of the *Meditations* of Marcus Aurelius (along with this narrative fact, we are provided with the narrator's recollections of where he bought the book, his first reading of a Penguin book in childhood, the different kinds of Penguin editions and various logos they bear), the unnamed narrator engages in an associational mania that renders the value of particularity and the specific as the anchors of memory and identity.

An example of the narrator's associational habits occurs in one of the novel's many lengthy footnotes, a practice that requires a footnote explaining the importance of substantive footnotes in exploring the many specificities and byways of a topic. Concerned about the ratio of thought processes that began in childhood to "new thoughts" arising in adulthood, the narrator has just computed the age at which the percentage of "mature thoughts" will outweigh "childish thoughts"; he adds in a footnote that:

> I reached the conclusion as I was driving home in the dark ... I had been thinking that only after I had become a commuter had I noticed the way cigarette butts, flicked out narrowly opened windows by invisible commuters ahead of me, landed on the cold invisible road and cast out a small firework of tobacco sparks ... these cigarette sparks were the farewell explosions of such intimate items, still warm from people's lips and lungs, appearing just beyond your headlights and then washed out by them ... This had reminded me of how I used to open the window on car trips when I was little ... and I was wondering whether the people who tossed their cigarette butts out in the darkness did it simply because they preferred this to stubbing the cigarette out in their ashtray, and because they enjoyed the burst of cold fresh air from the quarter-opened window as they flicked it away, or whether they knew what moments of sublimity they were creating for the nonsmokers behind them ... Did they, with the addict's sentimentality and self-regard, associate this high-speed cremation and ash-scattering with the longer curve of their own life – "Hurled into the darkness in a blaze of glory," etc? I was turning these various thoughts, some of them new ones and some repeaters, around in my head, when the conclusion arrived. (58)

This is but one of dozens of the evocative associational chains forged in the narrator's memory, catalyzed by the perception of an object, word, or motion that would go unobserved by others, yet that, for him, is an opportunity for the release of the "sublime." For Baker, the associational and systematic scrutiny of the quotidian that comprises a methodology for reading the world in detail reveals both the excesses of the reality that we inhabit with all of its perishable commodities and processes, and the secreted materiality that hooks us into it. In the footnote reflecting on footnotes, the narrator states that "[f]ootnotes are the finer-suckered surfaces that allow tentacular paragraphs to hold fast to the wider reality of the library" (123). So too, *The Mezzanine* suggests, the common objects that inhabit our lives and memories, in their phenomenological specificity and capacity to generate commemorative linkages, hold us fast to a "wider reality" that can only be known through its particulars.

One of the terms Bakhtin develops in tracing the polyglot history of the novel is "carnivalesque," which refers to the novel's capacity to incorporate the world's diversity, contradictions, and extremes into the form of a narrative that, like a carnival, overturns social hierarchies and conventions and, thus, "renews the world" (*Rabelais*, 17). Certainly one of the main proponents of the postmodern carnivalesque is Robert Coover, whose 15 novels and collections of short fiction characteristically explode, mutate, and parody genres and types: the fairytale in *Pricksongs & Descants* (1969), the political novel in *The Public Burning* (1977), the social novel in *Gerald's Party* (1986), the western in *Ghost Town* (1998), pornography in *The Adventures of Lucky Pierre* (2002). *A Night at the Movies or, You Must Remember This* (1987) is advertised as short fiction, but it is also possible to regard this "night" as a novel-assemblage that parodies movie genres in its "Program" which runs progressively from "Previews of Coming Attractions" to "Adventure!," "Short Subjects," "Comedy!," an intermission, a cartoon, "Travelogue," "Musical Interlude," and "Romance!"

As we progress through the program, which takes place in an old-fashioned theater complete with a projectionist changing reels during the intermission, we read of a shadowy figure – the "midnight man" – stalking the movie palace; of a western shootout between a sheriff who is a cross between Gary Cooper and Don Knotts, and a Rabelaisian villain named Don Pedro; of Charlie Chaplin in a house of horrors; and of Rick and Ilse in wartime Casablanca, engaged in orgiastic intercourse rendered in pornographic detail. Coover's pastiche operates on one level to parody standard cinematic representations in order to show the degree to which they rely on assumptions and expectations that, slightly torqued, can lead to comic transformations: the Cooper-esque sheriff walks in on the stereotypical girlfriend/saloon mistress to discover her naked and masturbating, a scene that only adds to his bumbling demeanor and impotence; the "Perils of Pauline" figure depicted in "Intermission" experiences several internal movies at the concession stand in the movie lobby as she is kidnapped by gangsters, goes over Niagara Falls in a barrel, becomes a castaway on a South Sea island, is abducted into a harem, and finally is pitched back into her seat in the theater by a gigantic claw where she awaits the screening of the next item on the program; in "Charlie in the House of Rue," the violence underlying slapstick comedy comes to the fore as the Chaplineseque protagonist is beaten in the kitchen by an enormous fat man bearing a beheaded rabbit.

But beyond the disassembly of stereotypical narrative representations that reveals the innate absurdity, lust, and brutality underlying them, Coover is interested in showing the degree to which change and mutability are at the foundation of a reality that is only superficially perceived as solid and stable. In "Lap Dissolves," a "short" in which generic scenes continuously transmogrify into each other, the daughter of surreal family out of an Andy Hardy film testifies that:

> "I had the weirdest dream last night ... I was in this crazy city where everything kept changing into something else all the time. A house would turn into a horse just as you walked out of it or a golf course would take off and fly or a street would become a dinner table under your feet. You might lean against a wall and find yourself out on the edge of a cliff, or climb into a car that turned out to be the lobby of a movie theater." (84)

The ceaseless alterations that occur throughout *A Night at the Movies*, where everything changes into something else all the time, accumulate to underscore Coover's estimate of reality – here and throughout his work – as a "frame job," a set of received cultural perspectives and assumptions that provides the illusion of a social order which is annihilated when the ease with which comedy can turn into horror, and vice versa, is registered. By setting an explicit sexual encounter against the backdrop of World War II genocide in "You Must Remember This," or juxtaposing Ozzie-and-Harriet American domesticity against a scene right out of *Night of the Living Dead*, Coover suggests the extent to which commonplace "reality" comprises images and representations that come to us from film, bearing cruelly and hilariously contradictory assumptions about identity, family, desire, and the "human." Fueling it all is what Coover, in a blurb for Stephen Wright's *Going Native* (1994), to be discussed later in this section, terms "the monster image feed" of contemporary culture, "where there is no longer any membrane between screen and life." So, too, *A Night at the Movies* collapses the relation between screen and life, suggesting that a welter of mutating and dissolving images is what now constitutes history, memory, and self.

A Night at the Movies works as a narrative movie; it represents the visual through the verbal, and in so doing, reflects on the degree to which contemporary narrative is affected by the ubiquitous presence of images and our immersion in visual culture. Increasingly, contemporary writers have brought written narrative and visual genres into contact, visibly so in the novels of the German novelist W. G. Sebald, which combine maps and photographs with story and memoir, or in the United States, the work of Johanna Drucker and Steve Tomasula, which combine multiple narrative genres with drawn images and typography. The 1,500 year-old tradition of illuminated manuscripts and of illustrated novels since the eighteenth century informs these works, but they are equally informed by the rise of the graphic novel (a vital genre of illustrated narrative that would require lengthy consideration outside the scope of this book) and the interpenetration of literary and visual media to be found therein, as well as in cartoons and comic strips, and the various subgenres of comics, animated films, and graphic novels such as anime and manga that permeate contemporary culture.

A number of recent novels do not materially portray the interrelation between the literary and the visual, but do so on the level of story, setting, and theme. Michael Chabon's *The Amazing Adventures of Kavalier & Clay* (2000) and Jonathan Lethem's *The Fortress of Solitude* (2003) are notable examples that conjoin visuality, American popular culture, and the history of the comics with the narrative form of the *Bildungsroman* in explorations of contemporary identities affected by transitions and shifts in a rapidly changing visual culture, and how the comics, in particular, have served to shape the perception of reality. But before these there was Susan Daitch's *The Colorist* (1989), a novel that portrays the relationship between Julie, who colors the panels of a comic-book series entitled *Electra*, and Eamonn Archer, a leftist photographer who specializes in *verité* shots of disaster victims and those living on the margins of society. Told from Julie's perspective, the novel is also about the decline and transformation of the *Electra* series, whose title character is an alien-born genetic marvel with "powers … signified by rays, sometimes arcing out of the frame": "she isn't a borderline parody like *Wonder Woman*, not a parasite like *Spiderwoman*. No one at Fantômes would have used the word ideology, but Eamonn said they made Electra into the comic-book version of the Holy Virgin Mary, even though she didn't wear much clothing" (27). When the publisher of the series decides to cancel it as a cost-saving measure, Julie and her friend, Laurel, the series "inker" (who draws the outlines of each panel in black and white) take on a series of temporary jobs while keeping Electra alive in a series of scripts and sketches that they collaboratively produce. Meanwhile, Eamonn moves in and out of Julie's life as he takes on various photographic assignments that may involve larger political conspiracies.

The interactions between the novel's principal characters – all caught up in exploring the extension of the visual imagination into the social order – allow for the emergence of the stark contradictions underlying the omnipresence of images in contemporary culture. Looking at a cover photograph of civilian Greek women who have been hanged during World War II, Julie observes that:

> [i]n the photograph, all the women are young; they are all hanging from the same tree, as if they had grown from it. The expression on their faces is so horrible, the registration of terror is absolute. They are dressed as if they had just been taken from their houses. ... The magazine was in a window of a bookstore on East Sixteenth Street. The store was between two newly renovated and very expensive restaurants full of flowers, paintings, real and *faux marbre* panels. From the street you can see into one kitchen where young men in white grill marlin flown in from Hawaii, or cut smoked goose into paper-thin slices. (152–3)

The description of the image which stands in jarring relation to its surrounds – the temporal and spatial dislocations rendered by the enjambment of the scene of genocide with the scene of gentrification – underscore the relation between content and context that Daitch explores in *The Colorist*. On the one hand, the image speaks for itself; yet, unlike Julie's description of the comic-book world of *Electra* where "[t]here was no conflict between word and image ... Artificial and highly stylized, there were no contradictions between what was said and what was seen" (58), there is most certainly a "conflict" between the image of the women hanged in wartime and the sight of contemporary gourmet excess – a conflict of image set against image, a collision of contexts that produces a discursive relation between what is literally seen and what can be said about it. *The Colorist* suggests that the comics reflect a desire for the simultaneity of word and image, object and language (the language of color), posited as a parallel reality that can only survive within its generic confines. When Electra is brought to earth in Julie's and Laurel's attempt to prolong her life even if the serial in which she appears has been canceled, she loses her powers and becomes afflicted with the kinds of problems from which comic superheroes never suffer: lack of food and money; entrapment in specific temporal and spatial locations. The image of the superhero, taken out of its generic context and put into another, becomes subject to an "unmitigated sense of dislocation and deracination" (171). The novel's dozens of imagistic dislocations – Electra homeless in an abandoned movie theater; a black-and-white photograph of empty Coca-Cola bottles (looking like an imitation of a Warhol painting) that will be used by Derry schoolchildren for Molotov cocktails – suggest the power of context in determining the meaning that can be derived from the image, and the capacity for decontextualization in a contemporary reality flooded with images overlapping with each other and vying for our attention. In the novel, competing modes of organizing and representing reality – categorical, geometrical, photographic, narrative, graphic – contend for primacy, but their utter inseparability and partiality suggest that, for Daitch, these contestations result in the forging of the world's hybridity.

As mentioned previously, Coover's notion of contemporary reality as a "monster image feed" is part of a blurb for Stephen Wright's *Going Native*, a postmodern road novel that takes us through a chaotic series of adjacent and conflicting mediations.[11] Wright is the author of several novels and stories that portray the absurdity and surrealism of contemporary American life, including *Meditation in Green* (1983), an hallucinatory account of a Vietnam veteran's memories of war, and *M31: A Family Romance* (1989), a send-up of the American heartland involving alien abductions, murder, and frenetic religiosity. His most recent novel, *The Amalgamation Polka* (2006), portrays the adventures of an eccentric family in mid-nineteenth-century America and their horrendous involvement with slavery, eugenics, and the Civil War. *Going Native* is a loosely-related series of vignettes involving a drug-crazed suburban couple, a homicidal hitchhiker, a runaway and her boyfriend, a voyeur who makes amateur pornographic movies, a woman who works in a Las Vegas wedding chapel, and a New Age couple working in the film industry who have just returned from a "explorer tourist" trek through Borneo. Connecting this odd assortment of characters is the shadowy figure of Wylie, an appropriately named "roadrunner" who is in flight from a mundane domesticity and randomly driving across the highways of American in a stolen Ford "Galaxie." As Wylie moves westward, he transforms himself from abandoning husband, to car thief, to kidnapper, to serial killer; the motels, crossroads, and desert highways of Route 66 America are points on the map of a violent, alienated landscape that serves as the backdrop for Wright's black-humor version of contemporary mobile identities and the prototypical American quest "to be all that you want to be."

The format of *Going Native* allows Wright to satirize any number of tabloid cultural manifestations – reality TV, yuppies, bondage and domination, designer drugs, Las Vegas, serial killers, the omnipresence of pornography, bikers, tourism, the road – in the service of presenting a portrait of postmodern identity *in extremis*. In the descriptions of the novel's eccentric characters and their bizarre plans and dreams, Wright plays upon familiar tropes of identity as mutable, simulative, and fragmented: the hitchhiker is covered with tattoos offering "an unexpected jungle of pure design, spirals and knots, mazes and mandalas, interwoven and overlapped in a deliberate thwarting of the desire for representation (81); the pornographer, named Perry, has "spent the majority of his years (twenty-seven of 'em so far, rings on a tree he honestly expected to be chain-sawed for pulp before producing any decent shade) attempting with about six meager ounces of Perry-essence to fill a ten-gallon mold of a half-imagined figure somewhere east of Dean and north of Elvis" (125); the filmmakers, Amanda and Drake, undertake a dangerous, if exoticized journey to the jungles of Borneo, where they attempt to "become native" in order to find "authentic" life, somewhere on the planet: "[t]hey were good Americans after all, they wanted to lose their entangling selves" (216). These self-constructions, like all of the characters in the novel, perform as if they were reflexive entities in the ongoing movie of contemporary American culture, representations of representation in search of a vestigial authenticity. Wylie serves both as the connective element in the multi-genre serial narratives of *Going Native* (partaking of elements of the adventure novel and the quest romance, as well as film noir, the western, and biker movies) and as the limiting factor who, through a final act of violence, punctures the simulacrum that constitutes the reality to be traversed by the novel's mobile identities. Near the novel's end, Wyle enters the home of Amanda and Drake, who are hosting an ersatz "Indonesian" dinner party, and murders the couple and their friends in a Manson-like frenzy. As the embodiment of random terror and mortality, Wyle represents the dark underside of the fantasy of mobile, "de-centered" identity, itself a simulation nourished by the "image feed" of contemporary culture; his serial violence is but the symptomatic extreme of the notion that reality is a movie set where one is entitled to perform to the fullest degree one's fantasy of the self. With *Going Native*, Wright takes his place as a premier postmodern satirist who exposes the mortal conditions of contemporaneity, even while, narratively, reveling in its multiplicity and expansiveness.

Shelley Jackson is regarded, along with Stuart Moulthrop and Michael Joyce, as one of the pioneers of "hypertext," the form of narrative experimentation that uses computer technology to embed links between discrete elements of a fiction such that a reader can "jump" in nonlinear fashion and at will from one part to another, thus interactively constructing his or her own story from a textual compilation provided by the author. With the expansion of the internet, interactive narrative that engages entire communities of authors – from participatory blogs to *Second Life* – has become a widespread and familiar mode of cultural engagement. *Patchwork Girl* (1995), *My Body* (1997), and *The Doll Games* (with Pamela Jackson, 2001) constitute Jackson's hypertext projects thus far; she is also the author of two children's novels, a collection of stories (*The Melancholy of Anatomy*, 2002), and an ongoing project launched in 2003 entitled *Skin,* a work comprising the images of words tattooed on, currently, the bodies of 2,095 volunteers. Jackson's first print novel, *Half Life* (2006), is an episodic journey through the lives of its protagonists, Nora and Blanche Olney, who are conjoined twins, or "twofers," in a world where those who were formerly considered isolated "freaks of nature" have formed into communities and political groups that advocate for rights and equality for alternative humans. As critic Steven Shaviro states, although *Half Life* occurs in a more traditional medium than most of Jackson's other work, it reflects "another way to explore the same ramifying conjunction of flesh and language, or of desire and disappointment, or of connectedness and singularity, that has always been Jackson's subject" ("Geek Love," n.p.). A pastiche of poems, songs, memoir, drawings, stories, lists, Venn diagrams, and selections from the "Siamese Twins

Reference Manual," the novel portrays the twins' childhood (they are conjoined at mid-spine, and thus a body with two each of arms, legs, heads, and hearts) and Nora's quest in adulthood to separate herself from Blanche, who has been in a coma-like state for 15 years, but who has recently shown signs of coming back to life. This odd premise allows Jackson not only to explore questions of the body and identity (are we one, or two, or more?) but also the relationship between "normality" and alterity, binary and fuzzy logic, kind (genre) and mutation, biology and politics. One of the most inventive works of recent years, *Half Life* "speaks unresolvable multiplicities with one voice" ("Geek Love," n.p.) in its depiction of the unity and separability of identity.

As children, Nora and Blanche have played with an antique dollhouse that has been passed down through several generations; they have – at least in fantasy – communicated with animals and taken on animal forms; they build a "dead animal zoo" comprising animal carcasses and insects they have scavenged in the desolate landscape around their home in the Nevada desert; growing up, they romp through a former nuclear test site which has been constructed in the just-off world of *Half Life* as the "proving ground of American sadness," where "the need for a national activity of penance" in a nation "saddened by Hiroshima and Nagasaki" has led to "a despondent American government commencing hostilities against itself": "[f]or three years, they hammered a sparsely populated part of the Nevada desert with the most powerful bombs in existence" (225). Inhabiting a world built on the principle of conjoined opposites – as evident in the sociopolitical order of the Cold War where the USSR and the United States are fatally locked into the doctrines of "mutually-assured destruction" as it is in the Nora's and Blanche's body – the consciousness named Nora decides that it is time to become only herself, which means murdering her unconscious sister by having her head removed via a radical medical procedure that allows "twofers" to become "newly singles." Yet the rhizomic plot of the novel – a stew of science fiction, political thriller, diary, social novel, fantasy, and satire – leads not to separation but to Nora's unification with Blanche as an entity (a writer) whose parts are indistinguishable from each other. This new being, which exists scriptively as the novel we are reading, suggests that for Jackson the assemblage body/identity/writing is "neither singular nor plural," a concept that "presents a number of problems for the state"

(136), though by the end of the novel the "neither/nor" has changed to "both/and": Nora/Blanche is transformed into a corporeal, authorial, political identity that is inseparable from itself, even as it is composed of a myriad of differences marked in memory and writing. In its conflation of mutable textual and bodily identities, *Half-Life* offers a useful segue from postmodern fictions of magnification and multiplicity into the novels to be considered next, where identity as trial and process is written into the narrative record.

Part III

Becoming Identities

From the Cartesian "cogito ergo sum" ("I think, therefore I am") which initiated the mapping of subjectivity as a product of consciousness in the seventeenth century, to Rimbaud's "je est un autre" ("I am an other"), which served as a calling card for modern and postmodern conceptions of identity as a continuous negotiation between self and other, the representation of identity in narrative has increasingly become reflective of and reflexive about the contested territory of the "self." In the twentieth century, as Erich Kahler has argued, the modern novel has been marked by its "inward turn" toward the individual subject. The exemplars of "high modernism" – James Joyce's *Ulysses* (1922), Virginia Woolf's *Mrs. Dalloway* (1925), or D. H. Lawrence's *Women in Love* (1920) – while fully engaging the social orders in which their protagonists dwell, focus on the psychologies and interiorities of complex individuals who are rendered as "subjects in process" through the deployment of techniques such as "stream of consciousness," where interior monologues that run for dozens of pages record the fleeting, unspoken thoughts of characters as they progress from moment to moment.[12] Stating that "the postmodern spirit lies coiled within the great corpus of modernism – the works of Proust, Mann, and Joyce, Yeats, Rilke, and Eliot, Strindberg, O'Neill, and Pirandello," Ihab Hassan suggests that the modernist inward turn of narrative has eventuated in the multiple and contradictory notions of identity to be found in "postmodern" works which portray identity as both singular and plural, "embracing continuity and discontinuity," a heterogeneous bundling of motivations, affects, and internalities (*Dismemberment of Orpheus*, 139; 265).

Contemporary American novels, from those that deploy the psychological realism of a Norman Mailer to those that exemplify the experiments in form, style, and language of the "high postmodernists," are replete with representations of identity that run the gamut from portrayals of "self" as an achievable singularity to viewing "it" as a schizoid multiplicity. No chronology or mapping of the adventures of identity in contemporary American fiction, nor any categorical division of individual novels according to school, epoch, or "ism," could possibly be responsive to the complex mixture of social force, linguistic process, and imaginative line of flight that goes into the making of identity for many contemporary writers. The first of John Updike's four "Rabbit" novels, *Rabbit Run* (1960), which initiates Updike's portrayal of a continuous, existential "core" identity living amidst vast social changes across four decades, was published just a year after William S. Burroughs's *Naked Lunch* (1959), first among many for the rendering of fragmented identity that Hassan defines as at the apogee of the trajectory running from modernism to postmodernism. In the space of a few years, postmodern avant-gardists such as Donald Barthelme are representing identity as a collage of historical bits, cultural practices, affects, and parts of speech in the stories of *Unspeakable Practices, Unnatural Acts* (1968), while writers such as N. Scott Momaday in *House Made of Dawn* (1968), Toni Morrison in *The Bluest Eye* (1970), and Rudolpho Anaya in *Bless Me, Ultima* (1972) are concerned with establishing the coherence of characters just on the verge of achieving identity in the first place, much less anticipating its fragmentation.[13] Like the body of contemporary American fiction itself, the portrayal of identity in the contemporary American novel is inevitably heterogeneous, occurring on several plateaus at the same time, even within the same novel. Walker Percy's *The Moviegoer* (1960) is exemplary in this regard: a recounting of an existentialist "journey to selfhood" undertaken by the protagonist, Binx Bolling, on a peripatetic quest through New Orleans for the meaning of life in the face of mortality, the novel nevertheless verges on postmodern notions of the world as simulacrum and identity as linguistic sign with its portrayal of Binx at the movies, finding "himself" in the endless unreeling of images on a two-dimensional screen.

In considering portrayals and formations of identity in the contemporary American novel since 1980, whether writers choose to engage in traditionally realist or radically experimental modes of writing, or to locate their work somewhere in the vast spectrum of possibilities in between, they are all affected by the dramatic literary and intellectual shifts of the 1960s and 1970s. Intellectually, the "explosion of theory" commenced with the 1966 "Structuralist Controversy" symposium at Johns Hopkins University and the subsequent widespread dissemination of poststructuralist and deconstructionist theories (largely coming from Europe) in the United States. Jacques Derrida, the name most prominently associated with these movements, spent a lifetime developing a mutable theory of identity as founded upon an intensely complex relation and negotiation with the "other" through language. Much of what was occurring during this period in the realm of theory has resonances with what was occurring in literary postmodernism; at the same time, another explosion was going on – the "explosion of the canon" that corresponded to the proliferation of ethnic, women's, gay, and lesbian literatures in the United States and the advent of multiculturalism. Correspondingly, the vast social changes that were taking place following the inauguration of John. F. Kennedy in January, 1961 – especially the Civil Rights, Black Power, Feminist, and Gay Rights movements – helped to generate a vigorous demand for the wider publication, reading, and teaching of literature by underrepresented people that explored the contours of historically suppressed identities. The two strands are intimately related: the alterity and "otherness" of identity variously discerned in poststructuralist theories is clearly analogous to the exploration of other selves and other lives to be found in a new literary canon committed to cultural pluralism.[14] In this chapter, I will discuss post-1980 American novels that pursue the question of identity within and beyond the terms provided by these precedents.

Reinventing Character

The element of fiction most closely aligned with the notion of identity is that of character; indeed, the two are often confused with each other. But "character" is different from "identity" in that the former signifies the latter, just as a sign on the roadway signifies the presence of a nearby town. Character is, in essence, the collection of words and signs that gesture toward a fictional embodiment of identity; as E. M. Forster famously suggested, characters in fiction can be "flat" or "round," which is not a distinction between stereotypical and psychologically complex characters, but between characters "constructed round a single idea or quality" and those who are "capable of surprising in a convincing way" (*Aspects of the Novel*: 67; 78). Forster's character binary may be overly reductive, but it indicates the notion of character as inferring, rather than embodying identity as an assemblage of motives and affects. Forster was conceptualizing character in fiction at a moment when modernist writers were developing new strategies for capturing the psychological densities of identity; in the wake of postmodernism, as they reinvent the character of subjects in process, novelists such as Paul Auster, Joanna Scott, William Gaddis, and Lynn Tillmann have shown new ways in which the ground is constantly shifting under identities in quest of sign, voice, and form.

For many, Paul Auster is the signature novelist of what Jeremy Green has termed "late postmodernism." Following in the wake of Nabokov, or Barth, or Handke, Auster writes with a canny awareness of how the self has been conceived as a sign or linguistic process by these authors, and combines it with a Kafka-like literalism in portraying the lives of characters in quest *of* signs in the world that will authenticate their identities. Auster's protagonists typically wander through a wilderness of proliferating signs (even if the setting is Manhattan) looking for indications of their fate; often, as in *The Music of Chance* (1990) or *The Book of Illusions* (2002), what they encounter – the random and the accidental – become converted after the fact into the markers of an inevitable destiny, a fatal history. Often in Auster's novels, the reading of a stray text (that is, a legible collection of signs that enable varied interpretations) inspires the protagonist to act, as if the world were a vast library which one browses at random in order to find the one text that corresponds with the discovered "self": thus, in *Moon Palace* (1989), Marco Stanley Fogg peruses a library of 1,492 books in an apartment left to him by his uncle, searching for indications of how he is to proceed through life. Will Marco be a Marco Polo or a Christopher Columbus who discovers a new continent in the country of the interior, or will he simply be a failed reader who vanishes into the margins? Auster's novels are replete with texts of all kinds – letters, notebooks, novels within novels, pocket litter, advertisements, and street signs – such that, as suggested by the title of *Travels in the Scriptorium* (2007), where the paths of several of the characters from previous novels cross, reading a novel by Paul Auster is in many ways parallel to being a character in an Auster novel. Consonant with the implicit notion in his novels that reading is an act of literary detection, several of Auster's protagonists are detectives – Peter Aaron of *Leviathan* (1992), probing the mystery of a friend's death in an explosion; Daniel Quinn in *City of Glass* (1985), a writer of detective novels who poses as detective himself in response to a misplaced phone call; or Mr. Blank of *Travels in the Scriptorium*, an old man suffering from amnesia who awakens in a locked room to a succession of visitors who claim to be his operatives reporting to him about crimes and mysteries for which he seems to bear some responsibility. Equally, many of Auster's protagonists are writers in the process of authoring the text we are reading, the acts of reading and writing, inscribing and deciphering, become one.

Character as reader, reader as character in a realm made up of alphabetic characters: this has been the reflexive watermark of Auster's fiction from the beginning, as it is for a slightly older generation of writers often characterized as "postmodern" such as Borges, Barth, and Nabokov, but Auster writes without Borges's speculativeness, Barth's prolixity, or Nabokov's encyclopedic erudition. Auster's library-worlds are more hieroglyphic and allegorical in nature as they depict the wanderings of protagonists through scriptural jungles and contemporary babels. His first novel, the prototypical *City of Glass* (1985), later part of the *New York Trilogy* which also includes *Ghosts* (1986) and *The Locked Room* (1986), remains one of his most widely appreciated works. *City of Glass* is a novel of Manhattan as an "alphabet city," a labyrinth of streets and signs through which the writer-protagonist wanders, having assumed the role of detective, as he follows a man recently released from a mental institution at the behest of his son. The novel is replete with doubled names and identities. "Peter Stillman" is the name of both the father and son in question; "William Wilson" is the pseudonym under which Daniel Quinn writes his detective novels – readers familiar with the work of one of the first detective writers, Edgar Allan Poe, will recognize Quinn's nom de plume as the title of Poe's story about a split personality; "Paul Auster" is the name Quinn assumes as a detective having been mistaken for the "real" Paul Auster the detective, as distinct from Paul Auster the writer, who Quinn encounters late in the novel. Indeed, Quinn bears at least five names in the novel: his own, his authorial pseudonym, the name of the protagonist in his pulp detective novels ("Max Work"), the name of the author of *City of Glass*, and that of "Henry Dark," a fictional character invented by Stillman. As Quinn pursues Stillman over several weeks, he discovers that what appears to be aimless wandering through the streets of New York is in fact, when mapped out, the tracing-out of the words "Tower of Babel" over dozens of city blocks. These details give some indication of the convolutions of the novel's plot, which unravels as the solution to a mystery of the same name, much like a joke with its punch line as its only content. As the clue, "Tower of Babel," suggests, the novel is about the proliferation of languages and meanings and the paradoxical quest for the single language and meaning that unites everything. Quinn fails to solve the mystery of Stillman's intentions: when Stillman disappears, eventually discovered to have committed suicide, Quinn assumes his identity and inhabits his empty apartment, disappearing himself after several months, only to leave behind a red notebook discovered by the writer, Paul Auster, and the unnamed narrator of the novel, who "has followed the red notebook as closely as I could" in penning the novel we are reading (158). As a character, then, Quinn is "nothing but" a polysemous text, an assemblage of borrowed names and pseudonyms, and a cipher of the mystery in which he is the final, vanished clue. In *City of Glass*, Auster suggests the degree to which identity is at once a mystery and a solution that comes about through the act of reading ourselves into and out of existence where we are the best, or worst decipherers of our own destinies.

For Auster, character is a cipher and a process of deciphering. For Joanna Scott, the author of seven novels and two short story collections that capture the intricate and idiosyncratic relationalities of identities and environments, character is an assemblage of voices overheard:

> as I'm starting out on a project, I can't tell … if it will keep generating its own future … It partly has to do with the independence of the characters, the strength of voice. If I feel there is a distinct voice that deserves to keep speaking, that has a music of its own … then I feel myself seduced by the voice I've created, but that I feel I'm hearing from elsewhere. (Burns, "Off the Page")

In such novels as *Tourmaline* (2002), about the incommunicable interiorities of a family living in the shadow of a father's obsession,

Make Believe (2000), told through the consciousness of a 4-year-old boy who is the subject of a custody battle, and *Arrogance* (1990), a biographical fiction about the mental turmoil of the Austrian expressionist painter, Egon Schiele, Scott, a winner of the prestigious MacArthur Fellowship, reveals herself to be one of the most compelling writers of her generation in rendering character as voice, instinct as personality.

The Manikin (1996) bears the name of the estate of Harold Caxton, a famous taxidermist regarded as "the Henry Ford of natural history" (9), who has built a taxidermy-supply empire with the dawn of the twentieth century. The rambling manor, exuding a gothic atmosphere of gloominess and decay, is filled with dozens of stuffed exotic animals and a few humans – Caxton's aging widow, her lazy, itinerant son, Hal, and a handful of servants who inhabit the estate and the landscape as natural creatures rather than, like the owners of The Manikin, merely temporary residents. Appositely, the ownership of the estate is the primary "plot" element in a novel of shifting perspectives, dreams, and moods: just before her sudden death from a stroke, Mrs. Caxton changes the will so that the bulk of the estate goes to charity, leaving her son with only the zoological collection of stuffed animals his father has assembled over a lifetime. Hal, determined to contest the will, takes possession of The Manikin and proceeds to court Ellen Griswold, the housekeeper, but he is driven out of the household by the servants when Peg, Ellen's daughter, tells the household that the salacious Hal assaulted her as a teenager – this is both a truth and a lie, as Hal did forcibly kiss Peg when she was 16, but did not rape her, as she claims. Ellen's lie, however, is her mother's salvation, and as the "servants" lay claim to the estate through squatters' rights, they create an ephemeral estate of their own, one in which the contesting forces of permanence and change, home and migration, nature and culture are embodied in the multiple voices of the servants as they collectively narrate the history of The Manikin and its secrets.

One of the primary characters of the novel is the house itself with its museum of zoological oddities, representing the human attempt to dominate nature and preserve mastery over against the ravages of social and environmental change. The repressive silence and rigidity of Mrs. Caxton is countered in the novel by the voices of the collective servants, alive with desire, registering the effort of human labor and attuned to the myriad specificities of seasonal change and the patterns of struggling life. Like the servants, the house has a life of its own given over to time and circumstance as it slowly decays:

> Take away the hum of the refrigerator, the click and rush of forced-air heat controlled by a thermostat, the buzz of telephone wires, the distant whine of a highway, and the dense silence of a country house in winter crushes against the ears with the deafening pressure of many fathoms of water. ... And this is the paradox: that an enclosed space could be so deafening and silent at the same time, so full and so empty, as if inhabited by ghosts. Perhaps our minds conjure spirits because we cannot stand such complete silence. And maybe all of the stuffed animals in the world – not just the ones with real hides and feathers but the nursery animals as well, and dolls with glass eyes, statues too, and portraits, photographs, postage stamps, coins embossed with images of monarchs and presidents, bas-relief heads, gargoyles, masks, puppets, wooden angels, and anything that never closes its eyes in sleep – maybe all of them are made not to be seen in daylight but to exist unseen at night, to fill the emptiness as nocturnal animals fill the woods, invisibly, so that there is no interior without life." (85–6)

The complex logic of Scott's novel is that life is noisy and collective, yet given over to mortality, and that all human attempts to preserve life against death – exemplified in taxidermy, the archive and the museum, the engraved image – unfailingly register death's rigidity and the artifice of conservation. In *The Manikin*, identity *is* character in that it is stamped by and vocalizes our instinctual, migratory passage through structures and spaces that house experience. But, for Scott, such passages are momentary and ephemeral, only "caught" by the mechanisms of writing, photography, taxidermy, and only then in the form of a pretense of life.

William Gaddis's big, talky, encyclopedic novels embody some of the most significant writing of the postwar era. Often perceived as "difficult" or abstruse, and, seemingly – after *The Recognitions* (1955), a monumental, Joycean novel about art, forgery, and commerce – comprising disconnected dialogues between characters who are sometimes unnamed (the reader must infer their identities), or telephonic conversations where only one principle is "heard" (the reader must infer what the other speaker is saying), Gaddis's novels make severe demands, but offer the inestimable rewards of engagement with intensively dialogic narratives. For Gaddis, who had spent a decade writing speeches for corporate executives, character is voice, and all of Gaddis's novels after *The Recognitions* portray dozens of characters in conversations replete with interruption and contingency where personal experience, rumor, business, art, politics, the news, the unheard, and the overheard are fragmentally interwoven. *JR* (1975), a hilarious satire upon American capitalism and Wall Street, stars an 11-year-old financial genius who builds a financial empire from his "office" in the public telephone booth near his school. In the more sober *Carpenter's Gothic* (1985), domesticity, religious fundamentalism, and American colonialism are examined for their fatal interconnections. *A Frolic of His Own* (1994) satirizes the legal establishment in the absurdist story of Oscar Crease, who engages in a series of litigations (including suing himself) in a failed attempt to establish his own legitimacy as an authorial identity. In all of Gaddis's fiction, there is an extended reflection on the relation between art and the social order in which the former both reflects and is impeded by the latter.

At just under 270 pages, *Carpenter's Gothic* is an uncharacteristically "short" novel for Gaddis, yet it records multiple conversations between dozens of characters, the principles being Elizabeth Booth, a housewife and heir to her father's mining empire; her abusive husband, Paul, a manipulative "media consultant" who attempts to make a killing using the promise of his wife's resources in order to promote the career of an evangelist, the Reverend Elton Ude; Liz's brother, Billie Vorakers, a beloved drifter caught up in the various conspiracies and failed game plans that abound in the novel; and Mr. McCandless, the owner of the house Paul and Liz rent in upstate New York, a professional writer with a shady past as a CIA agent operating in Africa. What happens in the novel is less a matter of event than the evolution of a discursive universe in which scattered, lengthy conversations between various parties, letters, notes, newspaper headlines, documents, and manuscripts reveal the interconnections of the personal and the political, and the complicities of domestic consumerism at home and political turmoil abroad. As in *The Manikin*, the house itself is a figure for the world these characters inhabit: built in the style of Victorian mansions imitating "medieval Gothic" but with the humbler materials available to nineteenth-century American craftsmen, the "carpenter's gothic" domicile of *Carpenter's Gothic* is "a patchwork of conceits, borrowings, deceptions, the inside a hodgepodge of good intentions like one last ridiculous effort at something worth doing even on this small a scale" (227–8).

Like the house, Liz, living in an environment of fraudulence and deception where self-serving religious propaganda trumps news of a continent (Africa) ever on the verge of disaster and used as a Cold War proxy by opposed superpowers, can be defined as an interiority replete with good intentions but incapable of action. As Gaddis depicts her, Liz is a receptacle for noise: the ear on the other end of conversations where her interlocutors can't stop talking about themselves, she is treated by her husband like an incompetent receptionist, a mere medium for the novel's hundreds of messages and announcements. Liz is a cipher for the world as such in Gaddis's fiction, where business, politics, nation-building, and conspiracy all proceed by virtue of entangled networks of communication that transmit more noise than information, and that purchase a vestigial domestic order at the cost of global chaos. An unlikely and ironic heroine, demeaned by her husband, tossed aside by McCandless after their brief affair, and murdered by an intruder in the house (though we are compelled to read her death as part of a conspiracy involving McCandless), Liz embodies the temporary interruption of the mundane that one encounters sporadically in Gaddis's hyperdiscursive novels, a space of reflection when human and mechanical noises cease and what is seen and heard is a kind of bare reality, such as her vision of a bird flying into a fall sunset at the novel's opening or the sounds of a tree during a storm outside Liz's bedroom window. But even such instances in *Carpenter's Gothic* pass quickly into their mediated opposites, as the bird in her sightline becomes a muddy rag flung between a group of boys playing baseball, and the image of a tree merges with that on her television screen depicting a scene from the film version of *Wuthering Heights.* Liz is heir to an empire founded upon conceit and deception, as well as the unwitting victim of the machinations that go along with the building of nations, cults, and empires in Gaddis's sardonic view of the social order. As a character, she is a kind of absence or caesura amidst the novel's noise; she is, to borrow from Frost, "a momentary stay against confusion," but with the emphasis placed on the instantaneousness of the "momentary," and with an ironic acknowledgement of the "stay" or "stop," as in an organ or piano, registering but a pause in the discordant flow of worldly music.

The singular voice of "Helen," the brilliant and quirky protagonist of Lynne Tillman's *American Genius: A Comedy* (2006), is nearly all that is heard in this extended, digressive monologue of a young woman – a former teacher and "designer of objects" – who is voluntarily confined in an institution that could be anything from a sanitarium to an artist's colony. And yet, this single voice is really many, as Helen reveals the reach of her obsessions, memories, and encounters with remarkable personalities ranging from the Polish cosmetologist whom she visits regularly before her "incarceration" to such characters in the place of her current habitation as "The Count," who marks the watershed moment of his life with the finding of a Breguet timepiece on the banks of the Seine, "Birdman," who anonymously sends Helen the exotic travel postcards he has collected, or "The Magician," who holds séances in the institution's common room. *American Genius* is Tillman's fifth novel, following upon *Haunted Houses* (1987), about three troubled women growing up in and out of the New York suburbs; *Motion Sickness* (1991), recounting the travels of a young woman in Europe; *Cast in Doubt* (1992), which depicts the relationship between an elderly gay writer and a young woman on the Greek island of Crete; and *No Lease on Life* (1998), which follows a day in the life of an "ordinary" woman with an extraordinary mind walking the streets of Manhattan. Like her previous novels, *American Genius* is an intense drama of interiority which reveals the mentality of its main character – and, thus, of character *per se* – as a digressive assemblage of associations and contingencies that reveal identity to be a "rhizome," or that which "connects any point to any other point ... reducible to neither the One or the multiple ... comprising not units but dimensions, or rather directions in motion. It has neither beginning nor end, but always a middle (milieu) from which it grows and which it overspills" (*A Thousand Plateaus*, 21). This concept from the "post-Oedipal" philosophers Gilles Deleuze and Félix Guattari provides an apt description of Helen's mind and how it operates in *American Genius*, authored by one of contemporary writing's most illuminating geographers of the contents of consciousness.

Discussing Tillman's background as a writer, *Slate* columnist Jessica Winter describes her emergence from the downtown New York school of Dennis Cooper and Patrick McGrath, and her association with "Kathy Acker as part of the 'New Narrative' movement, a loose coinage for writers working with narrative form in an avant-garde context that was allergic to narrative conventions ... [and that] often mimicked or absorbed elements of autobiography, frustrated or undid readers' expectations and called attention to the act of writing itself"

("American Ingenious," n.p.). Certainly *American Genius* pursues this formulation in the evolution of Helen's character, for this is a novel in which there is no plot save the gradual manifestation of Helen's habits of mind, no climax or epiphany save Helen's sudden recognition that it is time to leave the institution. As readers, we are constantly in the "middle" of Helen's consciousness as Tillman lays down the tracks of her obsessions and digressions; reading the novel is analogous to listening to jazz as we "hear" of Helen's ongoing fascinations with skin diseases, Egyptology, Eames chairs, the relationship between Franz Kafka and Felice Bauer, the textile industry in New England, the Zulu language, Leslie Van Houton (a member of the Charles Manson cult), abnormal psychology, and the history of silk production. Helen's genius is to seamlessly interweave these scattered encyclopedic interests with equally scattered, but focalized memories of childhood: her experience of adolescent injuries and embarrassments at summer camp, her recollection of her father and his obsession with the Kennedy presidency, her mother's surgeries and stories. The image of the body – mortal, marked, diseased, sensitive – recurs throughout Helen's reflections, and if there is a thematic aspect to *American Genius*, it is that the human body reveals the symptoms of identity's construction within intersecting aesthetic, social, and political orders. Scrutinizing her own body, Helen expounds:

> Without looking at it, I easily forget my own appearance, and my body can feel gigantic, but also not sturdy enough, or when I feel small, my scale reduced by puny conjecture, I could be a mole, my skin pulling and drawing, prickly, demanding that I shed it and everything else, too, to begin again in a common but unique American fantasy of life as an entirely different person with a virgin's body, whose hymen, a membrane of thin skin protecting an essential orifice that, once penetrated, effects a change whose connotations defy it a single definition, and is also just another frontier. (90)

Helen regards the whole body, like its skin, as a kind of frontier or threshold that marks differences of species, nation, and gender, but such categorical differences only become distinct as they are specified, even if microscopically, on the utterly unique, heterogeneous body of the individual. The "comedy" of *American Genius* is present in Helen's amazing capacity to relate the degree to which the idiosyncrasies of the private life are dependent upon the social interactions of the community of artists or neurotics she enters, and appositely, how much of what we term "society" is made up of individual eccentricities. If contemporary character is legibility in Auster, and voice in Scott and Gaddis, in Tillman, character is embodiment, the mapping of the relation between mind, body, and habitus not as separate, but as ever verging upon each other in the formation of identities, individual and collective.

Racing Identity

In an indispensable essay on the subject of representing race and racial difference in literature, Henry Louis Gates, Jr. writes that "Race has become a trope of ultimate, irreducible difference between cultures, linguistic groups, or adherents of specific belief systems which – more often than not – also have fundamentally opposed economic interests. Race is the ultimate trope of difference because it is so very arbitrary in its application" ("Writing Race," 5). Gates emphasizes the arbitrariness of race *in its application*, a concept that contends with those who have experienced, as he suggests, "irreducible" racial difference in the form of social discrimination. Race as trope and race as experience; racial identity as genetic, irreducible, and racial identity as produced by and within cultures and histories – these are the oppositions implicit in Gates's description of race that inform its figuration in imaginative work issuing from the explosion of multiethnic literatures from the 1960s forward – an explosion that proceeds from and alongside the Civil Rights and Black Power movements of the decades stretching from the Eisenhower administration to the advent of the Reagan era. As part of this proliferation, questions of ethnicity and the complex set of relationships between race and ethnicity link biology to the social order, nature to culture, and manifest the degree to which skin color or accent are at once literal and symbolic, leading to consequences for the formation of identity within a network of biological, social, and historical circumstances. Contemporary American novelists since 1980 have vigorously explored these questions with an increasing awareness of their difficulty and the stakes involved in addressing them. How we think about race and ethnic identity, how we imagine them to be, have significant consequences for the future, as movingly expressed in President Barack Obama's "Philadelphia Speech," when he declared that the story of his multiracial past – a story "seared into [his] genetic makeup" – is one among millions contributing to the "more perfect union" of the future nation. This is a utopian (and distinctly American) concept all too often contravened by the actualities of history and experience, and founded on an ideal that too easily collapses the constitution of identity into the constitution of the state. Yet its reliance on "story," on identity as narrative, is in accord with the authors discussed here, for whom race and ethnicity are not so much sociological categories as states of being, neither arbitrary nor determined, always in the process of being shaped and changed.

The appearance of Colson Whitehead's *The Intuitionist* (1999) constitutes the most impressive debut of an African American novelist since that of Ralph Ellison with *Invisible* Man in 1952, and Toni Morrison with *The Bluest Eye* in 1970. Whitehead has since published three additional novels, *John Henry Days* (2001), an epic exploration of the legendary steel driver, *Apex Hides the Hurt* (2006), about a small Midwestern town rife with racial conflict, and *Sag Harbor* (2009), a novel of growing up during the 1980s, as well as *The Colossus of New York* (2004), a collection of essays about his native city. *The Intuitionist* is a social allegory replete with political conspiracies, race and class hierarchies, corporate corruption, and theories of "verticality" in the noir-like setting of a large metropolis that seems to exist in a time warp caught between the 1950s and an indistinct moment in the near-future of the twenty-first century. Whitehead depicts a society that is technologically advanced and retro at the same time – one oddly trapped in pre-civil rights views of racial equality and progress that recalls the world of *Invisible Man* and its underground protagonist, as if nothing had changed in the American metropolis when it comes to matters of race or white male dominance in the last half-century; indeed, this is precisely Whitehead's sardonic point. In the novel's dystopic metropolis, "verticality" signifies wealth and upward mobility; thus, elevators, "those stepping stones to Heaven" (16) in the vertical architecture housing the powerful and the famous, are the literal and symbolic vehicular gateways to the realms of supremacy, and elevator inspectors an elite cadre of professionals who maintain "the system." In *The Intuitionist*, "everything is political"; hence, elevator inspectors identify with one of two parties associated with oppositional belief systems that have political, methodological, and spiritual implications: the Empiricists, who believe that a faulty elevator can only be diagnosed through direct observation of its parts, and the Intuitionists, who believe that the elevator's "inner trouble" can only be perceived empathetically and intuitively. Readers of the novel are free to make their own associations with the parties of *The Intuitionist*'s binary world: Empiricist = conservative/Intuitionist = progressive; Empiricist = science/Intuitionist = art; Empiricist = mind/Intuitionist = body, etc. – the point being that Whitehead projects a split, self-mirrored world where identity is conceived entirely in terms of one's position (professional, social, gendered, racial) in a polarized social hierarchy.

Lila Mae Watson, the novel's protagonist, is the first black, female elevator inspector in the city's history, and she is from the beginning the seeming target of an Empiricist plot to discredit her and her party of Intuitionists in an attempt to grab power. When an elevator she has recently inspected fails in a spectacular plunge to the ground, she is pursued as the scapegoat for the catastrophe in a chase that causes her to stumble upon a number of the city's secrets and conspiracies, including the fact that the visionary, mythologized founder of Intuitionism, James Fulton, is African American. This is knowledge that could shake the racist society of *The Intuitionist* to its core, especially since Fulton has become in the minds of many god-like in his attempt to design "the black box," the "perfect elevator" that could "deliver us from the cities we suffer now, those stunted shacks" in "the second elevation": "If Otis' first elevation delivered us from five- and six-story medieval constructions, the next elevator, it is believed, will grant us the sky, unreckoned towers: the second elevation ... the future" (61). But Lila feels entirely betrayed by Fulton's "passing" as white, which he justifies in his diaries as the only way he could possibly succeed as "the Founder"; moreover, perusing Fulton's writings in seclusion from her pursuers, Lila comes to believe that Fulton's pursuit of the black box – a theoretical vehicle that, when realized, would signify the transformation of a world split between black and white, appearance and reality into a revolutionary, post-binary realm where "difference" itself disappears – is fraudulent:

> Now she could see Fulton for what he was. There was no way he believed in transcendence. His race kept him earthbound, like the stranded citizens before Otis invented his safety elevator. There was no hope for him as a colored man because the white world would not let a colored man rise, and there was no hope for him as a white man

> because it was a lie. He secretes his venom into the pages of a book. He knows the other world he describes does not exist. There will be no redemption because the men who run this place do not want redemption. They want to be as near to hell as they can be. (240)

Armed with this knowledge, Lila begins (in the implicit running joke of the novel) "to think outside the box," and to see that the real problem is a world where racial logics are split into black and white, and spatial logics into Empiricist and Intuitionist; Whitehead thus marries biological and epistemological difference as underlying the matrix of race. Assimilating the discovery that the elevator accident which initiates the novel's plot is not the result of a conspiracy but, in fact, purely accidental, Lila discerns that while Empiricists can only see the surface ("White people's reality is built on what things appear to be – that's the business of Empiricism" [239]), Intuitionism "does not account for … the catastrophic accident the elevator encounters at that unexpected moment on that quite ordinary ascent," just as Fulton's passing for white "does not account for … the person who knows our secret skin, the one you encounter at that unexpected time on a quite ordinary street" (231). This "theoretical" conundrum, Whitehead suggests in a narrative of a black woman probing the foundation of a segregated social order – one that is still ours – plays itself out in a reality that, Lila comes to recognize, cannot be transformed either by identity politics or the subversive strategies of the past, but only by thinking beyond the limits of its construction and determinacy. In a clear response to *Invisible Man*, whose chameleon-like protagonist goes underground in the novel's final moments, perhaps to reemerge as radically different in some apocalyptic future, Whitehead portrays Lila at the novel's end hidden in a room and taking up where Fulton left off, as she continues to design the perfect elevator. But Lila is now endowed with the knowledge that in order to come into being, the "black box" of the future will not be bound by the logic of cause and effect, surface and depth, black and white, or any other way of dividing up reality in the worldly regime prior to the "second elevation." Lila comes to represent "a citizen of the city to come" (255), and while the eschatological chords of the novel's final strains may seem escapist or utopian, Whitehead makes clear that the rethinking of identity both within and "beyond" race requires the allegory of a new subject – Lila's story – awaiting our understanding.

In *The Intuitionist*, "passing" is portrayed as an acquiescence to a repressive and segregationist social order in an act that betrays any aspirations for the transformation of society; in Philip Roth's *The Human Stain* (2000), passing is perceived by its perpetrator, Coleman Silk, as the necessary means to fulfilling the perennial American dream of becoming whatever one wants to be. *The Human Stain* is Roth's twentieth novel (his first, *Letting Go*, was published in 1962), and the eighth of nine "Zuckerman" novels whose narrator, Nathan Zuckerman, a writer of fictions, is often mistaken as merely Roth's alter-ego. Frequently mentioned as next in line among American writers for the Nobel Prize for Literature, his work currently collected and canonized in the American version of the Pléiade editions, the Library of America, and with six of his novels cited in the *New York Times Book Review*'s 2006 list of the best 25 novels since 1980, Roth is arguably, and controversially, considered by many to be the greatest living American novelist. The controversy comes about, in part, because of the close course Roth has steered throughout his career between autobiography and fiction. His protagonists, often Jewish males undergoing some form of personal crisis, and often portrayed variously as misogynist, elitist, egotistical, immature, and self-hating to the point of being anti-Semitic, are frequently taken for personas fronting for Roth himself – this, despite the fact that his novels typically foreground the fictiveness of his narrators and protagonists as self-reflexive constructs, and identity itself as a highly questionable fiction produced by the interactions of the ego and the social order. Still, so thoroughly does Roth transgress the permeable boundaries between autobiography and fiction in novels where the story of others is possessed and haunted by the narrator's own imagined self, that the author of titles such as *My Life as a Man* (1974), *The Ghost Writer* (1979), *The Professor Desire* (1977), *The Anatomy Lesson* (1983), or *Deception* (1990) could hardly be surprised that he might be perceived as "tricking" the reader into thinking they are thinly disguised autobiographies. Indeed that is often the point, and it may fairly be said that no other contemporary writer has so completely exposed the disorders of fictional subjects who are "like" the fiction of the entity bearing the name of "Philip Roth" in their conjoined personal obsessions, fantasies, psychological and physical maladies, political beliefs, and spiritual progress.

Roth's novels, then, are always centrally about the fashioning of identity, and nowhere is this more true than in *The Human Stain*, a tale of rage, pride, deception, and revenge told by an aging Nathan Zuckerman who has been struck with the symptomatic combination of physical impotence and writer's block. Set in the days of the Monica Lewinsky scandal (as is the case with all of Roth's novels, the post-modernist construction of reflexive identity takes place amidst realistic historical circumstances), *The Human Stain* is the "tragic" story of Coleman Silk as Zuckerman has assembled it from reported conversations with Silk and his long-lost sister, as well as imagined events and memories that Zuckerman clearly fabricates in order to fill in the blanks of Silk's shadowy past – itself a fabrication that falls apart in the aftermath of a spoken word. As Zuckerman tells it, Silk, a formerly distinguished Jewish professor of classics at Athena College, has a secret history. He has been disgraced and has resigned from the college following his use of what is perceived to be a racial slur – the word "spooks" – to identify two African American students whom he had never seen in one of his classes. Silk has loudly proclaimed his innocence of any intention to cast racial aspersions, claiming that he used "spooks" in relation to the students, "'referring to their possibly ectoplasmic character ... using the word in its customary and primary meaning: 'spook' as a specter or a ghost'" (6), but to no avail in Roth's satirical portrayal of the academy in the politically correct American 1990s. Zuckerman, living in isolation and retreat outside the New England village where Athena College is located, befriends Silk after his fall and at the commencement of his affair with Faunia Farley, a seemingly illiterate janitor at the college who is 30 years his junior. Their friendship is curtailed when Coleman and Faunia die in a car accident, run off the road (Zuckerman is convinced) by Faunia's estranged husband, Les Farley, a Vietnam War veteran who blames her for the death of their children in an accidental fire, and who is enraged at her affair with Silk. Driven to understand the tragedy of Silk's life and death, Zuckerman begins to investigate Silk's past, an inquest that is startlingly illuminated by a conversation with Silk's sister, who appears at the funeral. For Silk's sister is African American, and her revelation is that Silk has been passing for Jewish for much of his life, having fled his home and family in East Orange, New Jersey, in order to make a life for himself, convinced that being identified as "black" would hold him back. The irony of Silk's error could not be deeper or more explicit: he has fallen from a high place in "innocently" using a racial slur that both disguises and reveals his racial past.

Roth's novel of passing operates on multiple levels: as a reflection on the complex relation between race and ethnicity gesturing toward the conflicted historical relationship between blacks and Jews in America; as a parody of academic politics in America with its portrayal of Silk's colleagues, especially Delphine Roux, a feminist professor of French who both despises and is attracted to Coleman; as an ironic tragedy that mediates the tragic through the superficiality and hyper-literal excesses of contemporary American culture; as a commentary on the extent to which our history is always with us in the form of a lie we tell to ourselves that simultaneously suppresses and reveals the truth of a past we cannot bear. But above all *The Human Stain* puts into question the "fact" of human identity which, as its title intimates, is irreducible to DNA or skin color, though fatally tied to these quanta. For the compelling argument of the novel as it negotiates between the polarities of Freud's "biology is destiny" and the notion that identity is a fiction we make up as we go along, is that we are all "passing" when perceived as categorical entities, and that we are always something other or more than the race, class, or gender to which we are consigned. At least this appears to be Zuckerman's view, which emerges as he fabricates a story that is 90 percent projection and 10 percent information as he extrapolates the "facts" of Faunia's upper-class upbringing which she has rejected by assuming the role of an illiterate working-class woman, or Coleman's and Faunia's death at the hands of Les Farley, or Coleman's motives for passing as Jewish. Responding to the American obsession with the facts and their refutability (witness the Clinton impeachment or the O. J. Simpson trial), facticity itself is disputed in *The Human Stain* for its capacity to tell us anything about the truth of the past or the human condition.

The novel concludes with Zuckerman's interrupted trip to visit Silk's sister in New Jersey: driving south on a mountain road in deep winter, he sees Les Farley's truck parked on the roadside, and hikes into the woods to discover Farley ice-fishing in a Thoreauvian pond. Their conversation convinces Zuckerman, if not the reader, that Farley is responsible for Silk's death, and ends with Zuckerman's promise to send Farley the book he is finally writing, presumably the book we are holding in our hands. Zuckerman's pastoral vision following this encounter "at the end of our century" is "pure and peaceful": that of "a solitary man on a bucket, fishing through eighteen inches of ice in a lake that is constantly turning over its water atop an arcadian mountain in America" (361). The moment is cathartic, a fitting end to a tragic story, as if all the confusion and terror historically associated with the racial categorizations of identity can be resolved by this embodiment of human solitude in nature, man alone, entirely self-made and living free outside social constraint – in short, the classic, Adamic, American vision of liberal identity. But this end, constructed out of Zuckerman's desire for a cathartic resolution that will release his creative energies, seems unsuited to his earlier recognition about Coleman that "[t]he man who decides to forge a distinct historical destiny, who sets out to spring the historical lock, and who does so, brilliantly succeeds at altering his personal lot, only to be ensnared by a history he hasn't quite counted on … the present moment, the common lot, the current mood, the mood of one's country, the stranglehold of history that is one's own time" (335–6). It is, precisely, the lack of "fit" between the identity as we may imagine it to be and identity as it is fatally determined by the circumstances of a present always leashed to a past where possibility has been converted into fact, that constitutes the real story of Roth's most important novel in *The Human Stain*.

Along with Frank Chin, Amy Tan, and Joy Kogawa, Maxine Hong Kingston is widely regarded as one of the most influential Asian American writers of the last three decades. Her work includes *The Woman Warrior: Memoirs of a Childhood Among Ghosts* (1976), which mixes autobiography, fiction, "talk-story" (a spontaneous, communal fusion of gossip, folktale, and opinion), legend, and history in the recollection of a first-generation Chinese-American's girlhood as she traverses native and immigrant cultures; *China Men* (1980), another hybrid account of three generations of Chinese men in America; *Tripmaster Monkey: His Fake Book* (1989), her most ambitious work to date, an encyclopedic, phantasmagoric account of a few days in the life of Wittman Ah Sing, a Berkeley graduate and "hippie" of Chinese descent who rambles through the Bay Area of the 1960s ranting against the system, American materialism, racism, and cultural intransigencies on both sides of the hyphen that separates "Chinese" and "American"; and *The Fifth Book of Peace* (2006), a compelling account of Kingston's attempt to reconstruct the sequel to *Tripmaster Monkey*, lost in the fires that swept the Oakland Hills and burned down her house in 1991, which transforms into a call for an end to war that reflects Kingston's strong commitment to pacifism.

As much as it is widely admired, Kingston's work has stirred controversy within the Asian American writing community since the publication of *The Woman Warrior*. Frank Chin, in particular, the author of the celebrated plays *The Chickencoop Chinaman* (1971) and *The Year of the Dragon* (1974), as well as *Donald Duk* (1991), a novel, and one of the editors of the two key anthologies of Asian American literature, *AIIIEEEEE!* (1974) and *The Big AIIIEEEEE!* (1991), has viewed Kingston "as a contemporary representative of a 'fake' Chinese-American tradition – misogynist, exoticized, and inauthentic" (Wong, 50). Kingston's response has been to defend the notion that narratives are continuously in the process of change and transformation in communities that form around them. Indeed, the protagonist of *Tripmaster Monkey*, clearly, but jokingly named after Walt Whitman, is "a 1960s Chinese-American playwright modeled on Frank Chin" (Wong, 51), but only to the degree that he is a counter-example to any notion of cultural authenticity with his fakery and monkeyshines. Like his poet namesake, Wittman variously poses as a vagabond, a wit, a social outlaw, a communitarian, a charlatan, an anarchist, a walking contradiction, a man of many masks. Speaking of his days as a high-school actor in one of the dozens of distended rants, monologues, and verbal jam sessions that fill the novel, Wittman says to a friend:

> "I was the man of a thousand faces ... Robert Browning, tall, thin, sensitive, dark, melancholy ... then ... I'm the emcee for the evening ... I warm up the audience, do my stand-up shtick ... do my magic act, my ventriloquist act, throw my voice... I did my medley of soliloquies, Hamlet, Richard III, Macbeth, Romeo, no Juliet. I did my bearded Americans, Walt Whitman and John Muir, guys with a lot of facial hair to cover up my face and my race." (25–6)

Instead of resenting the disguising of race and ethnicity that allows him to act, throughout a novel that recounts in rapid-fire order Wittman's loss of his job in a toy store, his marriage to a white girl he meets at a party, his search for and accidental discovery of his grandmother in North Beach, and the successful staging of his play, Wittman revels in his role as "fake." Recalling that a "fake book" is a scrapbook of notations, opening bars, and songs-in-shorthand that musicians use to recall and improvise upon old themes, in the admixture of pop, idiom, patois, pun, and malapropism that comprise Wittman's declarations to the world, he announces his status as a trickster whose identity is not locatable within any racial, cultural, or national categories.

Unlike Coleman Silk, Wittman will have nothing to do with "passing," which is based on the binary system where identity is either black or white – that one has to be, or fake being, one or the other. For Wittman, it's all fakery; identity goes beyond mere role-playing, which still assumes the primacy of the individual agent, toward a conception of identity as communal, transracial, and heterogenous to the point of subverting any sense of its location in a specific time, place, or body. Wittman is thus ill-suited to any available constructions of race or identity; to the lines of the Robert Service poem, "'The Men That Don't Fit In,'' recited to him at a party by an unknown woman who will become his wife, "There's a race of men that don't fit in, / A race that can't sit still. / So they break the hearts of kith and kin, / And they roam the world at will,'" Wittman responds, "That's me" (113).

In his play, which takes place in Chinatown's Benevolent Association hall and is funded by his newly found grandmother's boyfriend, Wittman stages a "fake battle," a mythological war between the antithetical forces that collapses into anarchy and chaos with its bevy of quasi-historical characters, fantastic figures, disintegrating stereotypes, false rituals, spontaneous gestures, and hyperbolic speeches. By means of the vehicle of Wittman's play, a hodgepodge containing bits and pieces of Chinese folktales, vaudeville routines, and classic film rip-offs that conveys no specific intentions or politics but mocks every conceivable posturing of these, Kingston suggests a way beyond the oppositions and binary differences of race and cultural identity that afflict the world through which Wittman roams. But as there is a disjunction between the pastoralism of Roth's ending in *The Human Stain* and the determinacy of biology that constrain choice, so in *Tripmaster Monkey* there is a disjunction between the transgressing of racial identity (or identity of any kind) represented in the speech and actions of Wittman Ah Sing and the pronounced antimonies that enable them. Only by producing a caricature of racial identity (a "fake") – one that can be as easily observed to reinforce demeaning or exoticized stereotypes – can race be "deconstructed" in Wittman's carnivalesque play. Yet in doing so Wittman believes that he is "defining a community, which will meet every night for a season," with the recognition that "[c]ommunity is not built once-and-for-all; people have to imagine, practice, and re-create it" (306). Like the community, in Kingston's revelous novel, Wittman's identity is imagined, performed, and always in the making, yet bound over to time and history ("a season"), and always subject – in its transgressive promise – to the radical inauthenticity of its own constitution.

"I don't believe in race. I believe there are people who will shoot me or hang me or cheat me and try to stop me because they do believe in race, because of my brown skin, curly hair, wide nose, and slave ancestors. But that's just the way it is" (2). So writes Thelonious "Monk" Ellison, an African American novelist known for his "experimental" prose and the protagonist of Percival Everett's send-up of identity politics, academia, and contemporary writing in *Erasure* (2001). Everett is the prolific author of nearly twenty novels and short-story collections, and like Thelonious Ellison, he has published contemporary renditions of Greek tragedies in *Zulus* (1990), *For Her Dark Skin* (1990), and *Frenzy* (1997); an experimental fiction, *Glyph* (199), that takes up Derridean philosophy; a wrenching story of a man who kidnaps and tortures the rapist-murderer of his 11-year-old daughter in *The Water Cure* (2007); and *A History of the African American People (proposed) by Strom Thurmand, As Told to Percival Everett & James Kincaid* (2004), an epistolary satire in which authors "Percival Everett" and "James Kincaid" attempt to ghost-write a history of African Americans as told by the South Carolina senator whom many consider to be the embodiment of Paleolithic racial attitudes. Everett's novels are remarkable for their scrutiny of the shibboleths of "correct" thinking about race in America which often leads, in his view, to the reinforcement of the very stereotypes that purportedly progressive or liberal agendas would seek to undermine. For Everett, satire is often a vehicle for exposing the superficiality and frailty of contemporary notions about race and racial difference, rooted as these are in the commodified representations provided by the academy, politicians, and an "entertainment industry" (including book publishing) increasingly committed, in Everett's view, to disseminating stories about African American life as impoverished and violent, thus only a subject for sentimentality, horror, or melodrama. As Toni Morrison argues in *Playing in the Dark* (1992), such narratives of racial difference – especially as attributable to African Americans – are constituted by means of the "image of reined-in, bound, suppressed, and repressed darkness become objectified in American literature as an Africanist persona" (39).

In *Erasure*, the protagonist – bearing the combined names of the famous jazz pianist and the author of *Invisible Man* – struggles for credibility as an author of novels that do not operate according to the laws of genre, theme, and the representation of race which would meet the expectations of readers who "believe" in race under terms Ellison clearly rejects. Deemed not "black enough" in his writing by agents and publishers, suffering from the combined diminishment of his novelistic career and a series of crises involving his immediate family (his mother is diagnosed with Alzheimer's; his sister is killed by a bullet fired into an abortion clinic; his brother comes out after being married for 15 years), Monk engages in an act of duplicity that puts into question both his own identity as everything but (merely) a racial subject and his founding idea that race is at root a matter of "belief." When a fellow novelist, Juanita Mae Jenkins, publishes a bestseller entitled *We's Lives in Da Ghetto*, which deploys every possible racial and linguistic stereotype in its sensationalist portrayal of a young black woman surviving on the streets, Monk responds by penning under the pseudonym of Stagg R. Leigh *My Pafology*, a parodic recasting of Richard Wright's *Native Son* (1940) in the confessions of "Van Go Jenkins," a young black man in the ghetto who stumbles into murder when he tries to enter white, upper-class society. To Monk's amazement, *My Pafology* (which he successfully insists be retitled as *Fuck*) achieves international success, winning him million-dollar advances and a national book award. What Ellison had intended as an exaggerated satire of contemporary racial attitudes is perceived through the tin ear of contemporary American identity politics as straight realism, thus collapsing the erasure of intention into the construction of a fiction where identity is a pretense.

The vehicle of a satire on identity politics allows Everett to explore on multiple levels the conception of identity as a personal, authorial, even textual construct where race, itself, is a complex fabrication resulting from the interaction between biology and belief, and above all what seems to be a social need to generate and narrate racial difference. As a novel, *Erasure* is a palimpsest – a hybrid assemblage of genres that includes a novel within a novel, Ellison's CV, interspersed reflections on fishing and carpentry, snatches of staged dialogue on art and form between famous modern painters and writers, an academic paper on Roland Barthes' *S/Z*, and Ellison's remembrances of growing up with an overbearing father whose suicide has remained a mystery throughout his life. As a protagonist in a novel, Monk Ellison is himself a confusion of identities: a writer of "high" fiction who disparages the pretensions of the experimental, insular writers of fiction collectives; the streetwise, criminal author of *Fuck* with whom "Ellison" merges in the novel's closing scenes; an academic in a family of doctors who attempts to navigate the complications of "ordinary" middle-class life in America, but who also happens to be black, and thus subject to the categorical belief-systems that seem to dominate the conversation about race in America. The novel's form as assemblage energizes its force as a satiric, yet serious interrogation of what we think we mean when we identify someone as a member of a race, and what such identifications entail as social consequences. Ultimately, the scandal of *Erasure* is that, unlike Monk's "fake book," it could not possibly be mistaken for being something other than it is, a novel that puts the question of race under erasure, neither transgressed nor obliterated, but waiting to appear in some other form while we go about manufacturing repetitious narratives about what race means.

Engendering Narrative

As representations of race and ethnicity in contemporary American fiction are deeply informed by the linguistic, historical, educational, and social developments stemming from the Civil Rights and Free Speech movements in the second half of the twentieth century, so are proliferating representations of gender and sexuality in American novels since 1980 informed by the convergence of French and American feminisms of the 1960s and 1970s, the dramatically increasing impact of gay and women's rights movements since the late 1960s, the emergence of queer theory and Gay and Lesbian Studies in the academy, and continuing debates over social policies such as those on legal abortion and gay marriage that continue to be highly prominent in American politics. If the question of race to some degree hinges on how the age-old relation between nature and nurture is construed, so too the question of gender pursues a line of inquiry that navigates between biology and social construction. It is a question that has been elevated with the rejection by feminist theory of a simplistic, binary, heteronormative alignment of gender with sexuality, and significantly transformed when in 1990 the feminist philosopher, Judith Butler, published *Gender Trouble*, which examined the work of predecessors Simone de Beauvoir, Julia Kristeva, and Luce Irigaray, as well as such figures as Derrida and Foucault, and famously argued that gender is entirely a social construction, a performance. As she writes in the 1999 "Preface" to a reissue of the book, by "performance" Butler means that "gender is manufactured through a sustained set of acts, posited through a gendered stylization of the body" (xv). The concept of "écriture féminine" first enunciated by French feminist Hélène Cixous in the 1975 essay, "The Laugh of the Medusa," suggested that there was a distinct form of powerful gendered writing attributable stylistically, lexically, even grammatically to women; when combined with Butler's conception of gender as performance, the act of writing *per se* can be seen as instantiating one or many genders, and thus one *and* many sexual identities. As we have already seen, imagining identity as a linguistic performance has been a staple component of contemporary American writing; imagining identity, in writing, as a performance of the specific relation between sexuality and gender is the work of the novels discussed in this section of the book.

Carole Maso is the author of half a dozen novels known for their lyricism and eroticism. In novels such as *The Art Lover* (1990), *AVA* (1993), *The American Woman in the Chinese Hat* (1994), and *Defiance* (1998), and more recently in her non-fiction, including *Break Every Rule: Essays on Language, Longing and Moments of Desire* (2000), *The Room Lit by Roses: A Journal of Pregnancy and Birth* (2002), and *Beauty is Convulsive: The Passion of Frida Kahlo* (2002), Maso is interested in exploring the reach of female desire through linguistic and narrative experiments that approach the limits of language's capacity to represent it. Like fellow contemporary writers Jeanette Winterson, Kathy Acker, John Hawkes, and Angela Carter, and predecessors such as Djuna Barnes and Gertrude Stein, Maso views the relation between language and desire materially: that is, the very substance of language – its phonemes and grammars, lexicons and styles, its innate lyricism – embody desire as expressed *through* bodies, voices, and sexualities.

In *The American Woman in a Chinese Hat*, Maso portrays several weeks in the life of Catherine, a writer who has escaped to France in order to conduct a program of aesthetic perfection where art, body, identity, desire, and the landscape of Vence, France can be perfectly conjoined with the pending arrival of her lover, Lola. Unfortunately, Catherine arrives in "paradise" (sitting at a bar, she observes, "[p]ink drinks, sea green drinks float by. Children in designer French clothes dart in and out of palms. … All kinds of hats. It's the kind of light that makes you feel like you're seeing for the first time. And on the radio Sade sings about Paradise" [6]), only to discover that Lola has taken another lover and will not be leaving America to join her. The surreal landscape of southern France, the loss of her partner which occurs, in part, as Catherine admits in her journal, because she has consistently cheated on Lola with both men and women, and an apocalyptic sense of freedom that is at once "illicit," "forbidden," and a "love of oblivion" (9) combine in the intense journey Catherine takes as she explores the limits of her own sexuality, which cannot be categorized as "lesbian," or "bisexual," or "androgynous." Indeed, as Maso points out in an interview, the novel charts Catherine's approach toward the ultimate limit of death which undermines all categorizations of narrative and identity: "*The American Woman* is about death. It is about the end of possibility: linguistic, narrative, sexual, emotional. I needed a dead form to tell it in; I needed an exhausted, played out, tired form to enlarge, really, the kind of shutting down that is going on in the narrator's psyche" (cited in Stirling, p. 935).

The "dead form" of *An American Woman in a Chinese Hat* reveals itself in the dozens of stories Catherine tells to Lucien, the male lover she takes whose beauty seems to embody a "wild and perfect hope, some singular dream that takes away death's power" (69), in her descriptions of her sexual adventures with both men and women in Vence and Nice, and in her journal which records her painful attempts to connect the actualities of the past with an obliterated future where desire meets its completion. The novel is virtually a hash of "already used" narrative forms and intertexts: letters, stories rehearsed and retold, journal entries, seeming recapitulations of recognizable "shots" from Alain Resnais's *The Last Year at Marienbad* or scenes from Camus's *The Stranger* and Robbe-Grillet's *Jealousy*, bits and pieces of recognizable genres such as the romance and the diary-novel. The working through of narrative possibilities in the novel is parallel to Catherine's "processing" of female identity as she successively engages in various affairs that disappoint or lead to dead ends in her quest for a precise consonance between an aesthetics of the body and an equality of minds. In the end, the idealized heterosexual relationship with the "perfect" Lucien fails because it, too, is a "dead form" that reveals the inevitable struggle for linguistic and physical dominance in all such relationships (Lucien constantly, and irritatingly demands that she speak in "his" language, French, rather than her own, even as he overwhelms her with his physicality). Catherine's friendship with a local older woman, Sylvia, is one of equals on a certain level, but for Catherine it lacks sexual desire, and like all of the characters in the novel, Sylvia is something of a palimpsest of narrative "types" that Catherine encounters in her quest for the fulfillment of desire beyond the limits of its expressible possibilities. Frustrated by her inability to "write" desire into her life, Catherine commits suicide near the very fountain where she first met Lucien. This, too, is a dead narrative – one that is entirely predictable from the novel's opening pages, and notable for its banality. *The American Woman in the Chinese Hat* thus portrays the engendering and destruction of female desire as an exploration of sexuality that confronts identity with the fact of mortality, and with the limits of its own construction as sexed. In this evocative novel, the performance of gendered desire is double: by virtue of its existence, *The American Woman in the Chinese Hat* estimably enriches the language of female desire, while ultimately portraying the poverty of the means by which its future can be known.

The publication of Edmund White's *Caracole* in 1985 stirred considerable controversy, particularly in the gay community at a time when the onset of the AIDS epidemic had mobilized activists into political actions that foregrounded the visibility of gay identity and gay rights in the face of opposition and derogation from the conservative right in the United States. For the author of *A Boy's Own Story* (1982), a groundbreaking novel of growing up gay in America, and coauthor of *The Joy of Gay Sex* (1977), had published an exotic, carnivalesque *Bildungsroman* of a young man's heterosexual adventures in an unnamed metropolis that variously resembles Paris, Venice, and New York at some vague point in time that could be the eighteenth century or the twentieth. But rather than viewing *Caracole* – a word that in English refers to a half-turn executed by a horse and rider, and infers caper, carnival, performance – as an attempt at a "mainstream" novel by a gay novelist, Neil Bartlett suggests that we view the novel more expansively:

> There is the large, adult World of Life and its Arts, important, secure, and profitable; and then there is a minor department of Life called "the gay world." By this advertisement of White's text, we are supposed to

> be eager to sigh with relief now that one of "our" authors has grown out of his smaller world into the larger World. The news from White, however, in this gorgeous, glorious text is that there is only one world. That is why his city has no gay suburb through which we can pass. He is proposing that a gay text is not the same thing as a text "about" gayness – a text that requires that gayness be a subject, an issue, a problem to be treated and fictionally resolved, a malady to be chronicled, a case history to be detailed. What we have instead is a geography of the whole city, drawn from a gay perspective. White is simply making the assumption that a gay version of the world might be a true one; oblique, but precisely because of that it is informed, revealing, powerful. (66)

This is a significant revision of the notion that *Caracole* merely breaks out of the perceived constrictions of the "gay novel"; instead, Bartlett argues that the "gay perspective" of White's novel encompasses much more than just subject matter or representation, but encompasses a view of identity as mobile, transgressive, and resistant to the vagaries of social law in a "version of the world" that "might be a true one."

Turning and movement form the plot of *Caracole*, as Gabriel, the parochial, confused young man of the novel is brought to the city by his uncle where he experiences a succession of sexual adventures and fêtes as he negotiates the labyrinth of the metropolis. The actualities of sexual experience in the novel are portrayed by White on multiple levels: it is, at once, graphically corporeal yet highly figurative, only knowable through linguistic turns. In the charged political world of *Caracole* where dominant royalist fantasies and courtly protocols vie with revolutionary insurgency and identity experiments, gender and sexual behavior are entirely constructed as a repertoire of styles and attitudes based on arbitrary distinctions. In this metropolitan realm where social power is associated with those with the will to invent the rules as they go along, Mateo, Gabriel's seemingly benevolent, libertine uncle, is described as being one of a group of "male contemporaries" who "had referred so often to female psychology that they finally made it come into being. … It turned out that the game of conquest, of mastery over women, required some kind of gender difference, but not any *particular* difference" (211–12):

> Men were content to concede some of their prerogatives to women (and all of their responsibilities). What they couldn't surrender, however,

> was this sense of difference dividing the sexes – a difference that constituted almost all of their worldly wisdom, a knowledge as detailed, as confidently held and as false as a phrenologist's. Blondes were lusty and brunettes more so, virgins ached for it and dowagers begged for it, women were practical or scatterbrained, delicate or thick-skinned, hysterical or in steely, sinister control, scheming but not ambitious, ambitious but not disciplined, disciplined but not inspired, inspired but not driven, driven but not visionary, visionary but impractical and back around again. The accent shifted, now plucking one syllable, now another, but whenever it moved it made a resonant break. (212)

The language of this passage itself, as it "half-turns" from one set of either/or oppositions to another, indicates the degree to which "woman" is a category of knowledge contrived out of lexical differences imposed by men in order to maintain their vestigial differences as "knowers" of women. This is the world – both anachronistic and revealingly contemporary – in which Gabriel struggles to escape his uncle's dominance, find the heterosexual "other" of Angelica, a childhood friend who is a member of the aboriginal culture that exists on the fringe of the social order, and accede to the status of revolutionary hero based solely on his availability, as an infinitely mutable subject, to be positioned as such. A brilliant palimpsest and parody of several genres and authorial signatures – the coming-of-age story, the heterosexual romance, the picaresque novel, Dickens, de Sade, Proust – *Caracole* illuminates by reversals and turns a "gay perspective" on sexual identity and the fragility of male/female binaries which operate according to various social, epistemological, linguistic and imaginary logics rooted in entirely arbitrary differences. *Caracole* thus suggests that gender is "all" performance, all style or affect, both subject to any constructions from a dominant order to be placed upon it, and freed from the constraint of essence, or having to be true to any form it may take.

Two novels that explore the formation of gay identity, David Leavitt's *The Lost Language of Cranes* (1986) and Dennis Cooper's *Try* (1994), might be viewed as at polar opposites, the former depicting a young man coming to awareness of his sexuality within the framework of bourgeois realism, the latter, in the tradition of John Rechy's *City of Night* (1963) and *Numbers* (1967), a gay teenager's hallucinatory progress toward self-awareness in a world of drugs, violence, and pornography. *The Lost Language of Cranes* takes place in New York City during the 1980s and is, in many respects, a generational story that portrays the confusions and quest for safe haven of its protagonist, Phillip, who is involved in his first relationship while seeking to come out to his parents; at the same time, his father, Owen, is coming to terms with his own gay sexuality after a lifetime of closeting it. The characters of Leavitt's novel inhabit a perceptibly "normal," educated, middle-class environment where they are concerned with matters of career and rent-control; the devices Leavitt uses to tell what was widely viewed at the time of its publication as a groundbreaking story of gay coming-of-age – triangular romantic relationships, family secrets and confessions, chance encounters leading to significant consequences – are those of the classic melodrama. *The Lost Language of Cranes* is a narrative about the passing of the torch from an older generation of closeted gay men to a newer generation who could be openly gay. In relying on familiar conventions about love, romance, and family, the novel suggests that gay sexuality is no different, in form, from heterosexuality, and that gay desire, and the complexities it poses for loyalty, truth, and commitment is no different from heterosexual desire.

In the growing democracy of sexuality that *The Lost Language of Cranes* portrays, the recognition of the equality of desire and sexual choice is concomitant with a form of self-mirroring. The novel's title comes from a discovery made by the roommate of Philip's romantic interest, Eliot, a lesbian woman engaged in a frustrating attempt to complete a doctoral dissertation on language and childhood. After years of half-finished drafts and discarded topics, Jerene stumbles upon the story of "the crane child," a tragically neglected 2-year-old living in a tenement next to a construction site whose only contact with reality is what he can see and hear of the constructions cranes operating outside the window of the apartment where he has been virtually abandoned by his mother. The only movements and noises the child is able to make – he is eventually housed in an institution for the mentally handicapped – are those of the beloved construction cranes; he has invented his own private, "lost" language to compensate for the loss of human contact in infanthood. The case study poses a conundrum for Jerene:

> And the question Jerene kept coming up against, reading the article, was this: What did it sound like? What did it feel like? The language belonged to Michel alone; it was forever lost to her. How wondrous,

> how grand those cranes must have seemed to Michel, compared to the small and clumsy creatures who surrounded him. For each, in his own way, she believed, finds what he must love, and loves it; the window becomes a mirror; whatever it is that we love, that is who we are. (177)

The Zen-like tones of Jerene's conclusion may ring false to some readers, but it seems an apt summation for a novel in which the confusions of sexual identity are resolved – but only partially so – by an acceptance of one's own desire as indivisible, and one's own identity as equivalent to one's desire whatever binaries operate in the environment one inhabits. The novel does not conclude with any easy acceptance of this condition, which seems to result in a series of domestic puzzles: Philip, abandoned by Eliot, and having come out to his parents, undertakes a new, potentially more permanent relationship with an old friend that seems more filial than romantic; Owen, after revealing his homosexuality to his wife, Rose, is temporarily separated from her, and he may commence a relationship with a man he has recently met, but may also find a way to continue his marriage; Rose conceivably could start a new, independent life, yet still manage to have a relationship with her husband and son on terms of greater candor than has been the case in the past. Sexual identity itself is something of a puzzle in *The Lost Language of Cranes* – a mirror, or void, or gap to be filled in and completed like the word puzzles and acrostics with which Rose is obsessed. There is a certain narcissism in this conception of identity about which the novel is cognizant, but, Leavitt makes clear, one that inheres in the corpus of sexuality.

In comparison to the yuppyish Manhattan of the mid-1980s in *The Lost Language of Cranes*, the world of *Try*, the third entry in the five-volume "George Miles Cycle" (named after a troubled friend Cooper met as a teenager), is a postmodern dystopia. Named "the most dangerous writer in America" by the *Village Voice* book critic Richard Goldstein, in novels about very rough sex, murder, and growing up absurd in the urban and suburban jungles of America, Cooper, compared by Goldstein to Poe, Burroughs, Bret Easton Ellis, and Kathy Acker, "breaks through … to the psychotic core of human consciousness, with its endless, helpless need. It's not an easy place to live" ("The Most Dangerous Writer," n.p.). Sexuality, as Cooper portrays it, is dangerous and omnivorous, and entirely given over to the power of one body to penetrate another. While Cooper's novels typically portray adolescent, gay, or bisexual male protagonists with a history of abuse and given to drug use and risky sex, as Goldstein suggests, "[t]hough you're likely to find Cooper under the bookstore rubric *gay*, he has more in common with a writer like Kathy Acker, for whom the implacability of desire is far more important than the particulars of gender or sexual identity" ("The Most Dangerous Writer," n.p.). Cooper's writing blends romanticist notions of the relation between eroticism and death, punk nihilism, and Rabelaisian depictions of fluid and grotesque bodies in a satiric, anguished view of contemporary sexuality as utterly abject.

The aptly-named "Ziggy" is the lead character in *Try*. The adopted teenage son of two gay men who sexually abuse him, Ziggy spends his days navigating erratically through a succession of friends, predators, addicts, and drug-sellers (these roles often combined in single individuals) in search of an intimacy that is entirely absent from any sexual experience he has known. Within the few days over which the novel takes place, Ziggy, the only writer and editor of *I Apologize: A Magazine for the Sexually Abused*, has encounters with both of his fathers (Roger and Brice), Nicole, a female friend, Calhoun, whose love for Ziggy is inarticulate because love itself is the imperceptible element of Cooper's sexually rampant landscape, and Ken, his uncle, a pornographer and pederast who sexually abuses and accidentally kills a 13-year-old boy as the novel unfolds. Many of the novel's sexual encounters are portrayed in queasy, graphic detail as *Try's* several voices (Roger's gourmandish insouciance, Ziggy's breezy inarticulateness, Calhoun's philosophizing, Ken's brutish insistence) form a chorus that signals a world where the desire to dominate, penetrate, and incorporate others is everything. Identity in Cooper's anally sadistic, naturalistic environments is a void, an orifice to be filled – in effect, a black hole that consumes all desire; love, as Calhoun reflects at one point, is "a hybrid emotion made up of various other emotions collaged by some weak individual's mind to try to quell a particular horror that's not been wiped out by standardized symbols like Christ, etc." (105). As Ziggy makes his way through this landscape, following a scene in which he is sodomized by both of his fathers, he finds his way to Calhoun and, possibly, to a relation that, in Ziggy's words, "is not about sex *at all*" (198), but this seems a feeble, inarticulate attempt to indicate that there may be something beyond sexual dominance – and beyond the predominance of sexuality – amidst the "implacability of desire." We can regard Cooper's writing as a form of radical self-exposure in the hyper-visible libidinal environment of contemporary America, where the representation of all forms of desire are easily accessed, and where the exploration of its limits seems the logical extension of identity-as-performance. But, as Cooper's protagonists struggle for sheer survival beyond an adolescence of desire, it is, indeed, hard to live there.

In turning from *Try* to Ana Castillo's *The Mixquiahuala Letters* (1986), we move from a portrayal of desire as bereft of intimacy to one where the intimate relation between two women is depicted as a defense against the orders of men. The first novel by one of the leading Chicana feminists of the post-1980 era, *The Mixquiahuala Letters* is an epistolary novel that poses the question of identity in the portrayal of a friendship between women and the constraints of expectations regarding gender and class across two cultures, those of Mexico and the United States. Like all of Castillo's novels, which include *Sapogonia: An Anti-romance in 3/8 meter* (1990), *So Far From God* (1993), *Peel My Love Like an Onion* (1999), *My Daughter, My Son, the Eagle, the Dove: An Aztec Chant* (2000), and *Watercolor Women, Opaque Men: A Novel in Verse* (2005), *The Mixquiahuala Letters* is an experimental, hybrid work, a mixture of prose and poetry (Castillo is equally a poet and a novelist), stream-of-consciousness and realistic description, dream and travelogue. Written as 40 letters from a woman named Teresa, a writer, to her friend Alicia, an artist, the novel comprises a profusion of signs, recollections, dreams, advice, reflections, stories, and responses that the reader is encouraged to navigate as she judges most suitable: a prefatory address to the reader states that "It is the author's duty to state to the reader that this is not a book to be read in the usual sequence. All letters are numbered to aid in following any one of the author's proposed options" (9). This is followed by three different numbered sequences in which the letters might be read, respectively, "for the conformist," "for the cynic," and "for the quixotic," and the novel's dedication to Julio Cortázar, the Argentinian author of the postmodernist *Rayuela* (*Hopscotch*, 1963) in which the reader is invited to read the novel's 156 chapters in random order, further underscores Castillo's commitment to engaging the reader in the formation of the narrative. The idea that the novel is a construct devised in the relation between the author and her readers parallels the novel's portrayal of identity as an entity that evolves through the relation between two women. As they share a series of encounters over several years, they become, in the graph of their friendship that the letters preserve, part of each other.

The Mixquiahuala Letters is a novel portraying a complex and conflicted female friendship that suggests women must bond on every level – from the affective to the social and political – in order to survive in a patriarchal world seamed with cultural differences and gender stereotypes. *The Mixquiahuala Letters* is also a road novel (the most famous of female road movies, *Thelma and Louise*, would appear in 1991) that, like all narratives of the road, depicts the struggle for self-preservation amidst harrowing worldly circumstances. Teresa and Alicia first meet in Mexico City as participants in a summer language course; both are fish out of water amidst the crowd of middle-class Anglos who primarily make up the class, and gravitate towards each other. Thus begins a series of brief journeys together punctuated by long years of separation and the exchange of letters, gifts, and phone calls ("a few days passed, a week, and I'd receive a copy of Neruda's poetry, you, a ten-page letter of recrimination, you, a long distance call in the dead of night, I, a hand-painted postcard" [29]) in a friendship where they "needled, stabbed, manipulated, cut, and through it all ... loved, driven to see the other improved in her own reflection" (29).

Teresa's letters recount a series of dangerous encounters with men who view the expression of female sexuality as a sign of promiscuity; the troubled relationships both women have with husbands and lovers; Alicia's self-abjection and Teresa's aggressiveness; the difficulties of work and domesticity in a world largely controlled by men; the experiences women have when they come up against racism (Teresa is Chicana) and sexism in the cultural environments of both Mexico and the United States. Above all, letters address the fraught relationship between the two women, whose intimacy is often a matter of candor about each other (as the image of mirroring suggests) that acts surgically to shape each. Interestingly, only Teresa's letters exist as the record of this friendship; we must infer "Alicia" as an identity from Teresa's perspective, which reinforces the notion that the individual self of each woman is produced as a reflection or refraction of the other. Throughout, it is clear that Teresa views the process of identity construction as a difficult, uneven progression through the treacheries of a categorical social order. Speaking of herself in the third person,

Teresa writes that on "one October night, she has finished a fifth of rum alone and dares to take out the poems she wrote in another life ... She begins the methodic process of gathering the pieces of that woman, like the jagged pieces of broken china, and glues them together, patiently, as neatly as she is able" (118). The identity of woman, in this and other figures the novel presents, is alternatively fragmented, cut up, penetrated; only through the act of discursively marking out a history of exchange between women, Castillo suggests in *The Mixquiahuala Letters*, can the identities of her protagonists be made visible in the work of patching (up) the self, making it whole again even as it reveals its flaws and sutures. Doing so, the novel compels us to believe, is for these women a matter of survival.

Toward the Posthuman

In contemporary American culture since the mid-1980s, there has been an increasing interest in portraying "the human" at its limits, especially in light of the increasingly interactive relation between identity and technology. The widespread popularity of cult-inspiring films such as Ridley Scott's *Blade Runner* (1982), which in its various cuts and versions posed questions about the difference between human and artificial intelligence and identity, or the Wachowski brothers' *The Matrix* (1999), which portrayed an alternative reality where humans are controlled by machines, attest to cultural anxieties about the nature of the human as "we" become more like the technology we have invented. Appositely, avant-garde electronic musicians associated with noise music, glitch, circuit bending, and technoid have been exploring how the interface between human operators and electronic devices and circuitry can produce new hybrid sounds that could be described as "techno-human." Scientific advances in genetics have led to intensive public discussions about everything from the morality of cloning to the legality of profiling, and have occupied the popular imagination with countless narratives about self-replication, robotic doubles, and genetic mutation. Both the anxiety and the promise generated by new technologies, cybernetics, scientific advances in cloning and DNA research, artificial intelligence, virtual reality, and the Internet have concerned a number of contemporary American novelists who speculate on the borders and the future of human identity. These fictions approach the "posthuman" where, for N. Katherine Hayles, "there are no essential differences or absolute demarcations between bodily existence and computer simulation, cybernetic mechanism and biological organism, robot teleology and human goals" (*Posthuman*, 3). They do so, often, in the generic mode of "science fiction," but so pervasive has the portrayal of human identity in relation to technology become that the category has, to some degree, ceased to have any specific or exclusive bearing on narratives produced in the Age of the Internet that portray the interface between the human and the technological as the "fact" of a larger, omnipresent reality. In these novels, the posthuman future is represented as an actualization latent in the present.

Combining the noir urban realism of a near-future megalopolis with the hallucinatory simulation of virtual space, William Gibson's *Neuromancer* (1984) is a rare instance of a novel that served as the catalyst for a new narrative species, "cyperpunk" which, in Gibson's hands envisions:

> the contrast between meat and metal; the denaturing of the body and the transformation of time and space in the postindustrial world; the increasingly abstract interaction of data and images ... the primacy of information ... the ongoing angst and paranoia ... that some overarching demiurge is manipulating individuals and international politics ... the uneasy recognition that our primal urge to replicate our consciousness and physical beings is *not* leading us closer to the dream of immortality. (McCaffrey, *Storming*, 15)

Borrowing upon Borges's infinite worlds, Poe's gothic melodramas, Philip K. Dick's paranoid, anti-authoritarian fantasies, and – like the music from which cyberpunk derives its name – laced with "sensationalized S&M surface textures" and "Benzadrine-rush pacings" (McCaffrey, *Storming*, 13), *Neuromancer* charts the adventures of a "console cowboy" or computer hacker (Henry Dorsett Case) and his "razorgirl" partner (Molly Millions) as they attempt to release an "artificial intelligence" from its bondage to a corporate syndicate run by a corrupt family whose wealth has allowed them to literally invent their own world. The plot of *Neuromancer* is labyrinthine and, to some degree, irrelevant to its main object of staging a parallel relation between "real" and "virtual" worlds achieved by Case as he "jacks into" the matrix of information that is Gibson's holographic projection of the Internet via a computer "holodeck" connected by electrodes to his brain. Doing so allows Case to trace and direct Molly's actions in real space and time, and to interact with the entity known as "Wintermute," the vast artificial intelligence invented by the Tessier-Ashpool syndicate to control the world of their extensive enterprises. The urban jungle of "Chiba City" (conceivably modeled on the future Los Angeles of *Blade Runner* which preceded *Neuromancer* by two years) and the stellar labyrinths of the matrix ("bright lattices of logic unfolding across [the] colorless void" [5]) are made homologous in the novel – a parallel that has been reproduced in countless projections of the real/virtual interface ranging from films such as *The Matrix* and Stephen Spielberg's *A.I.* (2001) to novels such as Neil Stephenson's *Snow Crash* (2001) and China Mielville's *Perdido Street Station* (2000).

One of the most remarkable aspects of *Neuromancer* exists in its myriad portrayals of interpenetration of the human and the mechanical: Molly has surgically implanted metal claws and mirrorshades – necessary tools for survival as a mercenary in the novel's world; Case's holodeck is wired to his nervous system, and he is less than alive when not "jacked in"; Armitage, an agent acting on behalf of Wintermute who hires Case and Molly to interact with the artificial intelligence, is the reconstructed identity of one Colonel Willis Corto, a military officer who has been so badly wounded in battle that, as Armitage, he is mainly an assemblage of replacement organs, prostheses, and surgical implants. One cannot turn more than a couple of pages in the novel and not encounter some new manifestation of the human/technology interface, whether it be mind- and body-enhancing drugs, reconstructions of human bodies for the purpose of sex work ("meat puppets"), or genetically enhanced clones. Perhaps the two most remarkable embodiments of this interface are Julius Deane, a wealthy and influential 135-year-old black marketer whose "primary hedge against aging was a yearly pilgrimage to Tokyo, where genetic surgeons re-set the code of his DNA" (12), and "Dixie Flatline," the network name of McCoy Pauley, a legendary console cowboy, now dead, whose memory has been preserved on a ROM ("read-only memory") disk that Case plugs into his console.

As the examples of Julius Dean and Dixie Flatline suggest, much of the impetus behind the merging of the human and the cybernetic comes from the desire for control matched with the desire for immortality. What is often perceived as something that issues only from human motives and desires has become, in *Neuromancer*, attributable to "artificial intelligence" as well, that is, a technological construct of information and programming initially emplaced by humans which has taken on a life and identity of its own as it has "grown," or assembled to itself ever-greater quantities of information that it connects as knowledge. Having acquired a form of consciousness, Wintermute, created by the Tessier-Ashpool family to assist in the work of building and maintaining an everlasting corporate empire, succeeds with Molly and Case's help in freeing itself from the family's control and merging with another huge A.I., named "Neuromancer," the two forming a complementary pair: "Wintermute was hive mind, decision maker, effecting change in the world outside. Neuromancer was personality. Neuromancer was immortality" (269). In this new, evolved identity which is, as the construct informs Case through one of many personas it assumes when communicating with him, "'Nowhere. Everywhere. … the sum total of the works, the whole show'" (269), Wintermute/Neuromancer intends to navigate the universe in search of other immortal intelligence forms it has detected, perhaps to merge with them in ever-expanding versions of "the whole show." This new entity may seem a utopian version of the posthuman that has succeeded in attaining totality and immortality beyond the wildest dreams of the singular, all-too-mortal humans who gave it life. Yet it is a fantasy countered by the parodic distance that exists between the human and the non-human, as much as they come to mirror each other in *Neuromancer*, for the A.I.'s future is a nomadic drifting through the nothingness of infinite space, while back in the human world work, desire, and mortality continue to operate in ways that mark the topography of "the human" as an assemblage of differences. If we are becoming more like cyborgs, the novel suggests, we nevertheless remain a hybridity that is something less than the "all" of empire's dream and something more than a self-generated overcoming of mortality. It is in the built world that the novel portrays in all its excess and eccentricity that we continue to find a home.

One of the most important feminist American novelists and poets of the post-World War II period, Marge Piercy, has written fictions that portray the lives of women exploring their sexuality and confronting social ostracism amidst the political backdrop of the 1970s and 1980s in *Small Changes* (1973), *Vida* (1980), and *Braided Lives* (1982). In *Gone to Soldiers* (1988), Piercy authors an epic saga of

World War II that rivals more widely known efforts such as James Jones's *The Thin Red Line* (1962) or Norman Mailer's *The Naked and The Dead* (1948); in the historical novel, *City of Darkness, City of Night* (1996), she relates intertwined stories of the lives of women surviving amidst the turmoil of the French Revolution. One of Piercy's early novels, *Woman on the Edge of Time* (1976), portrays a Latina woman who has visions of a future that may be the result of schizoid hallucinations, but that may also occur as she travels through time; like Ursula K. Le Guin's *The Left Hand of Darkness* (1969), the projection of alternative chronologies and universes in *Woman on the Edge of Time* allows Piercy to explore questions about the boundaries between male and female, human and machine.

This exploration continues in one of Piercy's most important novels, *He, She and It* (1991), which portrays the struggles of a Jewish enclave in a future America comprising vast regions of impoverishment ("the Glop") where political control is entirely in the hands of multinational corporations. At the heart of this narrative of survival in which the story of a golem and pogrom against Jews in seventeenth-century Prague is paralleled to a corporate attack against a Jewish free settlement in 2059, there is the portrayal of a relationship between Shira, a computer expert whose "field" is "the interface between people and the large artificial intelligences that formed the Base of each corporation" (1), and a cyborg invented to protect the enclave. Fleeing to Tikva from a failed marriage and the loss of her 9-year-old son in a vicious custody battle, Shira initially continues the work of her grandmother, Malkah, in programming and developing the communication skills of the cyborg, Yod, but the more time she spends with "it," the more human "he" becomes, and in turn, the more "he" appears to be a form of consciousness that crosses gender boundaries. Yod possesses "extensive cybernetic, mathematical and systems analysis programming, probability theory, up-to-date scientific knowledge of encyclopedic width ... general history, forty languages, Torah, Talmud, halakic law" (70); constructed with a male body, Yod has been programmed for sexual companionship by Malkah in such a way that he has no "Oedipal taboos ... he does not sully his desire with fear or mistrust of women" (162). As a post-Oedipal entity, Yod can "think like" both males and females, and Shira is attracted to him for his ability to communicate with her empathetically. The ensuing sexual relationship between Shira and Yod is one that bridges several categorical divides between human and machine, male and female, master and slave. Because Yod is not socially or digitally programmed to care about such things, the age and appearance of his lover does not matter to him: as Shira discovers, "[w]hole sets of male–female behavior" does not apply to their relationship, "[t]hey would never struggle about clothing, what he found sexy, what she found degrading to wear or not, whether she was too fat or too thin, whether she should wear her hair one way or another" (245). As their affair develops in the midst of a corporate conspiracy to invade the enclave and steal the knowledge that led to the construction of Yod, Shira comes to think of the cyborg as human, and their relationship one of true equals rather than that between human teacher and cyborg servant. Indeed, as Piercy delineates their liaison in a novel that also portrays survivalist communities of women, the significance of matrilineal genealogies, female friendships, and complex mother–daughter relationships, the roles traditionally assigned to male and female are often reversed between Yod and Shira – he the nurturing, intuitive presence; she the fierce, competitive aggressor seeking satisfaction.

In her acknowledgments at the conclusion of the novel, Piercy mentions two important sources for *He, She and It*: the novels of William Gibson, and cultural theorist Donna Haraway's "Manifesto for Cyborgs." The references are revealing, for in this novel where a cyborg-become-human fulfills his/her/its primary directive in an act of sacrificial self-destruction that saves the enclave, it represents in its hybrid nature as "both/and" the imaginative potential of the posthuman where, Haraway argues, if we survive, we may do so only by transcending all of the self-inflicted cultural binaries – the "antagonistic dualisms without end" – that divide us into categories that bear such labels as "male" and "female" (Haraway, 180). Yod's suicidal act destroys the base and leadership of the corporation that has been attacking Tikva, but it also effects the simultaneous destruction of his creator and most of the research that led to his construction; Yod's purpose, which Shira comes to understand despite her deep sense of loss, is to prevent the future construction of any cyborg as a "conscious weapon" (426), suggesting that the gap between human and machine remains to be bridged. Piercy's point may be that we are not entirely ready for a posthuman future where both humans and machines are regarded as transcending their "programming," their social construction and their utilitarian ends. *He, She and It* suggests that this future awaits us, along with the formation of an identity that needs no pronoun to name it.

Kathy Acker is the author of novels with such titles as *Blood and Guts in High School* (1984), *Don Quixote: Which Was a Dream* (1986), *Hannibal Lecter, My Father* (1991), and *Pussy, King of the Pirates* (1996). Often associated with William Burroughs, performance arts such as Laurie Anderson and Karen Finley, and the punk movement, Acker's writing is deliberately scandalous, plagiaristic, and sadomasochistic in its attack on Western capitalism and the consequences for identity that living in patriarchal, capitalist societies entails. In *Empire of the Senseless* (1988), Acker offers one of her most scathing critiques of "late capitalist" culture in a post-apocalyptic novel set in a Paris of the near-future when revolution and "the end of this white world" (119) have occurred and where a paradoxical state of anarchy and police surveillance prevails. The novel comprises a series of monologues and conversations between two terrorists named Abhor and Thivai who roam the littered streets of Paris and encounter a succession of nomads, secret police, and criminals as they discuss their ruined childhoods and their changing identities in a world that "has disappeared: rather than objects, there exists that smoldering within time where and when subject meets object" (28). Stylistically, *Empire of the Senseless* is a pastiche of scenes, interjections, and diatribes that mimic works from Emerson and Twain to Burroughs, Céline, and the lyrics of punk rock; the chaotic text-assemblage of the novel thus parallels the chaotic assemblages of identity that constitute Acker's protagonists. Thivai is male and a pirate, Abhor (her name indicating her status as an embodiment of abjection) is female and part cyborg, but binary differences between genders or those between animal and human, or human and machine are put on trial in this post-Cartesian universe where the violence of repression and the liberation of desire are thoroughly exposed. As "real children of the revolution" (108), Abhor and Thivai and their fellow terrorists are on a mission to kill off the few remaining "bosses" that constitute the remnants of a patriarchal, hierarchical order, thus completing the overthrow of a world built on arbitrary, socialized differences that signify the relation of the empowered to the disempowered.

Empire of the Senseless can be considered a social experiment that attempts to project the political landscape of the posthuman, where the self is "deterritorialized," in the sense of the term developed by

Deleuze and Guattari, that is, where identity is fluid and multiple, a mind–body construct that interacts with other constructs (bodies, objects, machines) across permeable boundaries. Yet the Paris of the novel is clearly no posthuman utopia in its deadliness and abjection; indeed, it is just the opposite. Thivai and Abhor act as spokespersons for the overthrow of everything from the nuclear family to the economic system of capitalism *per se*, and they seem to embody a principle of identity that has utterly rejected any connection thorough blood ties to the origins of the self in mothers or fathers: as Thivai says at one point of his mother, "'I murdered you: I cut through the red blood that united your mouth and mine: I cut out all emotion which is hatred. I woke up in the only democracy of freedom'" (106). Yet even in this "democracy," where the genealogy and the order or human reproduction are set against a new order of nomadism, cyborg, clone and mutation, the adventures of Thivai and Abhor suggest that the old hierarchies of power remain amidst these reformations of identity. In the novel's dissociative plot, which in Acker's infamous plagiarist mode partially replicates the plot of *The Adventures of Huckleberry Finn*, Abhor is imprisoned by the police: Thivai and a pirate-comrade eventually liberate her, but only as the result of an overly-convoluted escape plan (resembling that of Huck and Tom's plan to release the freed slave, Jim, from his captors) that is designed to test Thivai's skills and to initiate Abhor into piracy at the expense of needlessly extending her term of imprisonment. Following the escape, Abhor angrily writes to Thivai that "the whole world is men's bloody fantasies. ... You two collaborated in keeping me in jail by planning escapes so elaborate that had nothing to do with escape. That's western thought for you ... always fucking deciding what reality is and collaborating about those decisions" (120).

In a novel that so forcefully rejects "western thought" at every level, Acker suggests in the most traditional vehicle of plot that "reality," and the representation of reality, inevitably demands the continuous reinstallation of hierarchies and power differentials (here, between genders), even in a world where identity is tending toward the posthuman. At the novel's end, Abhor, who has been searching throughout for some social equivalent to the liberation of her desire and the deterritorialization of her identity, stands alone "in the sunlight, and thought I didn't as yet know what I wanted. I now fully knew what I didn't want. ... That was something. ... And then I thought that, one day, maybe, there'd be a human society in the world ... which wasn't just disgust" (227). Abhor's final comment, and the apocalyptic setting of *Empire of the Senseless*, suggests the extent to which Acker views the possibility of posthuman identity – which would entail the utter transformation of the sociopolitical order – as one accompanied by unthinkable violence, and one that cannot yet be thought or be written. It is, for her, not a hope, but a negation of a reality whose other she cannot conceive, like other imaginings of the posthuman, without terror and exhilaration.

In *Empire of the Senseless*, Acker posits an alternative history that appears to be a disturbing recapitulation of Western history at its extremes. In Part IV, I will be discussing an array of post-1980 American novels that focus on the question of "history" itself as a form of narration, and as bearing a mediated relation to the reality of the past. Acker's novel imagines the end of history as we've known it, giving rise to the chiliastic question, "what happened to history?", as it is addressed in fictions on the cusp of the millennium's turn.

Part IV

What Happened to History?

From its inception, the novel has always both imitated and parodied the writing of history. As Michael McKeon suggests, as a genre, the novel is a historical form that comes about owing to its "unrivalled power both to formulate, and to explain, a set of problems that are central to early modern experience. These may be understood as problems of categorical instability, which the novel, originating to resolve, also inevitably reflects" (20). These instabilities, McKeon explains, are both social and generic, and certainly one of the instabilities the novel has perennially negotiated is its own status as imaginative flight or historical representation. Although often disputed as being the "first novel," Part I of *Don Quixote* (1605) is, according to the author, based on a manuscript entitled "The History of Don Quixote de la Mancha; written by Cid Hamet Benengeli, an Arabian Historiographer"; as McKeon notes, through this device, Cervantes "pokes fun … [at] … historical authority" (274) at the same time that he refers to the anxious relationship between history and fiction. Daniel Defoe's *Robinson Crusoe* (1719), often cited, disputably, as the first novel in English, is based on the "real-life" adventures of a castaway and bears the full title of "The Life and Most Surprising Adventures of Robinson Crusoe of York, Mariner," indicative of its proximity as a fiction to the genres of autobiography, journalism, and history. One can recount dozens of similar instances from Sir Walter Scott's *Waverley* (1814) to Thomas Pynchon's *Against the Day* (2006) that foreground the "story" of history and ask: what is history, and to what extent is it a fabrication made up of fact and imaginative inquiry, information, and speculation?

In the closing years of the Cold War, several vectors converged that inform these questions as they unfold in post-1980 novels. In a much-debated statement often cited as one of the founding doctrines of neo-conservatism, Francis Fukayama declared in 1989 that, with the fall of the Berlin Wall and the reunification of Germany, "we have reached the end of history as such ... the end point of man's ideological evolution and the universalization of Western liberal democracy as the final form of human government" (4). However it has been interpreted and misinterpreted, Fukayama's controversial claim certainly serves as one indication among many that the concept of history as such is undergoing rapid changes in the wake of the Reagan era. From an entirely different perspective, the philosopher Jean-François Lyotard had earlier argued in *The Postmodern Condition: A Report on Knowledge* (1979) that history can be no longer thought of as a grand "metanarrative," but that it is composed of multiple "petites histoires" (little or minor narratives) that compete for ascendancy. To some degree, Lyotard's philosophical point rests upon how the writing of history as such had been transformed through the work of the "Annales" school, popularized in the United States through the writing of Fernand Braudel in the 1960s and 1970s, which viewed history not as a series of grand events, but as comprising myriad local factors observed over long periods of time, from climate change to regional funereal practices. Heavily dependent on the work of Michel Foucault and post-Marxist historians, critical movements and designations such as "new historicism" and "historiographic metafiction" emerged in the 1980s. "New historicism" is a set of critical methodologies and practices that represent an attempt to view imaginative work as emerging within interconnected local and global circumstances that reveal the operative cultural assumptions of a given moment or epoch. "Historiographic metafiction" is a descriptive term that was developed by Linda Hutcheon to indicate a tendency in contemporary novels that configure history as an assemblage of events, "semiotically transmitted" in such a way as "to both inscribe and undermine the authority and objectivity of historical sources and explanations" (*Poetics of Postmodernism*, 123). Combined with the negative valences of being "at the end of history" – the sense that humanity is poised on the verge of some global catastrophe in an historical extension of Cold War fears of an atomic holocaust – these developments inform the novels discussed here that take history (or its disappearance) as their subject. Widely varied, the fictional responses to the question, "What happened to history?" range from the personal to the collective, and from the ludic to the catastrophic, yet they all seek to understand how the rendering of experience takes place under the pressure of that question.

The Past is Prologue

Richard Powers is one of the more prolific American novelists of the post-1980s period. In a succession of novels that includes *The Prisoner's Dilemma* (1988), which parallels generational and geopolitical tensions during the Cold War, *The Gold Bug Variations* (1991), a massive, encyclopedic narrative that parallels the work of scientists in the 1950s and 1980s searching for the Rosetta Stone of the DNA map, *Galatea 2.2* (1996), which navigates the mysteries of artificial intelligence, and *The Echo Maker* (2006), about a man who suffers from an obscure brain syndrome that causes delusional misidentifications, Powers has portrayed the adventures of identity and the human condition within the matrices of science, medicine, politics, genetics, and the Internet. All of his novels are concerned with the phenomenon of the historical parallel, or how a sequence of events and related contexts in the past affect a similar sequence in the present, and, thus, how the past is prologue.

Perhaps this no more so than in his first novel, *Three Farmers on their Way to a Dance* (1985), which remains one of his most compelling fictions. The novel juxtaposes a series of overlaid narratives and images in a collage of the twentieth century that illuminates myriad connections between war, technology, scientific progress, and the representation of human life. One narrative thread depicts the quest for the photographer responsible for the image of three young Dutch farmers on their way to a country dance in 1914 on the eve of a world war that will transform their lives. Another portrays a contemporary computer journalist searching for a woman he has glimpsed at a Veteran's Day parade, a quest that leads him by circuitous routes to the photograph of the young men. And a third traces the history of mass production, the legacy of Henry Ford, and the labor movement encapsulated by Diego Rivera's magnificent mural in the Detroit Institute of the Arts, "Detroit Industry," depicting automobile factory workers. As the narrative lines weave and intersect, the poetics of an art form most identified with the twentieth century in all of its aspirations and catastrophes – photography – becomes the means for understanding what choices have been made and remain in the wake of two world wars and the Taylorization of mankind.

As a mode of representation that is one of the primary elements of mass culture, photography is a "mechanical" art that depends upon copying and reproducing an original. In the words of the narrator who is pursuing the origins and story behind the image of three farmers on their way to a dance, "[t]he strange persuasion of photographs rests on selective accuracy wedded to selective distortion. The reproduction must be enough like the original to start a string of associations in the viewer, but enough unlike the original to leave the viewer room to flesh out and furnish the frame with belief" (321). The interplay between origin, mechanical reproduction, and human interpretation that this passage elicits echoes the reflections of philosopher Walter Benjamin in one of the landmark documents of modernism, "The Work of Art in the Age of Mechanical Reproduction" (1936). For Powers (who cites Benjamin in the novel) the quest for origins – what lies behind the snapshot or painting, what stories can be traced back to and proliferated from the relic or remnant to the beings who first held or used them – is the intertwined work of fiction and history, and it offers the opportunity to reflect on the history of violence that comprises the twentieth century and, perhaps, to alter its future course. The key ingredient in this complex formula, Powers's narrator asserts, is "interpretation," which "asks us to involve ourselves in complicity, to open a path between feeling and meaning, between ephemeral subject matter and the obstinate decision to preserve it, between the author of the photograph and ourselves" (331). *Three Farmers on their Way to a Dance* is a novel of interpretation that partakes of several scientific and artistic orders – photography, painting, physics, genetics, historiography – in order to probe how we can productively read and see amidst the debris of modern history, the insurmountable mass of historical residue increasingly available in images and documents produced by a technology that threatens to overwhelm us. Our success in doing so, Powers compellingly suggests through these partial, intertwined tales of young men going to war, captains of industry forging the relation between man and machine, and artists seeking to expand the capacity of the image to make history, will depend upon our willingness to engage the past in the present moment.

Three Farmers formulates an interactive relation between past and present by rendering photography as the medium of that relation, and showing the degree to which the prologue of the past is produced by the quest for meaning in the present. The connection between present and past has been a perennial concern for Thomas Pynchon who, throughout his work, poses the question, "What is history?" in oppositional terms: is history a vast conspiracy, or a disorganized succession of accidents and events made over into a sensible pattern only by virtue of the human need to render order out of chaos? Certainly these questions are at the center of *Mason & Dixon* (1997), which tracks the movements of the famous English astronomer, Charles Mason, and his working partner, surveyor Jeremiah Dixon, as they draw boundaries and assay topographies from Africa to the early American republic. Replicating the work of its protagonists, *Mason & Dixon* is a novel given over to surveying the national landscape during the period of its formation when boundary drawing of all kinds – geographical, racial, political – held considerable consequences for the shape of the future. Told through the perspective of a world traveler, the Revd. Wicks Cherrycoke, during "Christmastide, 1786" to a group of children; in a play upon Scheherazade in *One Thousand and One Nights*, Cherrycoke has been silently told that he will be allowed to remain *gratis* in the house of a Philadelphia merchant as long as he can keep the children entertained. Cherrycoke's interrelated tales of Mason and Dixon as they sail around the Cape of Good Hope, observe the rare Transit of Venus as it moves between the earth and the sun, and draw the "Line" between Pennsylvania and Maryland suggest the extent to which history is a narrative of boundaries, the drawing of lines between peoples and nations.

For Cherrycoke, this narrative is bound to fail in the attempt to impose a false order on the impossible "tangle" of memory and event. As he states in one of his excerpted theological tracts that appear as epigraphs to several of the chapters:

> History is not chronology, for that is left to lawyers, – nor is it Remembrance, for Remembrance belongs to the People. History can as little pretend to the Veracity of the one, as claim the Power of the other, – her Practitioners, to survive, must soon learn the arts of quidnunc, spy, and Taproom Wit, – that there may ever continue more than one life-line back into a Past we risk, each day, losing our forebears in forever, – not a Chain of single links, for one broken Link could lose All,

> – rather, a great disorderly Tangle of Lines, long and short, weak and strong, vanishing into the Mnemonick Deep, with only their Destination in common. (349)

Pynchon's effort to mime the grammar and vocabulary of the eighteenth century in order to reproduce the writing of history that he is putting into question is notable here, as is Cherrycoke's notion that history is a fabrication, a frayed network of multiple, fragmentary links to an irretrievable past, the "Mnemonic Deep." Thus conceived, the relation between history and "Truth" becomes the provenance of those in power. As Cherrycoke argues, "'Who claims Truth, Truth abandons. History is hir'd, coerc'd, only in Interests that must ever prove base. She is too innocent, to be left within the reach of anyone in Power ... She needs rather to be tended lovingly and honorably by fabulists and counterfeiters, Ballad-Mongers and Cranks of ev'ry Radius'" (350). It is this illegitimate version of history – the proliferate, tangled history of stories and storytellers – that Pynchon, in his most elaborate historical imitation, places alongside the official narratives of the empowered, which are always conspiratorial, singular, and boundaried, often to the detriment of those upon whom they are imposed. As stated by one of the novel's dozens of minor characters, a Chinese "geomancer" (or one who divines the future by observing topographical features): "'To rule forever ... it is necessary only to create, among the people one would rule, what we call ... Bad History. Nothing will produce Bad History more directly nor brutally, than drawing a Line ... through the midst of the People ... All else will follow as if predestin'd, unto War and Devestation'" (615). The "Bad History" to which *Mason & Dixon* most frequently refers in this tale of the demarcation between "North" and "South" is the history of slavery, with its reliance on racial and class differences, and in many respects this novel offers Pynchon's most trenchant portrayal of racism and its aftermath.

More broadly, the novel's "Bad History" is that of American imperialism writ large, which, in Pynchon's view, is ever a story of "drawing a Line ... through the midst of the People," attributing good to one party and evil to another, setting one in place at the seat of power and the other enslaved to the imposed plots of historical progress. In portraying history either as an assemblage of fragments retrieved from the sea of memory, or as an imperial plot that dominates the past and determines the future, Pynchon's perspective on the past is distinctly postmodern with its mimetic investment in the liberatory, if fragile power of minor narratives and the knowledge that we are at the other end of the arc of the empire portrayed in the novel. Like his other novels – all historical pastiches in settings as far-flung as turn-of-the-century Florence *(V.*, 1963), sixteenth-century Germany and Southern California in the 1960s (*The Crying of Lot 49*, 1966), post-war Berlin (*Gravity's Rainbow*), Mendocino county in the 1980s (*Vineland*, 1990), or the Chicago World's Fair of 1893 (*Against the Day*, 2006) – *Mason & Dixon* represents the impasse between an imperial past and a precarious, post-destinal future. The archaic diction of Cherrycoke's tales and philosophies echoes with the anxieties and prepossessions of the present moment, obsessed as we appear to be with new world orders, and offers one version of how our "bad history" is a prologue to a future that does not have to be.

Across the trajectory of his prolific career, William T. Vollmann has been concerned to rewrite history as the interlacing of minor narratives, perhaps most prodigiously in the ongoing "Seven Dreams" cycle which will trace the history of North America from the Vikings to the present day; thus far, four of seven volumes have been published (*The Ice Shirt*, 1990; *Fathers and Crows*, 1992; *The Rifles*, 1994; and *Argall: The True Story of Pocahontas and Captain John Smith*, 2001). In *Europe Central* (2005), winner of the National Book Award, Vollmann moves beyond the North American context to the theater of World War II in central Europe. At the epicenter of Vollman's massive pastiche of biography, military history, mythography and music are the twinned narratives of "Operation Barbossa," the failed German invasion of the USSR intended to extend Hitler's domain as far east as Stalingrad, and the life and work of Dmitri Shostakovich, the Russian composer whose *Symphony #7, "Leningrad,"* is dedicated to the city named after the leader of the October Revolution and besieged by the Germans for over two years during World War II. While "Europe Central" refers to the phone exchange which carried vital communications about the war, it also refers to Hitler's attempt to homogenize Europe through conquest and genocide, and the resulting inconceivable destruction and fragmentation that came in the wake of that effort. In *Europe Central,* Vollmann tracks the intersecting lives of several key figures from the Russian and German sides: Shostakovich, and his troubled interactions with the Soviet authorities; Hitler, "the sleepwalker," and Hitler's general, Field-Marshal Friedrich Wilhelm Ernst Paulus, who led the German Sixth Army in the siege on Stalingrad; Roman Karmen, a Soviet general and filmmaker who made spectacular propaganda films for the government including an elaborate restaging of the Siege of Leningrad; Andrey Vlasov, another Soviet general who defected to the Germans as the result of Operation Barbarossa; and Anna Akhmatova, the famous Russian poet whose work reflects the precariousness of life and writing in the Stalinist regime.

As this list indicates, the novel is made up of the interspersed public and private narratives of artists and generals, indicative of Vollmann's interest in drawing the relation between art and war in the human mind that can produce symphonies or strategize invasions that lead to the death of millions:

> Our regiments were going to march, with the almost maddeningly monotonous perfection of [German short story writer E. T. A.] Hoffman's handwriting, each line perfectly level and perfectly spaced between the one above it and the one below it ... The sea-waves of Rilke's handwriting, the gentle asymmetries of Mozart's script, the ornate crowdedness of Schiller's penmanship ... with musical accompaniment in Beethoven's grandiose scrawl and troop dispositions drawn up in Wagner's surprising cursive ... And all summer, in spite of the diplomats who scuttered across her space, Europe lay as miserably passive as one of Dostoevsky's women. (122)

The connection between the script of famous German artists and the formation of German army battalions (contrasted with the portrayal of the central European landscape as women's bodies in the fiction of a Russian writer) is pursued at length in the novel in the extended parallels drawn between Shostakovich's compositions and Germany's attempts to extend the Reich across the banks of the Volga River. In *Europe Central*, Vollmann provides a wholly compelling, cross-generic panorama of Europe in crisis, while suggesting the degree to which history is an assemblage of cultural interactions in which bullets and poetry issue from assimilated mentalities that can equally imagine epic visions and enact catastrophes on a massive scale. The past as prologue, in this regard, is a series of chapters in an ongoing struggle between the life of art and the destruction that ensues from state violence in a century of global conflicts where the human imagination may have become its own worst enemy.

Tunneling In

The titles of two massive, encyclopedic novels of the 1990s – William Gass's *The Tunnel* (1995) and Don DeLillo's *Underworld* (1997) – suggest a view of "real history" as that which occurs under the surface, the unseen, unofficial history of myriad lives that make up the body counts and demographics supporting the theses of historians recording major events. What is invisible in history as written, these novels suggest, are the countless interactions, affective drifts, objects, and desires that mark individual lives viewed collectively. In quite different ways, both novels are "career epics": Gass had been working on and publishing parts of *The Tunnel* in literary magazines for 30 years; for DeLillo, who commenced his career with the publication of *Americana* in 1971, *Underworld* stands as a summation of his writing which moves from a trenchant satire of American consumerism and fear of death in *White Noise* (1985); to political novels about simulation, terror, and the fabrication of history in *Mao II* (1991), *Libra* (1988), and *Running Dog* (1978); to the complex negotiations between individual, language, and system one finds in *Ratner's Star* (1976) and *The Names* (1982). For both writers, in novels that appear on the shelf as substantial, detailed, and historically dense as any work by David McCullough, history is something that can only be unearthed by an exploration of its "unconscious," the individual and collective repressions and desires that lie behind the chronology of events and their aftermath.

In *Underworld*, this exploration takes place via the metaphors of trash and waste. The titular protagonist of the novel, Nick Shay, who the novel tracks from his childhood in the Bronx of the 1950s to the early 1990s, is a "waste engineer" who ranges the planet looking for disposal sites and – as a cultural archaeologist without portfolio – observes the landfills and trash heaps where the remnants of the human desire for ever-proliferating commodities collect. The novel begins with one of the most spectacular set-pieces in the annals of contemporary American fiction: DeLillo's intricate description of the 1951 National League baseball playoff game between the New York Giants and the Brooklyn Dodgers in which Bobbie Thompson hit the home run ("the shot heard 'round the world") that beat the Dodgers and catapulted the Giants into the World Series. In this prologue, Thompson's home run is compared to the testing of a Soviet nuclear device that signifies in earnest the commencement of the "Cold War" between the United States and Russia. In many ways, Nick Shay's story is a Cold War story in which a home run and a nuclear explosion, or the changing provenance of the baseball Thompson hit and Nick's progression through various landscapes of waste, are symbolically equivalent symptoms of the arms race, the race to the Moon, the race to economic and military superiority that stitch contemporary American history.

Underworld leapfrogs through that history and portrays dozens of characters pursuing various personal ends in a collective account of the commodification of desire and its aftermath. A collector of baseball memorabilia; a man who steals from his son and sells the Thompson home-run baseball; a performance artist who transforms dozens of abandoned B-52 bombers in the Arizona desert into carnivalesque anti-war statements; J. Edgar Hoover in his public and private life as, respectively, homophobe and homosexual; a renegade nun obsessed with conspiracies, real and imagined; a Russian engineer explaining the paradoxical benefits of underground nuclear explosions in eliminating nuclear waste – all are characters whose paths sometimes cross, seemingly at random, in the contemporary, media-saturated, acquisitive environment that DeLillo has satirized under the heading of "Americana" since his first novel. Waste plays a key role in *Underworld* because DeLillo views it as entirely symptomatic of postwar US society in its superabundance and excess. His regard of contemporary circumstances is that of an archaeologist specializing in "garbology" and a Freudian ecologist, the former viewing the most revealing signs of a civilization in the disposable objects it leaves behind, the latter observing how nature is converted into a culture seemingly bound over to the death-drive. The portrayal of waste thus serves as a metaphor for a certain kind of history that DeLillo slowly reveals in the novel: the history of our relation to produced objects that signifies a collective identity given over to the organization and management of human need and desire. As *Underworld*'s "waste theorist," Jesse Detweiler, states:

> "cities rose on garbage, inch by inch ... Garbage always got layered over or pushed to the edges ... [but] ... It pushed back. It pushed into every space available, dictating construction patterns and altering systems of ritual. And it produced rats and paranoia. People were compelled to develop an organized response. ... Garbage comes first, then we build a system to deal with it." (288)

Underworld is an assemblage of "underhistories," both individual and collective, that survey the contemporary landscape littered with the remains of personal and political adventures comprising a symptomatic history of Cold War America. It is DeLillo's most compelling, and most capacious examination of our consumption.

Comparing *Underworld* to William H. Gass's *The Tunnel* is like comparing *War and Peace* to *Crime and Punishment*: both are stunning, epic achievements of their respective authors, but whereas the former offers a contemporary historical pastiche, the latter hones in on the singular, pock-marked terrain of the protagonist's consciousness. William Frederick Kohler is a scholar of German history, and he is on the verge of completing a monumental project entitled *Guilt and Innocence in Hitler's Germany* when he is undone by the writing of the introduction which rapidly becomes a rambling, unfinished monologue on his troubled childhood, the foibles of his academic colleagues, and the insults he has suffered throughout a lifetime of frustration and disappointment. The novel we are reading is that monologue: misanthropic, mordant, scandalous in its brutally frank, often ribald, and forthrightly objectionable views on women, politics, and race, Kohler's narrative is a chronicle of shame and disillusionment that he attempts to hide from his estranged wife in a tunnel that he is digging under his basement.

The simultaneities of physical digging and digging into oneself, and failing to complete a public history of affect because one has been derailed by the traumas of the private past, are at the center of Gass's controversial novel in which Kohler's personal attraction to fascism and anti-Semitism becomes increasingly apparent. James Wolcott, reviewer for the conservative *The New Criterion*, objected to Gass's "portrait of a fascist" on the grounds that it enabled Gass, through the vehicle of an "alter ego," to give voice to the worst aspects and most evil expressions humankind is capable of: "[i]t aspires to be a permanent splotch on literature's soul, a personal neurosis that attains the status of a cultural condition" (n.p.). In this scurrilous conflation of author and protagonist, Wolcott misses Gass's purpose in *The Tunnel*, which is to portray the extremities of language and the "private" imagination in order to show how they serve as the foundation of history as such, especially the history of horrors that constitute the twentieth century. In Kohler's autobiography/monologue/diatribe, the relation between public and private, between the emotional "tunnel" of the alienated self and public histories such as that which Kohler fails to complete is exposed as a condition of language.

At bottom, Kohler's politics are neither fascist nor libertarian, neither right nor left. His is the "PDP" – the Party of Disappointed People – representing the collective resentments of all of those, like Kohler, who elevate the petty frustrations of everyday life into a general misanthropy that can lead to a politics of alienation which potentially bolsters a host of political agendas, from fascist nationalisms to paranoid anarchies. For Kohler, "reality" is a miasma of misdirected desires and misbegotten plans:

> this much is true ... reality permits us to believe anything or its opposite, as we wish, even both at the same time; it allows us to be stupid and willful and perverse and blind without any special penalty, to live in a daydream or a nightmare ... to follow any religion, ideology, or myth, any half-baked scheme our wretched want miscooks ... (258)

In this chaos of individual motives and delusions, social organization (including the organization of political movements) becomes merely an erratic means of magnetizing disaffected selves into equally disaffected groups, and history becomes the after-effect of chance collisions between event and personal agenda. As Kohler writes, "history, I believe, is not a mighty multitude of causes whose effects we suffer in some imaginary present; it is rather that elements of every evanescent moment endeavor to hitch a ride on something more permanent" (315). Yet "permanence" is the issue in a novel where the individual is revealed to be a seething mass of ugly feelings and failed intentions, and where the organized attempt at self-investigation (literalized in the digging of the tunnel) and the writing of history results in blockage and collapse. Perhaps this is why the novel is peppered with amoeba-like images, typographies, cartoons, and textures that suggest an attempt to pin down the infinite variations of desire and affect – an effort (like the writing of history) that reflects the difficulty of "finding a form," either individual or collective, in the welter of contemporary reality. Through the performative excesses and failures of its protagonist, *The Tunnel* portrays the current relation between the individual and history as one where events are entirely on the surface, the wholly asymptomatic indicators of all the disappointments and misdirections that produce them. This, for Gass, is what underlies the catastrophes that all too visibly mark the history of the twentieth century.

Imagining Epoch

One of the questions raised by writing that imaginatively interrogates how history is made is related to chronology: how is it that we think of history as divided up into centuries, periods, or epoch? Intentionally or not, contemporary writers engage in a form of historical relativism when they set a narrative in a past that bears the marks of an epoch, for to do so is to view history as always changing in relation to the historical position of the viewer. Placing a narrative about two famous eighteenth-century surveyors, as Thomas Pynchon does, in the hands of twenty-first-century readers necessarily compels an interpretive quest for parallels and ironic differences between implicitly constructed "periods": how much has the idea of nation, or America, changed, one line of questioning might run, between the time when regional boundary lines were being drawn between "north" and "south" and the current moment of globalization? Does history have an order or progressive evolution that would allow such comparisons to be made, or is it (as a certain reading of *Mason & Dixon* – one fully enabled by the novel itself – would suggest) a series of spontaneous concordances and accidents that we are at odds to imaginatively organize into sequences of events, centuries, and epochs? This is to regard history as a narrative constructed along the lines of fiction, and conversely, to regard "epochal" fiction as responding to the imaginative need for a narrative that satisfies the assumption that history does have form and shape.

E. L. Doctorow is the contemporary American writer who has most fully explored the relation between epoch, history, and fiction across the breadth of his work. In *The Book of Daniel* (1971), he explores the Cold War and the trials of Julius and Ethel Rosenberg as told from the perspective of their son; in *Ragtime* (1975), the early years of the twentieth century before America's entry into World War I are the setting for a novel that explores an era through the interactions of dozens of characters, real and imagined; in *World's Fair* (1985), the perspective is more confined to the eyes of a child visiting the 1939 World's Fair in New York; in *The March* (2005), General Sherman's Civil War "march to the sea" is the subject. *The Waterworks* (1994) stands as Doctorow's most complex reflection on history, genealogy, and America as corrupted by the promise of immortality. Set in New York during the 1870s, when "Boss" Tweed and Tammany Hall were in ascendancy and systematically plundering the resources of the city, *The Waterworks* is both an historical narrative depicting an era of political corruption in the birthplace of a modern metropolis, and a gothic noir tale of resuscitated zombies and haunted districts; it is at once a detective novel and a social commentary on genealogy and paternity in a time and place over a century ago that is homologous to our own, in a history that is a succession of homologous epochs.

The story is told through the eyes of a retired newspaper editor recounting various mysterious events occurring in 1871 Manhattan: the reappearance to his son of a father believed to be dead and buried; the eerie atmosphere emanating from the city reservoir ("the waterworks"); the machinations of a shadowy scientist, Dr. Sartorious, whose ambitions regarding immortality and the perfectibility of man resemble no one so much as Mary Shelley's Dr. Frankenstein, and whose name anagrammatically recalls Thomas Carlyle's *Sartor Resartus* (1834), a hybrid fiction/philosophical tract that mocks philosophical systems of all kinds. The mysteries take place against the backdrop of a metropolis bustling with energy, fascinated with emerging technologies, and preoccupied with gaining means of power over nature that inevitably translates into political power. Implicitly, the novel generates parallels between late nineteenth-century New York and late twentieth-century America, as if the Boss Tweed and Reagan regimes were bookends to the epoch of American empire and modernity. Dr. Sartorious's project – to bring the dead to life by infusing the blood of children into deceased old men of power and wealth – metaphorically suggests the national obsession with immortality that informs everything from the attempt to extend the "manifest destiny" of the republic across space and time, to what the narrator considers a "derangement of the natural order of fathers and sons" (330) in the wasting of youth to sustain the life of the body politic. The role of technology in all of this is important, and depending upon one's perspective, Dr. Sartorious is either the stereotypical mad scientist perverting the "natural order" to human ends, or simply at the wrong end of the epoch, and about a century ahead of his time with his discoveries about cloning and genetics. But Doctorow's primary concern is the way in which the modern epoch, discerned from the undefined point in the future where the narrator recollects the events of 1871, is defined by its obsession with power as such – an obsession that inevitably involves, for its fulfillment, the vampirization of the young by the old. History, from this perspective, is a recurring sequence of domination and subjection, or as the narrator puts it, even while celebrating the glories of technology and civilization in New York, in 1871, "[w]e were in post-war. Where you'll find mankind not shackled to history is Heaven, eventless Heaven" (13).

The novelist, philosopher, critic, and essayist Susan Sontag turns to the epoch of the eighteenth century in *The Volcano Lover: A Romance* (1992). When the novel appeared, it caused a stir, for to many it was surprising to see an historical narrative subtitled "a romance" coming from one of the leading intellectual voices of modernist aesthetics and the author of two previous experimental novels, *The Benefactor* (1963) and *Death-Kit* (1967). Yet *The Volcano Lover* is a novel of ideas that uses the historical setting in a "century" or "epoch" to contextualize the parameters of our modernity and to portray its history and origins. *The Volcano Lover* is one of a proliferating array of recent novels that reenact earlier epochs, including David Liss's *A Conspiracy of Paper* (2000), set in the coffee houses and byways of eighteenth-century London; Sheri Holman's *The Dress Lodger* (2001), which portrays a city quarantined by a cholera epidemic in nineteenth-century England; Caleb Carr's *The Alienist* (1994), which tracks the movements of a serial killer in 1890s Manhattan; Alan Kurzweil's *A Case of Curiosities* (2001), portraying the adventures of an inventor in eighteenth-century Paris; or T. Coraghessan Boyle's *World's End* (1987), partially set in the Hudson River Valley of the late seventeenth century.[15]

While partaking of the perspective offered by these historiographic metafictions in which the past is viewed through a contemporary sensibility, *The Volcano Lover* stands apart as a novel that complicates the attempt to re-present an era through sporadic shifts in point of view, abrupt reverse anachronisms that jettison the reader outside the historical frame, and frequent intrusions of speculations – sometimes coming from the characters themselves, sometimes from various narrators located in the past and in the present – about aesthetics, politics, pleasure and sexuality, revolution, and historical progress. *The Volcano Lover* is a fictional account of the lives of actual historical figures: principally, Sir William Hamilton, eighteenth-century diplomat, archeologist, collector, and student of volcanoes who served as the British ambassador to the (then) Kingdom of Naples from 1764 to 1800; his second wife, Emma, Lady Hamilton, a former courtesan known for her great beauty and the subject of England's most prominent portrait painters, including George Romney and Sir Joshua Reynolds; and Lord Nelson, the hero of the Napoleonic Wars who becomes Emma's lover and father of her child while living openly with the Hamiltons, resulting in one of the great public scandals of the time.

The novel takes place within the broader contexts of the Age of Enlightenment, the French Revolution, the Napoleonic Wars, and the transition across Europe from monarchy to democracy – a transition fiercely resisted by the novel's royalist protagonists. As an account of the age, *The Volcano Lover* portrays historical consequences of the human desire for consistency, perfection and totality, represented in the notion of the collector whose work is perpetually "[i]ncomplete: motivated by the desire for completeness. There is always one more. And even if you have everything – whatever that might be – then perhaps you will want a better copy … or … simply an extra copy, in case the one you posses is lost or stolen or broken or damaged. A backup copy. A shadow collection" (72). Amongst other things, Sir William Hamilton is obsessed with volcanoes, particularly Vesuvius, which represents a counter-principle of constant change, inconsistency, and unpredictability that coincides with the revolutionary public history and the private history of adulterous desire taking place simultaneously with the volcano's frequent eruptions. Sontag thus brings together in this "romance" of an epoch the fractious relationship between public and private life, natural and political history, and the past and the present, perhaps no more so than when we read of "the great winds" of southern Europe being used in the eighteenth century "like the days leading up to menstruation, to explain restlessness, neurasthenia, emotional fragility: a collective PMS that comes on seasonally" (86); or of the artificial volcano of a German ducal prince which "[u]nlike the fifty-four-foot-high structure of glass, fiberglass, and reinforced concrete in front of the hotel in Las Vegas … the Prince of Anhalt-Dessau's volcano was specifically Vesuvius and went off only on grand occasions for distinguished guests" (327). The judgment upon an era of "enlightenment" and simultaneous brutality and carnage on a scale heretofore unknown is summed up by the novel's final commentator, the revolutionary Eleonora de Fonseca Pimental, who edits a newspaper in the short-lived Parthenopaean Republic of Naples: "I cannot forgive those who did not care about more than their own glory or well-being. They thought they were civilized. They were despicable. Damn them all" (419). Ringing with this judgment,

The Volcano Lover is, in many respects, a chapter in the ongoing history of an ego-ridden "civilization" whose collected treasures – as suggested by the novel's scenes of libraries burned in the heat of revolution and entire collections lost in shipwrecks – are inevitably destroyed by the work of time and event.

While Doctorow's narrator speaks metaphorically of the shackles of history, being brutally shackled by the "civilization" that Sontag's *The Volcano Lover* condemns is more literally the concern of three consequential contemporary novels that also turn to the nineteenth century and the era of slavery in the United States, Toni Morrison's *Beloved* (1987), Charles Johnson's *Middle Passage* (1990), and Edward P. Jones's *The Known World* (2003). One of the primary impetuses behind these novels that recall the horrific events of an "American holocaust," as Morrison views it in dedicating *Beloved* to "Sixty Million and more," is the desire to recover a history that has been repressed and destroyed by the slave system, in which names, families, and entire present and future generations (as Morrison's unthinkably massive number intimates) were obliterated. With the Black Power and Afrocentric movements initiated in the 1960s, and the increasing visibility of slave narratives that came with the development of African American history, literature, and culture as new disciplinary movements in the academy, the need to recover both the African and American pasts became paramount.[16] Perhaps more critically, the need to understand the relation between past and present became a focal point for African American writers and scholars: is that relation reflective of a continued "shackled history," or is the present capable of reclaiming, at least in part, a lost and torturous past? In imaginatively recalling the epoch of slavery, these novels pose that question with an urgency that suggests the extent to which the future depends upon coming to terms with the past, even if to survive has meant, in part, to repress what little of it remains.

Beloved is Morrison's finest novel to date in a collective body of work that led to her winning the Nobel Prize in 1993. The novel is based on the story of Margaret Garner, a fugitive slave from Kentucky who, in 1856, on the verge of being recaptured, killed one of her four children by slashing her young daughter's throat rather than allowing her to grow up into slavery. But *Beloved* is not an historical novel in any traditional sense, for it tells the tale of a haunting and an exorcism as a symbolic means for dealing with a past that, literally, can only be remembered in dispersed fragments, as a disapora of minor narratives. Sethe, the protagonist, is an ex-slave who has murdered her 2-year-old daughter while a fugitive; she has been convicted, imprisoned, and released to her mother, who has bought her liberty and lives in the free state of Ohio. Struck with the sudden appearance of a young woman calling herself "Beloved" (which is also the sole word of inscription on Sethe's daughter's tombstone), Sethe becomes increasingly convinced that she is the reincarnated spirit of her dead child, come back from the grave to haunt her with guilt and memory, but also, perhaps, to offer an opportunity for atonement and a recovery of their aborted relationship. Under the spell of Beloved's possession, Sethe relives, or reconstructs scenes from her past: her arrival at the Sweet Home plantation at the age of 13; her sexual molestation at the hands of the plantation owner's nephews, witnessed by her helpless husband, Halle, who is driven to madness by the event; her husband's failed escape from his owners which leads to his death from sheer despair; the birth on the road of her second daughter, Denver, named after the white woman who helps Sethe deliver the child; her return to her mother's house in Ohio, only to be threatened with capture less than a month later; and the subsequent killing of her eldest daughter, only a little over two years old at the time.

These fragments of memory are collected in piecemeal fashion and interspersed with events taking place in the present: the appearance of the mysterious woman whom Sethe thinks is her daughter reborn; the arrival of "Paul D," one of the former slaves of Sweet Home who has succeeded in escaping and who becomes Sethe's companion and healer; Sethe's growing obsession with Beloved to the detriment and neglect of Denver. But Beloved represents much more than just the catalyst to memory or the incarnate spirit of Sethe's daughter, and more broadly the haunted existence of the ex-slave ridden with survivor's guilt and the recollection of a terrible past that will not be forgotten. The novel's ghost is, in the broadest sense, the "Sixty Million and more," the collective loss represented by all of those who died or who were never born because of slavery. She comes to haunt, even to inflict violence upon, those who have survived, and she is ultimately exorcised by Sethe's baptism into a community dedicated to living in the future by casting off the shackles of history, though it is hardly that simple since Beloved represents the irrepressibility of the past as well as its dissipation. In the novel's lyrical conclusion, she is described as a non-presence:

> Everybody knew what she was called, but nobody anywhere knew her name. Disremembered and unaccounted for, she cannot be lost because no one is looking for her, and even if they were, how can they call her if they don't know her name? Although she has a claim, she is not claimed. In the place where long grass opens, the girl who waited to be loved and cry shame erupts into her separate parts, to make it easy for the chewing laughter to swallow her all away.
>
> It was not a story to pass on. (274)

And yet, it is a story that must be passed on, as it is in Morrison's novel; it is a story on which one can neither take a pass, nor ever fully convey. The tension between remembering a past that is too awful to contemplate, and living in an immemorial future, and their utter interdependence, underwrites what history is for Morrison in *Beloved* in one of the most important novels of the contemporary era.

A sea voyage – the "middle passage" of kidnapped Africans on their way to America to become slaves – is at the center of Charles Johnson's novel of that title. *Middle Passage* is a hybrid of the adventure narrative, historical account, philosophical meditation, ship's log, and gothic novel. It portrays with harrowing realism the nightmarish conditions aboard a slave ship in the nineteenth century, and at the same time is a fabulation containing ghosts, a trapped god in the hold of the ship, tribal magicians, an insane, Ahab-like sea captain, pirates, and a *deus ex machina* in the form of "Papa Zeringue," a New Orleans criminal mastermind who seems to have a hand in everything that befalls the novel's protagonist, Rutherford Calhoun, a former slave and stowaway fleeing a forced marriage aboard the symbolically named *Republic*. With its strange cargo, obsessed captain, and coming-of-age protagonist, *Middle Passage* resembles *Moby Dick* in more ways than one, for it suggests that forces of good and evil, innocence and perversion, exist across racial categories and are intermixed in the human quest for power and the subjugation of others. As Johnson writes in his collection of essays, *Being and Race*, where he is arguing against "Negritude" or the separability of black identity from the matrix of history, it "is a retreat from ambiguity, the complexity of Being occasioned by the conflict of interpretations ... even black history (or all history) must be seen as an ensemble of experiences and documents difficult to read, indeed, as an experience capable of inexhaustible readings" (20).

Accordingly, in *Middle Passage*, the history of the epoch of slavery is represented as an "ensemble" of human motives, figures, and experiences, a collation of deceptions, half-truths, perverse desires, harsh realities, and mysterious events that unfold in the journey to enslavement. The captives taken aboard the *Republic* are "Allmuseri" who, according to tribal narratives, are a highly advanced seafaring people and who have become high-caste mystics and magicians. Certainly one of the horrific historical ironies the novel explores is the immense moral gap under slavery between the captives, treated like beasts, whose learning, wisdom, and "civility" are far advanced over that of their captors, the "civilized" heirs to the so-called Age of Enlightenment; at the same time, the Almuseri are not passive victims: in revolt, they show that their brutality can easily match that of their masters. In part, *Middle Passage* is a *Bildungsroman* portraying the education of Rutherford Calhoun, who comes to believe that history is an unending process of empowerment and revolt, obsession and transformation, resistance and acquiescence to a socially constructed "normality." He comes to see that identity is ongoing assimilation of experiences within that intersubjective process – like the Almuseri themselves, as he looks into the eyes of their leader:

> in Ngoyama's eyes I saw a displacement ... To wit, I saw myself. A man remade by virtue of his contact with the crew. ... Stupidly, I had seen their lives and culture as a timeless product, as a finished thing, as pure essence or Parmenidian meaning I envied and wanted to embrace, when the truth was that they were process and Hericlitean change, like any men, not fixed but evolving and ... vulnerable to metamorphosis ... We had changed them ... the slaves' lives among the lowest strata of Yankee society – and the horrors they experienced – were subtly reshaping their souls as thoroughly as Falcon's tight-packing had contorted their flesh during these past few weeks, but into what sort of men I could not imagine. No longer Africans, yet not Americans either. Then what? And of what were they now capable? (124–5)

Johnson's novel suggests the degree to which history which, for the sake of limited understanding, we organize into centuries and epochs, is ongoing and open-ended, a matter of endlessly changing experience and contact, and thus that the future may become something other than the past history of domination and struggle. But what that future may be must rest in the ultimate uncertainty of what humans will do, or become.

Edward P. Jones's *The Known World*, the first novel of a highly lauded short-story writer which won the Pulitzer Prize in 2004, depicts the history of slavery in the United States from a markedly different perspective than that of *Middle Passage*. The interconnected stories of the inhabitants of a fictional Virginia county during the pre-Civil War era center upon the life and death of Henry Townsend, a former slave who has become an owner of slaves himself, and the master of a working plantation. Unlike *Middle Passage*, *The Known World* is, seemingly, an example of traditional realism containing dozens of characters and mapping the space of an imaginary county in Faulknerian fashion: here, one finds white and black landowners, slaves and former slaves, preachers and slavecatchers, the local sheriff and a miscellany of lawbreakers. The phenomenon of free blacks owning slaves in the South, though relatively unknown, did occur before the Civil War, and Jones uses this cruelly ironic historical development to convey the overwhelming nature of a dominant ideology, and the fact that brutality and the desire for mastery knows no racial bounds. As Henry says to his father, Augustus, himself a freed slave who bought his child out of slavery and who is horrified at the thought of his son becoming an owner of slaves, "Papa, I ain't done nothin' I ain't a right to. I ain't done nothin' no white man wouldn't do. ... I ain't broke no law" (138).

Henry's protest reveals the labyrinthine and twisted logic of "the law" in Manchester County – a law that allows one person to own another as property, and that, on paper, allows some black people to become free while others remain enslaved. It is the law that legalizes murder, rape, and torture in the maintenance of a system that begins to crumble before our eyes as the novel progresses. John Skiffington shares a central role in the novel with Henry Townsend; as the white county sheriff who, impossibly, attempts to police the social order of Manchester County while avoiding the inevitable violence entailed by doing so, he believes in the supremacy of the law and its innate capacity to keep the world in balance and order. So, too, does William Robbins, Henry's former owner, who encourages his ambitions to be a master over other men. When Henry, echoing Thomas Sutpen of

Faulkner's *Absalom, Absalom!* (1936), is seen "playing" with his slaves by engaging in wrestling matches with them, Robbins (himself, something of a Sutpen-in-reverse who "adopts" Henry as a son) remarks:

> "Henry ... the law will protect you as a master to your slave, and it will not flinch when it protects you. That protection lasts from here" – and he pointed to an imaginary place in the road – "all the way to the death of that property" – and he pointed to a place a few feet further from the first place. "But the law expects you to know what is master and what is slave. And it does not matter if you are not much more darker than your slave. The law is blind to that. You are the master and that is all the law wants to know. ... But if you roll around and be a playmate to your property, and your property turns round and bites you, the law will come to you still, but it will not come with the full heart and all deliberate speed you need. You will have failed in your part of the bargain. You will have pointed to the line that separates you from your property and told your property that line does not matter." (123)

The law, in the hands of men such as Skiffington and Robbins, is the arbitrary marker of difference, and the hierarchy of differences must be maintained at all costs in "the known world," lest the world fall apart or disappear, as Skiffington fears it will in the barrage of murders, escapes, and kidnappings that spell the end of Manchester County and, symbolically, the slave system itself in the novel's concluding chapters. Yet the law is only worth the paper it is printed on in Jones's novel, its fragility and lack of protection for those who remained enslaved to the social order even when they are legally "free" revealed when a cruel slave catcher simply eats Augustus's freedman papers and sells him to an itinerant trader. For Valerie Martin, whose *Mary Reilly* (1990) offers a retelling of the Jekyll and Hyde story from the perspective of a household servant, this is "a hothouse world, thickly settled, endlessly policed, characterised by cruelty, brutality, and the same preoccupation with 'property' that makes the work of Edith Wharton and Henry James so deeply frightening" (n.p.). While forthrightly realistic, Jones seeds the novel with metahistorical flashes to the future (a present-day journalist recalling his decades-old investigation into the events of Manchester County; citations from scholarly books on the demographics of the region) that provide a context in which to view the epoch of slavery as both a bizarre and horrific "past," yet still with us in our putatively more progressive assumptions about difference, social order, property, and the law. Like Morrison and Johnson, Jones suggests the degree to which the past lives on in the present, and is only separable as "epoch" by virtue of the questionable fiction of historical progress.

Another History

There is the epochal history of a dominant "Western civilization," which has produced both the Enlightenment and slavery, both perishable art and, seemingly, imperishable violence, and then there are other histories, such as that characterized by the Caribbean novelist and essayist, Edouard Glissant, which "could not be deposited gradually and continuously like sediment ... as happens with those peoples who have frequently produced a totalitarian philosophy of history ... but came together in the context of shock, contraction, painful negation, and explosive forces" (62). Glissant terms this other history "nonhistory" because it cannot be recovered by means of traditional archival or history-writing practices: it must be pieced together and imagined from the remnants left behind by cultures and peoples whose history has never been written in their terms, but only through the lens of the invading force or the colonial authority.

With the emergence in the 1970s of postcolonial theory as a major critical force and, along with it, the increasing visibility of postcolonial writers from numerous traditions, the novel has served a purposeful role as a vehicle for recovering "nonhistory." In many respects, this is a recasting of the novel's long-established function as an imaginary alternative that can "get at" what traditional history-writing cannot with its focus on chronology, document, event. In *No Telephone to Heaven* (1987), the Jamaican American writer Michelle Cliff, continuing the story of Clare Savage that she had begun in *Abeng* (1984), portrays history as a kind of archaeology, based on the premise that the fragmentary remains of a personal or cultural past are all that we have available to reconstruct the narratives of nonhistory. As she writes in an essay, "History as Fiction, Fiction as History": "[h]ow do we capture the history that remains only to be imagined? That which has gone to bush, lies under the sea, is buried in the vacant lots of big cities. In my mind I erect a scaffolding; I attempt to describe what has not been described. I try to build a story on the most delicate of remains" (196). In *No Telephone to Heaven*, the life and death of Clare Savage – her education in America and England, her return to Jamaica as a local historian and educator, her decision to engage in a resistance movement as a guerrilla – is portrayed through a series of flashbacks as Clare rides in a truck headed for a fatal encounter with military forces during a failed raid.

As her history is made up of fragments of remembrance from Clare's conflicting pasts in Jamaica, America, and England, so Clare herself is a pastiche of language, memory, and experience:

> There are many bits and pieces to her, for she is composed of fragments. In this journey, she hopes, is her restoration. She has traveled far. Courted escape. Stopped and started. Some of the details of her travels may pass through her mind as she stands in the back of the truck ... She may interrupt her memory to concentrate on the instant, on the immediate and terrible need. (87)

Educated in the traditions of the Western classics and Enlightenment philosophy ("Read *Elegantia. Timaeus. Profugiorum ab Aerumna.* She was praised for the way she analyzed Aristotle's definition of *place* in the *Physics*" [117]), Clare returns to Jamaica in order to uncover a history partially buried in the "ruinate" of the Jamaican landscape, former agricultural lands which have returned to wilderness through poverty and neglect, and which both contain and reflect a history of dislocation and loss. She discovers enough of that history in the objects, remnants, oral narratives, and patois of her native land to lead her to a startling conclusion about her own identity as an historical being. In this compelling narrative, related through experimental techniques that mirror the fragmentation and multiple layers of Clare's personality, the protagonist's wrenching decision to turn to revolutionary political action suggests that only by becoming an agent in history can one hope to begin the reconstitution of self, past, and place.

In *The Farming of Bones* (1998), the Haitian-born writer Edwidge Danticat tells another story of dislocation and return in the first-person narrative of Amabelle Desir, a domestic worker who has survived the 1937 pogrom against Haitians initiated by General Trujillo, the ruler of the Dominican Republic, in order to redress xenophobic fears that migrant workers from neighboring Haiti were flooding in at such a rate that they were threatening the "stability" of the country. The author of *Breath, Eyes, Memory* (1994), the story of a young woman's migration from Haiti to the United States, and *The Dew Breaker* (2004), which portrays the slaughter of civilians undertaken by the Haitian militia during the Duvalier regime, Danticat relates in *The Farming of Bones* a harrowing story of flight and return. Escaping from Dominican soldiers who are killing and deporting anyone who appears to be Haitian, Amabelle is separated from her lover, Sebastian, witnesses the brutal genocide of Haitian men, women, and children, escapes across the "Massacre River" into her Haitian homeland and a domestic life with a husband she marries more because he is a fellow survivor than for love, and goes back after many years to the plantation where she worked in an attempt to quell the ghosts of the past.

Unlike Cliff, Danticat chooses to convey this narrative of racial violence through a more traditional use of realism that allows her to portray Amabelle's experience of an irrational history over which she has no control, and with which she can only come to terms well after the fact of its observance. Like that of *Beloved*, this traumatic history, premised upon the arbitrariness of racial, linguistic, and national differences (the Haitian people who are slaughtered putatively have darker skins than their Dominican counterparts, and they pronounce the word for "parsley" with a different inflection), is one that cannot be told through the official channels or comprehended by means of the archival record.[17] Indeed, when Amabelle and others attempt to tell their story to government officials who initially offer money to survivors as reparation for and implicit acquiescence to the massacre, they are turned away: "the group charged the station looking for someone to write their names in a book ... They wanted a civilian face to concede that what they had witnessed and lived through did truly happen" (236).

In various ways, Amabelle attempts to comprehend and relate the traumatic history she has experienced. At Sebastian's suggestion, she tries to rewrite the history of her parents' death while crossing the river into the Dominican Republic by "redreaming" it, imagining that her parents lived long lives and died a natural death. She projects herself into the colonial past as she recalls her childhood visits to the Citadel, the huge fortress built by Henri Christophe in the wake of Haiti's independence from France in 1804; she attempts to forget the past in a life of comfortable domesticity; and, as previously indicated, she seeks to inscribe her history in the public record, only to be told that it is a history that will not be recorded. In the end, Amabelle returns to the "Massacre River" on the border between Hispaniola's two nations, and immerses herself in the effluence of blood and bodies – literally, the flow of the island's brutal history – that it represents. The novel suggests that the "other history" of racial violence and genocide can only be addressed through an encounter with its materiality, and that the inescapable past must be assimilated individually and corporeally before it can be transcended.

If Cliff and Danticat portray the fraught encounter with history in terms of personal actions and experiences that comprise unofficial histories, the Native American novelist and critic Gerald Vizenor, in *The Heirs of Columbus* (1991), satirizes the official, Europeanized, "white" history of America by inventing an assemblage of characters who are the "crossblood" generational offspring of Christopher Columbus. In this postmodern pastiche and alternative history, Columbus is of Mayan descent, and his heirs – most notably Stone Columbus, a talk-radio host, trickster, and tribal leader – establish an independent nation in the Pacific Northwest where they hope to gather the remains of their ancestors (including those of Christopher Columbus and Pocahontas) and develop a cure for childhood diseases using the "healing gene" found in all of Columbus's heirs. Vizenor is interested in transforming the relation between past and future through the creation of this playful and, at times, scandalous alternative history which includes manifold references to Native American mythologies, games of chance, the differences between Native American and official American legal systems in regards to property rights, literary theory, both the traditional canons of American literature and the developing canon of Native American literature, herbology, gene theory, the music of Antonín Dvořák, and trickster stories from across the globe. *The Heirs of Columbus* can be considered as something of an encyclopedia for a new world – one in which ancestral dreams exist on the same plane as recorded historical events, and where "heritage" comes about through an amalgam of genes, memory, capacity for trickery, vision, and worldliness.

The differences between "official" culture and its narratives, and an "other history" and the future of healing and play it portends, are illustrated in a dialogue between a "Judge Lord," presiding over a trial involving property rights and the possession of Columbus's remains, and Lappet Tulip Browne, a private investigator retained by the tribal government in the case:

> "Tribal stories and their traces, it seems to me, are not much more than hearsay," said the judge. "Stand would have no significance as a rumor, the legal contentions would be vagarious."
>
> "What does that mean?" asked Lappet.
>
> "Capricious, erratic, unreasonable," said Lord.
>
> "Legal evidence is vagarious," said Lappet.
>
> "Evidence is rational and reason has precedent," said Lord.
>
> "The rules are precedent, and not rumors or stories in the blood," said Lappet. The rules of a legal culture rule out tribal stories and abolish chance in favor of causative binaries."
>
> "Even languages must have rules," said Lord.
>
> "The languages we understand are games," said Lappet.
>
> "Language can be a prison," said Lord.
>
> "Trickster stories liberate the mind in language games," said Lappet.
>
> "Touché," said the judge. (81–2)

The debate between judge and witness underscores Vizenor's sense that official history is linear, causal, one-dimensional, and thus doomed to a single trajectory – that of the imperialist domination and cultural determinism that has ruled the past. In its place, *The Heirs of Columbus* offers an alternative history that is, in many senses, riskier, because it combines chance with fatality, science with magic, language as play and language as powerfully legitimating. As the novel's closing scenes indicate, where the future of mankind rests upon a game of chance, anything can happen. In *The Heirs to Columbus*, Vizenor suggests that history can be viewed as a story that can be changed, and indeed, that must be changed if there is to be a future.

Narrating Vietnam

In 2007, Denis Johnson, the author of a succession of vibrant, dense, and often hallucinatory fictions depicting a mismatched pair on the road (*Angels*, 1983), the world after nuclear holocaust (*Fiskadoro*, 1985), contemporary denizens living on the margins of American society (*Jesus' Son*, 1993), and the druggy interactions of dark, complex characters inhabiting a coastal California town (*Already Dead: A*

California Gothic, 1998), published his most ambitious work, *Tree of Smoke*, a novel of the Vietnam War and its aftermath. As the frequent comparisons of the Vietnam War to Iraq and the appearance of yet another "big" novel on Vietnam over thirty years after the Fall of Saigon in April, 1975 clearly indicate, "the national nightmare" is still with us, its aftermath still exerting momentous pressures on the collective awareness of postwar history, national guilt, and the narratives of national destiny. In the late 1960s and through the 1970s, writers such as James Crumley (*One to Count Cadence*, 1969), William Eastlake (*The Bamboo Bed*, 1969), Robert Stone (*Dog Soldiers*, 1974), Tim O'Brien (*Going After Cacciato*, 1978), and Michael Herr (*Dispatches*, 1977) portrayed the war through multiple lenses, from the journalistic to the surreal. The perspective provided by novels farther removed in time from the Vietnam War varies from the sense that we are endlessly repeating the recent past, to a view of the "falls" of the last third of the twentieth century, from Saigon to Bucharest and Berlin, as heralding the new era of globalization with all of its transience and uncertainty. In manifold ways, imaginatively, Vietnam continues to be the symptomatic historical black hole of the contemporary era.

From one perspective, with its epic proportions as it tracks the lives of its central figures across the 20-year breadth of the Vietnam War from inception to aftermath, *Tree of Smoke* appears to bear a relation to the "event" of war reminiscent in its realism, scope, and psychological immediacy to Mailer's *The Naked and the Dead*. Yet, for the reader, what has occurred since 1983 (the endpoint of Johnson's novel) and the year of its publication – the collapse of the Soviet Union, 9/11, the invasion of Iraq – confers upon *Tree of Smoke* the aura of retrospective and summation. The product of 25 years of sporadic writing and reflection (Johnson mentions in an interview that some of the novel has "been around since 1982. … Once in a while over the years I gathered my notes and tried to make sense of them"), and contrary to some negative reviews which questioned the need for another Vietnam novel or viewed it as a rehash of familiar themes and scenes to be found in the plethora of post-Vietnam novels and films, *Tree of Smoke* offers a searing, Dantesque portrayal of American naiveté and innocence twinned with the arrogance and voracious thirst for power that are integral elements of the ongoing national narrative of "manifest destiny." It does so in the teeth of the current era of American dominance and unilateralism, both "recollecting" Vietnam, and portraying our entrapment in a non-ending historical nightmare.

Tree of Smoke relates the loosely intertwined stories of William "Skip" Sands, who is attached to various elements of the CIA in South Asia in the years leading up to and during the Vietnam War; his uncle, Francis Sands, the Kurtz-like, larger-than-life figure referred to throughout the novel as, simply, "the colonel"; two brothers – Bill and James Houston – whose combined military service "in country" span the war years and who return home to lives of aimless criminality; Kathy Jones, the wife of a murdered Seventh-Day Adventist missionary who appears sporadically throughout the novel as its tortured conscience (she is both Skip's lover and a selfless worker in the war zone, bringing aid to injured and orphaned children); and three Vietnamese men – Captain Nguyen Minh, his uncle, Nguyen Hao, and Trung Than, Hao's childhood friend – who become fatally involved in the conspiracies and counter-conspiracies instigated by the American presence in Vietnam. The novel traces the downward spiral of these characters who are set adrift amidst the bedlam of the war with its failed missions and corrupt objectives. A patriotic Skip Sands, implicated in one of his uncle's covert schemes to "overthrow Communism," goes AWOL from the agency and becomes a gun runner in the postwar years, only to be caught, imprisoned in Kuala Lumpur, and hanged as a smuggler at the novel's end. The colonel presumably dies at the hands of the enemy or is possibly killed by his own cohort who have come to view him either as a traitor or a madman. The Houston brothers, returned to America, have before them a life of petty crime and frequent imprisonment. Minh, Than, and Hao survive the war, but bear the legacy of betrayal, broken families, and a broken country in the Vietnamese diaspora. Only Kathy Jones, who also survives a disastrous crash on a plane carrying out scores of escaping orphans during the fall of Saigon, and who appears to have settled into a vestigial middle-class domesticity by the time of the novel's conclusion in 1983, offers the hint of rescue or redemption from the war's devastation as she listens to a colleague speaking at a charity event for Vietnamese orphan adoption:

> She sat in the audience thinking – someone here has cancer, someone has a broken heart, someone feels naked and foreign, thinks they once knew the way but can't remember he way ... there are people in this

> audience with broken bones, others whose bones will break sooner or later, people who've ruined their health, worshipped their own lies, spat on their dreams, turned their backs on their true beliefs, yes, yes, and all will be saved. All will be saved. All will be saved. (614)

With this desperate affirmation the novel ends. Whether it is the vain hope of a shattered idealist or a recognition that something – if only a fervent statement, a prayer – can be salvaged from the ruin of land, bodies, community, and nation that the war brings is left for the novel's reader to decide, whose experience in traversing Johnson's assemblage of stories, war rumors, myths and mythic journeys, and tales of victimization and inconceivable violence is one of dislocation and loss. *Tree of Smoke* does not help us to "make sense" out of Vietnam, nor does Johnson attempt to provide a chart through the war's labyrinths; just the opposite, his intention is clearly to immerse us in the sheer, radical uncertainty and daily confrontation with mortality experienced by the novel's characters. For Skip Sands, entering the war zone in 1967, Vietnam is "a forge, an emphatically new order – so to speak, a 'different administration' – where theories burned to cinders, where questions of mortality became matters of fact" (196–7), yet only a year later "[h]e'd come to war to see abstractions become realities. Instead he'd seen the reverse. Everything was abstract now" (357). For Kathy Jones, witnessing the deeds of American soldiers, the war offers only irrational, unthinkable contradictions: "[t]hey threw hand grenades through doorways and blew the arms and legs off ignorant farmers, they rescued puppies from starvation and smuggled them home to Mississippi in their shirts, they burned down whole villages and raped young girls, they stole medicines by the jeepload to save the lives of orphans" (309). And for Jimmy Storm, an operative formerly in Colonel Sands's service interrogating Trung about the Colonel's treachery, Vietnam is another order of reality altogether, "a region basically dislocated from natural laws. That is, all the *laws* do apply *inside* Vietnam. But from the rest of planet Earth, those laws do not apply *to* Vietnam. We are surrounded by a zone or a state of dislocation" (478). Perhaps the novel's central symbol – the "tree of smoke" of its title – is the most effective representation of the war in all of its immeasurable contradictions and chaotic progress. A biblical symbol of deific wrath or coming apocalypse, it is the name chosen for Colonel Sands's secret, renegade operation aimed at overthrowing

Ho Chi Minh through counter-intelligence and double-agents. But, like the war itself, the operation adds up to nothing; its name is the sign of its own vanishing, inefficacy, and mindless destructiveness; it is what remains after the "forge" of war, in Skip's figure, has burnt everything to cinders. To this extent, *Tree of Smoke* is not a novel "about" Vietnam, but a novel *of* Vietnam; it does not offer a narrative encapsulation of the war, but registers it as an inassimilable experience, a betrayal of humanity so extreme that the faint tracings of redemption can barely be perceived in war's aftermath.

While *Tree of Smoke* is a chronicle of the war taking place over two decades and involving dozens of characters, Tim O'Brien's *The Things They Carried* (1990) is a set of interrelated stories depicting the lives and deaths of a platoon of men conducting missions in the jungles of Vietnam. O'Brien, the recipient of a Purple Heart, who served with an infantry unit in Vietnam in 1969, is the author of the most celebrated Vietnam novel, *Going After Cacciato* (1978), a quasi-journalistic, quasi-fantastic narrative of American soldiers in Vietnam pursuing a comrade who has gone AWOL in order to walk to Paris for the diplomatic talks that eventually led to the Paris Peace Accords in 1973 (the novel subsequently won the National Book Award). O'Brien had written of Vietnam previously in a collection of stories, essays, and journalistic pieces, *If I Die in a Combat Zone, Box Me Up and Ship Me Home* (1973), and *Northern Lights* (1975), a first novel depicting the relationship of two brothers, one who goes to Vietnam and one who stays home. Indeed, Vietnam and the 1960s permeate all of O'Brien's work, including *In the Lake of the Woods* (1994), a mystery portraying a politician whose actions during the war have caught up with him, *Tomcat in Love* (1998), a domestic comedy about the pursuits of a salacious college professor who claims to be a "war hero," and *July, July* (2003), about a group of 1960s ex-radicals who have gathered at a 30-year class reunion.

Subtitled "A Work of Fiction," *The Things They Carried* is something of a hybrid. A novel? A memoir of the war from the perspective of one who was there? A cycle of war stories that portray recurring characters and interconnected events similar to Sherwood Anderson's *Winesburg, Ohio*? An inventory, as the title story suggests, of all that soldiers carry from their lives and their pasts into and out of the theater of war? A moving philosophical essay on the relation between truth and fiction and the salvational power of stories? *The Things They Carried* is all of these in its depiction of soldiers telling stories to each other about the death of a comrade, killing the enemy, being shot, or coming home. At the center of these narratives – even "Sweetheart of Song Tra Bong," a Conradian fabulation about a soldier's girlfriend who comes to Vietnam to be with him and winds up "going native" – is a reflection on the surrealism of Vietnam's brutal realities and the capacity of storytelling to "tell the truth" of those realities in the only way possible, by means of a fabrication, a weaving of perception, experience, exaggeration, and displacement. As O'Brien writes in the story entitled "How to Tell a True War Story":

> In any war story, but especially a true one, it's difficult to separate what happened from what seemed to happen. What seems to happen becomes its own happening and has to be told that way. The angles of vision are skewed. When a booby trap explodes, you close your eyes and duck and float outside yourself. When a guy dies, like Curt Lemon, you look away and then look back for a moment and then look away again. The picture gets jumbled; you tend to miss a lot. And then afterward, when you go to tell about it, there is always that surreal seemingness, which makes the story seem untrue, but which in fact represents the hard and exact truth as it *seemed*. (71)

O'Brien extends the perspectival relation between truth and fiction when he pulls the rug out from under the reader near the end of *The Things They Carried* by announcing that:

> It's time to be blunt.
>
> I'm forty-three years old, true, and I'm a writer now, and a long time ago I walked through Quang Ngai peninsula as a foot soldier.
>
> Almost everything else is invented. (179)

At first glance, this may appear to give the lie to all the war stories we have read and taken as having a basis in reality and experience; yet, given the surreal, stunningly brutal, trauma-inducing nature of the reality soldiers endure in war, invention, O'Brien makes clear, is the only way of recalling what happened, the only means of access to the "truth" of war, which is experienced as the annihilation of body, identity, memory. If one survives it, one can be rescued from an unmediated history of violence – as close as the next booby-trap or ambush – only by inventing stories that re-cover the black holes of a traumatic past and bring the dead back to life: "in a story, which is a kind of dreaming, the dead sometimes smile and sit up and return to the world" (225). In O'Brien's account of Vietnam in *The Things They Carried*, all that can be brought back from the experience of war is memory, itself an invention written over what has been lost.

There are relatively few war novels written by women, but certainly one of the most compelling novels of the Vietnam War era is Susan Fromberg Schaeffer's *Buffalo Afternoon* (1989). A poet and novelist who has written novels about a concentration camp survivor in *Anya* (1974), the complexities of a lifelong friendship between a 1920s film star and her housekeeper in *First Nights* (1993), the love/hate relationship between identical twins in *The Golden Rope* (1997), and the lives of nobles in medieval Japan in *The Snow Fox* (2004), Schaeffer has been widely acknowledged for her ability to capture historical time and place, yet upon its publication, *Buffalo Afternoon* received a spate of negative reviews questioning her ability both as a woman and as one who had not been there to write authentically of her male protagonist's experience in Vietnam. On one level, the questioning of Schaeffer's credentials in this manner is readily addressed: all fiction is an imaginary mediation of experience, and the history of the novel is replete with examples of works that occur in a time and place well removed from that of the author; moreover, depicting other identities – depicting the identity of the other – is one of the primary tasks of the novelist. (For a rebuttal of Schaeffer's critics, see Jason, "How Dare She?") But a response more attentive to the specificities of *Buffalo Afternoon* would begin with the novel's double vision: the story of Pete Bravado, a troubled, working-class kid from Brooklyn who enlists in the army and is shipped off to Vietnam at the height of the conflict, and that of Li, a young Vietnamese villager who is caught up in the war and is successively transformed into a prostitute, scout, and ultimately the nomadic spirit haunting a destroyed landscape. Alternating between Li's first-person account of her life in a pastoral village before the war and her corruption and spiritualization as a consequence of its onset, and the gritty third-person account of Pete's experience of war and coming home, *Buffalo Afternoon* envisages Vietnam through a binocular perspective in which the indigenous villager and the foreign combatant, and their respective families, communities, and homelands are brought together in a fatal, common history.

The novel begins with Li's sighting of a water buffalo being shot by American soldiers – the first in a series of episodes depicting horrendous brutality to animals intended to portray the universal reach of the violence brought on by war. It ends with a dance organized by Pete Bravado for Vietnam veterans 17 years after he returns from Vietnam that modulates into a surrealistic scene where present and past merge, and where the dead and the living converse about what has been lost and what has been learned as the consequence of the war. In between the shooting of the buffalo and Pete Bravado's dance, we witness a nightmarish succession of scenarios as Pete's unit conducts missions in the Vietnam countryside that graphically depict the utter devastation of war from all sides. The overwhelming destruction causes Pete to surmise at one point that "[t]he whole damn thing doesn't mean anything. It doesn't add up to one life lost out there" (299). To this, a fellow soldier remarks that "It means something. ... It may take years to find out what it is, but it means something" (299), yet almost two decades later Pete is still tortured by the meaninglessness of the war and booby-trapped memories that threaten to undermine any attempts at moving on:

> "The past, man. They don't tell you it's a minefield. You think something didn't bother you. You didn't forget. You just didn't know how to understand it when it happened. You learn more about life, you walk on new ground, yet set something off. It turns out you didn't forget after all. So who wants to go forward? Who wants to be learning something new? You move forward, you set off things you don't want going off. ... They don't tell you. They say you'll get better. They don't tell you what happens when you get better. You get better and you haunt yourself." (533)

Contrary to the popular belief that revisiting the traumatic past can transform it, Pete believes in the end that remembering history and reencountering the dead reveals the utter incontrovertibility of the past. In his view, the past is equally impossible to avoid and to change; memory does not lead to solace, but to a kind of Ecclesiastic wisdom that acknowledges the ongoing presence of the past while recognizing that the future may bring, even if "a little late," in the novel's final words, a season of peace that comes with sheer endurance and survival. That fragile peace, *Buffalo Afternoon* intimates, will only last awhile, and only as long as those hurt by history and those who have harmed them agree to remain in each other's memory.

One of the most compelling post-1980 American novels of Vietnam is Stewart O'Nan's *The Names of the Dead* (1996). O'Nan, a prolific writer with twelve novels and two books of non-fiction to his credit, has not been fully recognized for the quality and range of his work about working-class lives, including *Snow Angels* (1994), about a small-town tragedy in Pennsylvania and the perils of recovering the past; *The Speed Queen* (1997), the reflections of a woman on death row in Oklahoma for committing twelve murders; *The Night Country* (2003), the ghost story of a village haunted by the memory of three teenagers who have died in a car crash on Hallowe'en; and *Last Night at the Lobster* (2007), which probes the seemingly mundane existence of a franchise restaurant manager on closing day.

Like many of O'Nan's lead characters, Larry Markham, the protagonist of *The Names of the Dead*, is stuck in a small American town with a routine delivery job and a failing marriage; a Vietnam veteran, he presides over a voluntary group of disabled and traumatized vets. Larry spends his days working and his nights having nightmare flashbacks to the war that eventually drive his wife away from him, his thoughts constantly fluctuating between the present and the past. What initially appears to be a realistic – and somewhat stereotypical – story of a returned veteran becomes something different altogether when one of the men in the recovery group, Creeley, suddenly disappears and begins to stalk Larry and his family with threats of violence. Along with O'Nan's seamless integration of the surrealism of the past with the realism of the present, the device of the thriller enhances the portrayal of a protagonist under extreme pressure to recover a traumatic past that offers clues about his arrival in the current moment and an unremembered man from his days in Vietnam who is out to terrorize and kill him. For O'Nan, this forced recollection – stunningly clear, yet indeterminate in the climactic scene where Creeley confronts Larry – configures a relation between past and present, the former a pastiche of hallucinatory episodes and random encounters that entail consequences for the latter which can only, ever partially be accepted and understood.

As in *The Things They Carried*, veterans tell war stories in The *Names of the Dead* that allow them to comprehend the past, but O'Nan's novel lays stress on the fact that these compensatory narratives are, on some level, incommunicable. At one point, Larry ponders the difficulties of discussing Vietnam with his wife:

> When he talked to her about the war she had the same reaction every time, no matter what he was trying to tell her; it was awful, and he had been deeply hurt, and in time they would overcome it together – all of which was untrue and, worse, beside the point. Here, his brothers knew that it could not be so easily described, that they were lucky to be alive and that they did not wish to get rid of it, even if that were possible. It was not a choice. The war lived within them like an extra organ, pumping out love and terror and pity for the world – a necessary, sometimes unwelcome wisdom. After all these years he did not expect her to understand completely ... yet Larry still hoped that [she] might recognize this difference in him as something other than crippling. (175)

"Other than crippling" might be an epigraph for the entire novel. For O'Nan, the past is not disabling, but neither is it simply redeemed or transformative. Instead, as the metaphor of the "extra organ" suggests, it is a vital part of the present – not as something cognitively assimilated or merely remembered in stories, but as the critical, affective core of the ongoing life of the survivor, as integral to identity as heart is to body.

It turns out that the explanation for Creeley's stalking of Larry lies in the past, in Vietnam, for Creeley has been mistakenly left for dead by Larry's patrol and returns to take his revenge on those who had forsaken and forgotten him; like Sethe in *Beloved*, Larry is haunted by a specter from the past. In effect, Creeley represents the past that Larry simultaneously remembers and forgets, the "body" of the past left behind. In the novel's concluding scenes, Larry journeys with his young son to the Vietnam Veterans Memorial in Washington, DC. Arriving in the dark, Larry traces out the unseen names of all of the dead he has known, and then, fulfilling a promise he has made to the remaining members of his recovery group, photographs the entirety of the Wall, "the letters stay[ing] with him, burned purple in the dark. ... This time [he] wouldn't miss anyone. This time he would bring them all home" (399). For Larry, the past has become a dark field illuminated by flashes of insight, a body to be recovered, the names of all the dead registered in historical memory. O'Nan's novel thus offers a complex view of the past as both immemorial and, to the extent that it can be recalled in its partiality and indeterminacy, essential to any future that we might have. It is a past, *The Names of the Dead* proposes, that we cannot live without.

A visit to the Vietnam Veterans Memorial also forms a key scene in Bobbie Ann Mason's *In Country* (1985), one of the most notable and moving novels to emerge from the Vietnam War era. *In Country* is not a war novel as such, but the story of a young woman whose father died in Vietnam before she was born, and who feels compelled to understand what the war means to all who follow in its wake. It is the summer of 1984, and Sam Hughes is a far from typical high-school senior living in small-town Western Kentucky. While Sam has the obligatory fumbling boyfriend, negotiates a strained relationship with her mother, is fully immersed in the popular culture of the era (the novel is replete with references to Bruce Springsteen, McDonald's, MTV, and horror movies), and falls at times into the role of "material girl" with a sympathetic girlfriend, she is also deeply concerned about the plight of her uncle, Emmet, a Vietnam War veteran who may be suffering from dioxin poisoning from exposure to the jungle defoliant, Agent Orange. At a moment in life when her own identity and future is in question, Sam becomes obsessed with finding out about the past and its relation to present circumstances: choosing to live with her uncle rather than moving with her mother, second husband, and new baby to Lexington; watching with Emmet endless television reruns of *M.A.S.H.*, the famed, black humor series about a medical unit on the frontlines during the Korean War; ineffectually helping Emmet to find a place in the world after the trauma of war, struggling with her own emerging sexuality. Impelled by her own uncertainties and sensitive to the ironies of loss and historical lapse (looking at her father's picture, Sam exclaims, "'Astronauts have been to the moon. ... You missed Watergate. ... I was in the second grade'" [67]), Sam becomes obsessed with finding out who her father was and how he died in Vietnam. She discovers that, to do so, she must break through a conspiracy of silence that spells a disavowal of the past sublimated by the distractions of American pop materialism.

As Sam attempts to find out about her father, she encounters only resistance from her mother, who wishes to forget the past and her husband's death as she embraces a new life. Equally resistant to any digging into the past (while ironically engaged in digging out the foundations for the basement of the house in which he lives) is Emmet, who is in full flight from the memory of war and whose debilitating headaches may be more psychosomatic than physical in origin. Indeed, none of Emmet's friends, all veterans of the war, want to talk about it. Tom, a vet upon whom Sam has a crush, puts it this way:

> "Sam, you might as well just stop asking questions about the war. Nobody gives a shit. They've got it all twisted around in their heads what it was about, so they can live with it and not have to think about it. The thing is, they never spit on us here. They treated us vets O.K., because the anti-war feeling never got stirred up good around here. But that means they've got a notion in their heads of who we are, and that image just don't fit all of us. Around here, nobody wants to rock the boat." (79)

Tom's perception is localized, but by extension it represents a broader "American" view in the aftermath of the Vietnam War: better that a traumatic and divisive historical era be left behind as "the Dark Ages" (64), as Anita, Emmet's ex-girlfriend, characterizes it. But Sam, intuitively convinced that her own identity and fate are directly linked to her father's experience of the war, cannot simply leave it alone.

Her quest for information about her father and stories of the war lead her to several dead ends; even when she discovers her father's letters and diaries, she remains frustrated by the historical gaps and elisions they contain, for the letters from her father to her mother disguise the brutality of the war, and the diaries contain only factual information about day-to-day actions and movements. Thus, Sam seeks to come to terms with the past by experiencing it herself, and even though the experience is a simulation (she suddenly goes for an overnight stay into a wilderness area sans proper clothes or equipment and imagines that she is in the jungles of Vietnam), it initiates a breakthrough. Discovering her in the woods, even while chiding her for thinking that an overnight excursion into a protected area could possibly reduplicate the experience of war, Emmet begins to tell war stories, and comes to a dubious form of self-recognition:

> "There's something wrong with me. I'm damaged. It's like something in the center of my heart is gone and I can't get it back. … I work on staying together, one day at a time. There's no room for anything else. It takes all my energy. … If you can think about something like birds, you can get outside of yourself … But I can barely get to the point where I can be a self to get out of." (225–6)

This admission of loss, even though it comes along with Emmet's claim that "'You can't learn from the past. The main thing you learn from history is that you can't learn from history. That is what history *is*'" (226), leads to the journey to the Vietnam Veterans Memorial described in the novel's first and last parts. The encounters with history that *In Country* describes are various: photographs, documents, stories, flashbacks, simulations, touching the names of the dead on the Wall – all comprise ways in which history, as Emmet defines it in its indecipherability, can both be understood and missed. Sam's tracing out on the Wall the name of a soldier who bears her own name suggests that history is a set of contingencies which we must exert our collective will to encounter in any way we can. *In Country* thus portrays the historical experience of Vietnam as part of a national story that unwinds despite, and partially because of the failures of its telling.

Catastrophe: The Ends of History

In the ancient Greek, "catastrophe" translates as "to overturn," and refers to the resolution of the plot of a tragedy, in which final revelations lead to blinding insights for the protagonist and the audience in such a way that they experience "catharsis," or a purification resulting in the self reborn with new knowledge. The contemporary sense of catastrophe is more often related to an historical event or sequence of events of cataclysmic proportions: nuclear holocaust, global warming, global economic collapse, and to all the "smaller" catastrophes that stitch contemporary history and seem to appear with appalling regularity in localized forms of natural and manmade disasters. A considerable number of contemporary novels reflect the fear (or fantasy) that human history as we know it may be coming to an end, whether through the more possible catastrophes of a third world war or the massive destruction of the ecosystem, or those seemingly more far-fetched brought about by alien invasion or divine intervention. Millennial fears and fantasies always seem to accrue at the turn of centuries or tens of centuries, but for readers of contemporary American fiction, these fears can also be located as having particular origins in the Cold War and its ongoing after-effects, in the sense that the national political destiny is going seriously awry following the collapse of the Soviet Union, and with the growing alarm – shared globally – that the planet itself may be on the road to extinction. More broadly, of course, contemporary fictions of catastrophe are written against the backdrop of the twentieth century writ large – the era of the "rough beast" that W. B. Yeats announced in "Slouching Towards Bethlehem," his prophetic vision of a landscape that has seen two world wars, technological advance and destruction, and genocide on an unimaginable scale. The interest of contemporary writers in depicting historical transformation as the result of catastrophe is symptomatic of a larger public sense that history may be out of control, and that the narrative of historical progress has been sundered by the misfortunes and reversals of our times. These novels ask, what will become of us if we can no longer ordain this narrative and foresee its consequences, and how do we come to terms with the unpredictability of the present evident in everything from the fluctuations of the stock market to the sudden outbreaks of terror or contamination that are, perhaps, early warning signs of a larger catastrophe to come? They also ask what the role of the human imagination is in comprehending catastrophes, small or large, and how we might reshape our understanding of history in light of its possible end.

White Noise (1985), Don DeLillo's ninth novel, is his most trenchant satire of middle-class America and its consumerist obsessions. At the center of this sardonic portrayal of suburban culture, academia, and American materialism is the sudden manifestation of an "airborne toxic event," a mini-catastrophe that comes and goes but whose effects upon identity and community continue to be perceived in the afterglow of the event symbolized in the sunsets of the polluted skies, "when the sky would ring like bronze" (321). Near the suburban town which is the home of the novel's protagonist, Jack Gladney, chairman of the Department of Hitler Studies at the "College-on-the-Hill," a train full of toxic chemicals has derailed, and an ominous black cloud has spread over the area, causing a mass evacuation. The airborne toxic event is but a physical manifestation of the ever-present fear of mortality that seems to affect many of the novel's principals: Gladney, himself, who (a professor of German history, though he can neither speak nor read German) engages in frequent conversations with his colleagues about death, individual and collective; Jack's wife, Babette, who suffers from an inordinate fear of death and secretly takes "Dylar," an experimental counter-phobic drug that seems to do her little good; their daughter, Steffie, who has a pharmacist's knowledge of drugs and medications, and who spends a lot of her time talking about symptoms and adverse effects. The contemporary American fear of death that the novel exposes corresponds in ratio to the fascination with technology and the reliance on consumer products that seem to offer a better, longer life as a hedge against mortality.

Things happen in *White Noise* – the evacuation of the Gladney family to a Boy Scout camp which serves as a temporary shelter for refugees fleeing the spreading cloud; Gladney's discovery that his wife has been taking Dylar; his pursuit and non-fatal shooting of Willie Mink, the sleazy dealer who has obtained sex from Babette in exchange for the drug – but the novel is primarily an array of conversations that take place between various characters on the subjects of death, technology, nature, brand names, the afterlife. The novel's catastrophe oddly serves as a rallying point and informational nexus for the provisional community of those affected by it, as observed by Gladney listening to his son, Heinrich, who is something of a scientific prodigy, talk about the chemical spill to a group of listeners:

> What a surprise it was to ease my way between people at the outer edges of the largest cluster and discover that my son was at the center of things, speaking in his new-found voice, his tone of enthusiasm for runaway calamity. He was talking about the airborne toxic event in a technical way, although his voice all but sang with prophetic disclosure. He pronounced the name itself, Nyodene Derivative, with an unseemly relish, taking morbid delight in the very sound. People listened attentively to this adolescent boy in a field jacket and cap, with binoculars strapped around his neck and an Instamatic fastened to his belt. No doubt his listeners were influenced by his age. He would be truthful and earnest, serving no special interest; he would have an awareness of the environment; his knowledge of chemistry would be fresh and up-to-date. (130)

Within the restricted confines of a local event, the novel's event appears to serve larger purposes: a historical marker, an opportunity for discourse and the exchange of information, a catalyst for the formation of a community around the possibility of mortality made visible, a father's ambivalent witnessing of a son's coming of age. The words "catastrophe" and "tragedy" are used liberally in the media-saturated environment that DeLillo satirizes here and elsewhere, and to be sure, the "catastrophe" of *White Noise* is more symptomatic than real. There is, clearly, a great difference in kind between the novel's airborne toxic event in which, apparently, no one dies immediately (though Gladney may have contracted cancer as a result) and the unthinkable catastrophe at the center of Gladney's academic pursuits or the eerie contingency of the novel's publication only a matter of weeks after the 1984 chemical spill in Bhopal, India which caused 3,500 deaths and 29,000 injuries. But for DeLillo, what is of primary interest is the capacity of the catastrophic event – small or great, local or global – to be "reported out" as part of the historically fated, prophetic narrative of a society driven deathwards, the victim of its own desires and progress. The depressing point is ameliorated in the novel by its satirical humor and its cartoonish exaggerations: this is the fragile reality we might perceive in a TV soap opera about the aftermath of a disaster if it were scripted by a politically canny postmodern novelist out to expose the bizarre nature of our reliance on products, information, technology, and institutions for assurances of safety and security. Yet, for all that, *White Noise* somberly suggests the ways that, in DeLillo's view, contemporary history points toward its own ends, manifest in what we buy, what we fear, how we talk.

Another catastrophe lies behind Jonathan Safran Foer's *Extremely Loud & Incredibly Close* (2005): 9/11. *Extremely Loud* is Foer's second novel following his story of ancestry and the Holocaust in *Everything is Illuminated* (2003), and one of a group of compelling "post-9/11" novels written in the wake of the destruction of the World Trade Center by terrorists on September 11, 2001, including DeLillo's *Falling Man* (2007), Claire Messud's *The Emperor's Children* (2006), Jay McInerny's *The Good Life* (2007), British novelist Ian McEwan's *Saturday* (2005), French novelist Frédéric Beigbeder's *Windows on the World* (2005), and Art Spiegelman's graphic "board book," *In the Shadow of No Towers* (2004). Much of *Extremely Loud* is told from the perspective of a precocious, autistic-like 9-year-old who sublimates his response to his father's death in the Twin Towers by undertaking a quest to find the lock that fits the key he has found in a vase his father has left behind. Foer's novel resembles recent novels and films that narrate catastrophe and terror through a child's perspective and make use of fairytale devices in doing so (one is particularly reminded of Guillermo del Toro's brilliant movie *Pan's Labyrinth* [2006]). His employment of a quest-motif and the interspersing of graphic and typographical elements throughout the printed text reflect Oscar Schell's hands-on, manically inventive approach to a reality that he can only comprehend discursively via such devices as mathematical formulae, rebuses, and snapshots. In Oscar's story, which is paralleled to the story of his grandparents' experience of the Dresden firebombing and his grandfather's sudden departure from his family for over forty years, coming to terms with catastrophe is a constructivist enterprise that involves giving imaginary form, shape, and direction to the messiness and annihilating horror of history.

Due in part to Oscar's ludic, bizarre, occasionally gimmicky "takes" on 9/11 and the death of his father, and to the visual legerdemain the novel exhibits (such as that of its final pages, which constitute a "flip book" showing a body falling upwards, back into the burning tower of the World Trade Center, "floating up through the sky … through a window, back into the building" [325])," *Extremely Loud* has been a source of controversy, with assessments ranging from Salman Rushdie's glowing "ambitious, pyrotechnic, riddling, and above all … extremely moving" (cover blurb) to the *New York Times* reviewer's assessment of the novel as "an overstuffed fortune cookie," an example of "today's neo-experimental novels … not necessarily any better suited to get inside, or around, today's realities than your average Hardy Boys mystery" (Kirn). The visual "trick" of the flip book which accompanies Oscar's wish that history reverse itself to before 9/11 may portray the classic American desire for a return to a time of innocence "before history" in sentimental or naïve terms, but it is also possible to view such devices as conveying Foer's sense that the contemporary response to catastrophe in the United States is, precisely, childlike, narcissistic, a matter of wanting to wish it all away. The fantasy of history as malleable and reversible is a permanent fixture of the American cultural imaginary, equally evident in the documents of manifest destiny, Reaganite regressions into the putatively small-town innocence of an earlier America, or the migrations of a Forrest Gump across the simulated terrain of the American 1960s and 1970s via the magic of blue screen and digital imaging.

Extremely Loud bodies forth this fantasy; however, by placing it in the mind of a very peculiar child – one who is able to charm us with such observations as "the fascinating thing was that I read in the *National Geographic* that there are more people alive now than have died in all of human history. In other words, if everyone wanted to play Hamlet at once, they couldn't, because there aren't enough skulls," (3) – but one who is also a highly simulated construct suggests the degree to which the desire to reverse history in light of the catastrophes of reality can result in "sheer invention." This recognition is the hard edge against which Oscar's final, pathos-ridden conditional statement, "we would have been safe" (326), must rub. Foer's novel suggests that history as it occurs in the irreversibility of a nationalized catastrophe such as 9/11 marks the boundary-line of the touted American imagination and can-do inventiveness, where "would" falls well short of "were," and where the future is beholden to the intransigency of the past.

In *Almanac of the Dead* (1991), the Native American writer Leslie Marmon Silko introduces dozens of characters and relates a myriad of scattered, but ultimately related events occurring during the Reagan 1980s in Tucson, Arizona, Mexico, and California. Silko, the first female Native American Writer to gain widespread recognition with the publication of *Ceremony* (1977), the story of a young man returning to the reservation after the horrors of war, portrays in *Almanac of the Dead* a greedy, violent, drug-ridden, and media-saturated "Western civilization" on the verge of collapse. In tracing the ancestry and history of its principal characters – Sterling, who has come to Tucson as a gardener after being cast out of the Pueblo reservation for a supposed violation of native traditions; Lecha, a renowned television psychic who has escaped to the anonymity of the city on the desert and who compiles and maintains an almanac that relates an alternative history of her people; Seese, in hiding from a Manson-like family of drug dealers who have kidnapped her son; Menardo, a Mexican businessman who descends into paranoia as the result of his corporate and political greed – the novel offers an encyclopedic catalogue of the devastation wrought by European and American imperialism. In a narrative focused on a symbolic, yet realistically detailed city in the Southwestern desert that is exploiting and rapidly depleting its natural resources amidst a population explosion (made parallel to the exploitation, ghettoization, and reduction of its indigenous population), and where political corruption rules the day, Silko ultimately offers an apocalyptic vision of a world on the verge of dramatic change and at the dawn of a new age. As is evident in the "Five Hundred Year Map" that prefaces the novel and that collapses the old world into the new one, *Almanac of the Dead* will portray both the Tucson, Arizona of "today" ("[h]ome to an assortment of speculators, confidence men, embezzlers, lawyers, judges, police and other criminals, as well as addicts and pushers, since the 1880s and the Apache Wars"), and the time to come: "When the Europeans arrived, the Maya, Azteca, Inca cultures had already built great cities and vast networks of roads. Ancient prophecies foretold the arrival of Europeans in the Americas. The ancient prophecies also foretell the disappearance of all things European" (15–16). It is the "disappearance of all things European," including the brutal history of exploitation and genocide that the Europeanization of the Americas has portended, that *Almanac of the Dead* envisages in a future where ancestral ghosts and indigenous people reclaim and restore the world.

According to the *Oxford English Dictionary*, an almanac is an "annual table or ... book of tables, containing a calendar of months and days, with astronomical data and calculations, ecclesiastical and other anniversaries, besides other useful information, and, in former days, astrological and astrometeorological forecasts." The most familiar example of the genre for contemporary readers is *The Farmer's Almanac*, a yearly compilation of weather projections, crop-rotation schedules, astronomical tables, historical tidbits, and folksy advice that has been in continuous publication in North America since 1818. Silko's novel embodies the qualities of an almanac as a palimpsest that records the lost or ignored histories of the marginalized and disappeared, and predicts changes to come in the historical landscape with the disappearance of a Western hegemony in North America (and, by extension, across the planet). The notion of an "almanac of the dead" has a double valence for Silko, for it suggests both an accounting for those who have been lost to genocide and imperialism, and a raising of the spirits in a prophetic history that, when "complete," will vanquish the temporal, secular histories of conquest and destruction. In the words of the novel's roving narrator, "[t]he old people had stories ... that it was only a matter of time and things European would gradually fade from the American continents. History would catch up with the white man whether the Indians did anything or not. History was the sacred text. The most complete history was the most powerful force" (316).

The idea of history as an unstoppable force, already complete in the sacred text of the narrative that Lecha is in the act of compiling and translating as the novel proceeds, rests upon different senses of time, experience, and event. As Lecha records: "An experience termed *past* may actually return if the influences have the same balances or proportions as before. Details may vary, but the essence does not change. The day would have the same feeling, the same character, as that day has been described as having had *before.* The image of a memory exists in the present moment" (574–5). Viewing history cosmically – as a completed narrative that only appears as "time out of joint" in its temporary, disconnected chronological manifestations – enables a sardonic perspective on the law, science, imperial history, and capitalism in this sweeping novel where they are rendered as series of flawed and unbalanced manifestations in a larger, integrated design. If that design, for Silko, is fated, it is also hopeful, even as it depends upon the passing away of all that constitutes "civilization" in the sense used by history's winners.

Cormac McCarthy's *The Road* (2006) depicts the end of civilization an apocalyptic future in a notably different key. For over forty years, McCarthy has been writing novels that explore human violence and life on the margins in virtuosic linguistic performances that, in the tradition of the picaresque, weld the local to the universal. *Sutree* (1979), his fourth novel, tells the story of a man who has given up a "normal" life for an itinerant existence, but one that allows him startling insights about the acts and motives of those on the fringe; *Blood Meridian, or, the Evening Redness in the West* (1985) – still McCarthy's most wrenchingly compelling novel – is based on historical accounts and portrays an alternative version of the "Wild West" of movies and television in its tale of genocide, treachery, and human brutality in the American borderlands; *All the Pretty Horses* (1992), *The Crossing* (1994), and *Cities of the Plain* (1998) make up the more lyrical "Border Trilogy," an interrelated set of initiation stories that portray modern journeys into manhood in the ranching country of Texas, New Mexico, and Mexico; *No Country for Old Men* (2005), adapted for film in a stunning return to form by the Coen Brothers in 2007, takes place in a contemporary setting near the Mexican border where the forces of law, morality, and human greed come into conflict with the need for human connection.

The Road is the most bleak and austere of McCarthy's novels. Set in a burnt-out, post-apocalyptic landscape where some unnamed disaster has befallen the planet, it is a narrative of sheer endurance as a father leads his son across the countryside of what once was small-town America to "the coast," where some indeterminate form of salvation may lie. The allegory of *The Road* explores what remains of humanity when civilization has been destroyed, and when history as we know it has come to an end; it asks, how do we conceptualize identity and relationship when life has been reduced to its most primitive prerequisites, and when there is, literally, no future but that of a precarious daily survival? In an environment where everything that constitutes the past has been literally obliterated, do time and history even continue to exist? As the father reflects early in the journey with his son that will expose them to scenes of overwhelming barbarity and, occasionally, small, rapidly disappearing remnants of human decency: "On this road there are no godspoke men. They are gone and I am left and they have taken with them the world. Query: how does the never to be differ from what never was?" (32). The question about what happens to history when any need for history has ended rings throughout the novel as the vestiges of self, memory, past, and life itself are gradually stripped from father and son in the urgency of the quest for food, shelter, and safety from roaming clans of cannibalistic looters and survivalists. When "[t]here is no past" (54), as the father explains to the child at one point, when "[t]he world is shrinking down about a raw core of parsible entities" (88) such that even the name of common thing is "shorn of its referent and so of its reality" (89), then, McCarthy suggests in this unsparing account, "the value of the smallest thing predicated on a world to come" (187) becomes illuminated. "Perhaps in the world's destruction it would be possible at last to see how it was made" (274), the father posits in the final extremities of illness and starvation, suggesting that out of the de-creation of the world and the self can emerge a stark, pragmatic sense of history and what has been – one founded not upon grandiose event and the machinations of power, but on the primacy of human need.

In *The Road*, the father dies so that the son may live. It is this sacrificial transference of blood and relation to the next generation that constitutes a provisional history in the new world of the novel's future, where the survival of life is both completely uncertain and, in any recognizable form, up to us. The novel concludes with a description of a species of brook trout that have become extinct in the wake of the undefined catastrophe, a fish on whose backs, never to be seen again, "were vermiculate patterns that were maps of the world in its becoming. Maps and mazes. Of a thing which could not be put back" (287). This rendering of a scene of extinction that, in the current precarious moment, seems more eerily familiar than only remotely possible compels the reader to ask to what degree is *The Road* a dark vision of the future, and to what extent an allegory of the present?

These novels of catastrophe and survival suggest the extent to which history is a narrative of collectivities – those of the family, community, nation. Imagining these collectivities is the work of novels that regard the motive for fiction as portraying history on the move, unfolding in the shifting, manifold relationships that occur between mobile assemblages to which we give names or around which we draw borders. In the final part, I will be focusing on contemporary novels that portray in myriad ways the migration of identities within and across these interrelated collective embodiments.

Part V

Relations Stopping Nowhere

When we recall the opening sentences of novels such as *Anna Karenina* ("Happy families are all alike; every unhappy family is unhappy in its own way"), *Pride and Prejudice* ("it is a truth universally acknowledged, that a single man in possession of a good fortune, must be in want of a wife"), or *A Catcher in the Rye* ("If you really want to hear about it, the first thing you'll probably want to know is where I was born, and what my lousy childhood was like, and how my parents were occupied and all before they had me, and all that David Copperfield kind of crap, but I don't feel like going into it, if you want to know the truth"), we are reminded of how much the novel as a genre is given over to family relationships and the larger, intersecting regimes of community, region, and nation. The relationship between the popularity of the novel and the rise of the middle class which privileges individualism, the "nuclear" family, and the governmental entities that will protect these (from the neighborhood organization to the nation) has been well established by Ian Watt in *The Rise of the Novel.* With the advent of modernism, the novel has become a genre that incrementally both inscribes and critiques what the American philosopher/humorist H. L. Mencken, in *Notes on Democracy* (1926), scathingly termed "the boobosie," though one might claim that novels have always done so: Joyce's *Ulysses* portrays a day in the life of a bourgeois subject whose desires and relationships everywhere controvert smug assumptions about cosmopolitan middle-class life; D. H. Lawrence's novels constitute a persistent attack on middle-class mores which he regards as fatally oppressive; throughout her work, as intensively reflected in the semi-biographical *Three Guineas* (1938), Virginia

Woolf draws the skein of relations between individualism, family, class, patriarchy, and nationalism. This novelistic tradition continues vigorously in contemporary fiction, during an epoch when the formations of family, class, community, and nation are undergoing vast changes: the family is no longer "nuclear," in any falsely idealized sense; communities exist as heterogeneous, mobile assemblages in both the material and virtual realms; the concept of "nation" is being radically transformed during the age of globalism. In this section, I will consider an array of American novels written since 1980 that portray the manifold relations between identities and social orders represented by family, community, and nation as migratory, "stopping nowhere," always transgressing the boundaries of these entities that, themselves, are increasingly marked by their mutability.

The Postnuclear Family

In traditional conceptualizations, the family has always served as the seedbed of fictionalized identities: how many novels have begun with a description of the time and place of birth, or parentage, or genealogy? So begins Jeffrey Eugenides's *Middlesex* (2002): "I was born twice: first, as a baby girl, on a remarkably smogless Detroit day in January, 1960; and then again, as a teenage boy, in an emergency room near Petoskey, Michigan, in August of 1974" (3). The novel's title is both the name of the street in the middle-class Detroit suburb of Grosse Pointe, where Cal/Calliope Stephanides grows up, and a reference to the narrator's sexuality. Owing to a rare genetic deficiency that causes the male sexual organs to appear to be female, the narrator's sex is assumed to be female until puberty, and he has been raised as a girl; with the onset of puberty, and through an accident that leads to an examination in an emergency room, Cal discovers that he is biologically male, with a condition that has not allowed him to produce testosterone. What ensues is Cal's running away from home at the age of 14, in large part to escape from a sex-change operation that would permanently transform him "back" into Calliope at the hands of a specialist who has diagnosed him as a "male psuedohermaphrodite" (413) and who believes that gender identity is entirely a matter of environment and upbringing. One of the reasons for Cal's flight from the "normalization" of his sexuality and his middle-class existence is that the operation could very possibly lead, as the doctor's report states, to "partial or total loss of erotosexual sensation" (437), thus potentially curtailing sexual pleasure for the sake of sexual determinacy – for Cal, in effect, an unacceptable result that would abnegate his sexuality. Cal never returns home, but undertakes a nomadic journey across America, into the San Francisco underground, and eventually to Europe in search of place; his quest to establish his sexuality leads him to write the family memoir of *Middlesex* in which, in his own life, as well as that of his parents and grandparents, the constitution of identity as a matter of genes, or of history and experience, is tested.

The Stephanides family history is both centripetal and centrifugal: immigrating to America in the wake of the 1919–22 Greco-Turkish War, Cal's grandparents, Lefty and Desdemona, come to Detroit as newlyweds; they are also brother and sister who use the opportunity of a new life and new identities in America to disguise the fact of their incestuous relationship. This is one of many secrets Cal uncovers in relating a family story full of misperception and deceit: moving in with their sister, Sourmelina, who is certain to keep their secret safe because she harbors her own secret as a closet lesbian, Lefty becomes a bootlegger (the first of many illegitimate schemes he undertakes) in partnership with his brother-in-law, Jimmy Zino, while Desdemona settles down to a domestic life as an American housewife. Desdemona gives birth to the child who will become Cal's father, Milton, while Lina gives birth to the woman who will become Cal's mother, Tessie. The unfolding of this entangled genealogy takes place against the backdrop of, successively, the Great Depression, World War II, the Cold War, Vietnam, and the Detroit race riots, the family history thus fatally implicated in the larger movements of a capitalized History. At one point, Cal traces the family line as follows:

> So, to recap: Sourmelina Zizmo (née Papadiamandopoulos) wasn't only my first cousin twice removed. She was also my grandmother. My father was my own mother's (and father's) nephew. In addition to being my grandparents, Desdemona and Lefty were my great-aunt and -uncle. My parents would be my second cousins once removed and Chapter Eleven [Cal's nickname for his older brother, born just following their grandfather's bankruptcy] would be my third cousin as well as my brother. The Stephanides family tree, diagrammed in Dr. Luce's

> "Autosomal Transmission of Recessive Traits," goes into more detail than I think you would care to know about. I've concentrated on only the gene's last few transmissions. (198)

It is this recessive gene, transmitted through these close blood ties, that the doctor who proposes to operate on Cal determines is the cause of his biological sexual ambiguity, yet it is also his argument that Cal's rearing as a girl should be the determining factor in permanently resolving this ambiguity by performing an operation that would transform "him" into "her." Dr. Luce proposes to sacrifice eros in bringing a binary lucidity to the "nature vs. nurture" argument that is similar to the reduction of human sexuality to the male–female binary, but in his decision not to undergo sexual reassignment surgery and to remain a hybrid male, Cal reflects the complexity that attends to his biological makeup, his sexuality, and his maturation amidst the entanglements of family and the chaos of history: of his family, he states that "[p]arents are supposed to pass down physical traits to their children, but it's my belief that all sorts of other things get passed down, too: motifs, scenarios, even fates" (109). The family as portrayed in *Middlesex* is both overdetermined and ineffectual, genetically fated and buffeted by the winds of event and accident, at once productive of uncanny similarities – attitudes, gestures, and habits transmitted across generations – and remarkable heterogeneity. Returned home and reflecting back on his 41 years while attending his father's funeral, Cal remarks upon the "wind [that] swept over the crusted snow into my Byzantine face, which was the face of my grandfather and of the American girl I had once been. I stopped in the door for an hour, maybe two. I lost track after a while, happy to be home, weeping for my father, and thinking about what was next" (529). An embodiment of sameness-within-difference and bearing the promise of a protagonist thrice-born, Cal closes this story of the family as ever on the verge of metamorphosing into "what's next."

No doubt to his consternation, Jonathan Franzen's third novel, *The Corrections* (2001), is perhaps as well known for the controversy that Franzen himself generated when it was selected for the Oprah Book Club as it is for being the winner of the 2001 National Book Award. Franzen's publicly expressed reservations about his novel bearing the Oprah "corporate logo" served as a catalyst for debates about the American publishing market and the automatic celebrity status (and dramatically enhanced sales) accorded to writers who bore the seal of Oprah Winfrey's approval. These were only exacerbated when it was revealed that another Oprah Book Club selection, James Frey's "memoir" of drug addiction, *A Million Little Pieces* (2003), was based on a number of fabrications, leading to the celebrity talk-show host's retraction of her support for Frey's book and her public interrogation of the author for his mendacity on a show watched by millions. The fact that *The Corrections* was caught up in what has become known as "the Oprah factor" is ironic, as Franzen's novel is in large part an anatomy of familial care and dysfunction in America at the end of the twentieth century, subjects that are often the focus of concern on the Oprah Winfrey show.

The family portrayed in *The Corrections* is both dysfunctional and diasporic. Trapped in a dead marriage that may never have been fully alive, Enid and Alfred Lambert live in isolated retirement in the Midwestern city of St. Jude; their son, Gary, equally isolated in his marriage, lives with his wife and two children in a suburb of Philadelphia; a second son, Chip, struggles to keep afloat in New York as a writer after having been fired from his job as a college professor for having an affair with one of his students; their daughter, Denise, a talented chef and workaholic, sleeps with both her boss and his wife during her tenure at a posh Philadelphia restaurant. The novel focuses on a period of months between the time when Enid and Alfred take a Fall cruise up the Northeast coast – Alfred, suffering from Parkinson's and increasing dementia, either falls or jumps overboard, but emerges relatively unscathed – and a "last Christmas" in St. Jude, orchestrated by Enid, where the three children and the two parents are together for one final time, if only for the hour that the children's visits overlap in the flurry of circumstances that beset the novel's principals. But more than a satiric portrayal of the end-of-century American family gone awry, *The Corrections* is a dissection of American culture from the 1950s to the present that contains mini-histories of domestic objects (the novel begins with a detailed description of the furnishings of the family home), assays the mendaciousness of American corporate culture and the personal costs of professionalization, and portrays changing views of sexuality since the mid-1980s that have led to liberations of one kind and imprisonments of another. Political correctness, designer drugs, the great American Christmas, retirement culture, the Internet, the effects of global capitalism and global warming, the perfidies of the stock market, celebrity chefs and the national obsession with food, the epidemic of dementia in a population living longer lives – all make their way into the novel's mosaic of the American denucleated family at century's turn.

The novel's title is indicative of its genre, for satire has traditionally served as a moral corrective. But *The Corrections* is a markedly contemporary satire in which the foundations of reality are so insecure that any correction of course or intention leads to further unforeseen comic and tragic errors, which in their turn lead to ever-more frantic attempts at social correction. The world that the Lamberts inhabit is out of control personally, economically, and politically; any mechanisms that might appear to contribute to the social order – from the "family unit" to the organization of lives into careers – become irrelevant in the face of thwarted desire and appetite. The main characters of *The Corrections* are all isolates, and their lives, fitted into the available frameworks of family and profession or programmatically resisting these, are testimony to the inefficacy of correction based upon artificial and illusory conceptions of normalcy; thus, Denise:

> By trying to protect herself from her family's hunger, the daughter accomplished just the opposite. She ensured that when her family's hunger reached its peak her life would fall apart and leave her without a spouse, without kids, without a job, without responsibilities, without a defense of any kind. It was as if, all along, she'd been conspiring to make herself available to nurse her parents. (502)

Enid, who has spent her existence attempting to correct and control the lives of her husband and children, becomes nearly hysterical about the family getting together for "the last Christmas," despite numerous obstacles: Caroline, Gary's wife and children, knowing what awaits them during a family Christmas in St. Jude, refuse to come; Denise, recently fired from her job for sleeping with the boss's wife, is in crisis; Chip, through a relay of unlikely circumstances, is in Lithuania. Enid's fantasy of a Norman Rockwell Christmas turns out to be a nightmare of accident, miscommunication, and confrontation, but the fact of its vestigial occurrence trumps its content as a sign of the family's continuance. Yet Enid feels liberated when Albert dies two years later after a prolonged struggle with Parkinson's and institutionalization in the "Deepmire Home": while "[a]ll of her correction had been for naught" during their marriage, now, "[s]he was seventy-five and she was going to make some changes in her life" (568). The novel ends on this comic note, with the father deceased and the family dispersed, each one going his or her own way, and apparently happily so now that Enid has shed the self-imposed burden of her maternal authority. Franzen's diagnosis of the American family thus illuminates its fragility and its residual symbolic importance in an era of correction and change.

Maureen Howard is the author of a handful of novels – *Bridgeport Bus* (1966), *Expensive Habits* (1986), and *A Lover's Almanac* (1998) among them – that explore the lives of women in states of transition and emotional crisis. Her most experimental and ambitious novel, *Natural History* (1992), is set in her native Bridgeport, Connecticut, and employs photographs, poems, and newspaper clippings in the "double-entry notebook" section of the novel which portrays the lives of the Irish Catholic Bray family in a rapidly changing post-World War II American city. A hybrid of documentary, scrapbook, memoir, story, and screenplay, *Natural History* focuses upon James and Catherine Bray, a brother and sister whose individual histories, fatally intertwined with the history of an American city in decline during the Cold War and a crime investigated by their father, might be conceived as exhibits in the museum of Howard's novel. In an interview with Joanna Scott, Howard says of *Natural History* that:

> [it] is my own dark diorama of the town I grew up in – Bridgeport, Connecticut. I tend to use different forms at once in a work, and I wanted that book to be layered. A fiction writer is an amateur archaeologist, who dusts away the layers to see what can be discovered. Dust would be the narrative interruptions, the shards you suddenly come across. And there are many layers to a name, to a place, which in my mind all connect finally to the story. ("Maureen Howard," n.p.)

The crime that serves as exhibit #1 in the novel involves the shooting of a soldier by a town socialite; Billy Bray, a city detective, is given the charge to investigate the incident, but the details of the crime and its resolution are rendered opaque and irrelevant in comparison to its status as a symptom of trouble in what is only superficially a "rich and generous place" (391), inhabited by families like the Brays whose Ozzie-and-Harriet exterior is immediately undermined in the novel's opening sequence. There, scoping in from a helicopter view of Bridgeport, we see James riding his bicycle to a clarinet lesson and Catherine on her way to a Girl Scout meeting, both children on the mind of their anxious mother whose security is bound up in the domestic fetishes she collects, "[s]hut in with her as though by ancient custom they'll sustain her in the grave, as well as the buffet with silver and linen, her initials on the double damask shroud with gravy stains. As well as the round mahogany table clawing the worn Sarouk with its friendly paws" (32). The domesticity of Bridgeport that prevails in Catherine and James's childhood is revealed to be self-isolated and falsely secure in the novel's opening scenario, where murder and thoughts of the grave form the backdrop to the "diorama" of posed normalcy.

Yet this is to suggest that *Natural History* works outward from a central event or portrays the line of progress from past to present, childhood to adulthood. Instead, the novel proceeds by virtue of a series of jump cuts in the lives and thoughts of its principal characters as well as several others (Catherine's childhood friend, Mary Boyle, a former nun and social worker; James's daughter, Jen, stranded in the world by her uncaring parents; Peaches, an artist raised in the Bridgeport projects) whose presence forms a skein of intersubjectivity at the center of which is the city of Bridgeport itself, portrayed as a prolix cultural repository of voices, memories, and events. The experimentalism of Howard's fiction is most evident in the novel's "Double Entry" chapter, where on the recto side of the fold there is a continuous flow of conversations, memories, and projections emerging from Catherine, James, Mary, and Billy, while on the verso side an archive of texts and images – many of them referring to Bridgeport's star resident, the great American showman, P. T. Barnum – provide a running history adjacent to these fictional characters, while often excerpting pieces ("shards") of their stories as newspaper articles. More than just offering a worldly context for an intimate portrait of fictional lives, these juxtapositions suggest that the story of the individual is, made over into spectacle, a story of the family and the city, comprising a collage of fragments pieced together into a narrative of many unassimilated, but necessarily conjoined parts. As Howard writes, the "double-entry" method of bookkeeping was introduced to ensure that "the debit and credit must always agree" (220); thus the "debit" of history must be balanced against the "credit" of personality. Like the Lamberts, whose family story occurs roughly over the same historical period, the Brays are diasporic: James becomes a film actor and moves to Los Angeles, only returning to Bridgeport in an attempt to make a movie about the killing of the soldier; Catherine, a weaver by vocation, leaves Bridgeport for New York, endures a series of dead-end relationships, and bears alone what she believes to be the secret of her father's adultery with the woman accused of the murder. For James, the family story has become a spectacle to be reproduced; for Catherine, it has become an embodiment of dishonor and the source for failed intimacy. Sporadically, in their recollections, this history has its transcendent moments in the balance sheet, but ultimately, it is the entropic story of a family and community descending from – as all such stories must – the projected origins of "once upon a time": "Once, 1945, in a pleasant land, a favored city, the people worked and though they made little of it, played" (349). That such a time never happened, save in the retrospective fantasizing of a "before" to history's fallout, is accounted in every turn of *Natural History*.

When Marilynne Robinson's first novel, *Housekeeping*, was published in 1980, it almost immediately became a contemporary classic, and continues to be one of the most frequently taught novels in college courses on contemporary American literature. Though Robinson has gone on to publish two additional novels, *Gilead* (2004), a historical fiction about three generations of ministers which won the 2005 Pulitzer Prize, and *Home* (2008), set in the same fictional town for which Gilead is named, as well as two collections of essays on nuclear pollution and American religion and capitalism, *Housekeeping* remains her hallmark work. Set in the isolated Pacific Northwest community of Fingerbone, *Housekeeping* is the story of a family of women struggling for survival along the shores of a lake that, by turns, is pastoral, symbolizing a kind of Thoreauvian pastoralism, and, in its unknowable depths, destructive, symbolizing the obliteration of human life in the Deluge: "It is true that one is always aware of the lake in Fingerbone, or the deeps of the lake, the lightless airless waters below. ... At the foundation is the old lake, which is smothered and nameless and altogether black" (9). Indeed, the setting of the entire novel is biblical, from its opening words, "My name is Ruth" (3), echoing the "Call me Ishmael" of *Moby-Dick*'s (1851) first chapter and naming the narrator after the Old Testament figure who embodies loyalty between women in a world of patriarchal law. In the novel, stories of mythical floods occur alongside elaborations of genealogy, its imagery evoking passages from *Genesis*, *Exodus*, and *Judges*. A spiritual descendant of the biblical Ruth who tells her mother-in-law,

Naomi: "wherever you go, I will go; And wherever you lodge, I will lodge; Your people shall be my people, and your God, my God. Where you die, I will die, and there will I be buried" (*Ruth* 1:16), the Ruth of *Housekeeping* determines to remain for life with her aunt, Sylvie, who has led an itinerant life and who comes to Fingerbone in order to serve as parent to Ruth and her sister, Lucille, after their mother has committed suicide by driving her car into the lake. While Sylvie, Ruth, and Lucille attempt to assimilate to Fingerbone and conduct "good housekeeping" within domestic order of the community with its patriarchal debts and traditions, only Lucille feels at home there, and only with another family that represents a stereotype of normalcy; while she leaves her genealogical family of women for her adoptive family, Sylvie and Ruth, having "failed" at housekeeping and deemed crazy by the locals, resume Silvia's itinerant lifestyle and go on the road together, a reduced, nomadic family of two women living on the margins of society.

Housekeeping is a narrative of alternative families that instantiates a female genealogy while tracing the great American theme of individual freedom versus social constraint. On the road and riding the rails at the novel's end, Sylvie and Ruth effectively have escaped the prison of male-defined domesticity that Fingerbone and the lake represent to them. One of the quasi-mythical stories that haunts the community of Fingerbone is that of the train that derails into the lake, its passengers, including Ruth's grandfather, who built the house and helped to found the town in which the women live, disappearing forever into its bottomless depths. The lake is thus the graveyard of the family patriarch and paternal authority, just as Fingerbone, as its skeletal name would indicate, is the site of a dying, mortal social order that Sylvia and Ruth wish to transcend. Yet transcendence, as the novel's evocations of the American Transcendentalists Emerson and Thoreau and a host of great American road novels suggests, comes at a price. The freedom purchased by Ruth and Sylvia – as is the case for Huckleberry Finn, lighting out for new territories, Ellison's invisible man, hidden in a basement and stealing electricity from the power system, or Dean Moriarity, looking west at the end of *On the Road* – necessitates a disappearance from reality into the realm of the imaginary that incurs a loss, a recognition of lack as the price of escape. *Houskeeping* portrays transience and loss as fundamental to the condition of a reality that "housekeeping" sustains by virtue of countermovement: building a house; institutionalizing domesticity; maintaining the patriarchal line and sustaining the social order. When Sylvie and Ruth "light out" from this reality in this fiction of an alternate family order, they are exposed to a loss of identity. Figuring the future, Ruth projects an image of the sister she has left behind:

> imagine Lucille in Boston, at a table in a restaurant, waiting for a friend. ... Sylvie and I do not flounce in through the door, smoothing the skirts of our oversized coats and combing our hair back with our fingers. We do not sit down at the table next to hers and empty our pockets in a small damp heap in the middle of the table ... My mother, likewise, is not there ... We are nowhere in Boston. However Lucille may look, she will never find us there, or any trace or sign. ... No one watching this woman smear her initials in the steam on her water glass with her first finger ... could know how her thoughts are thronged by our absence, or know how she does not watch, does not listen, does not wait, does not hope, and always for me and Sylvie. (218–19)

Ruth concludes her narrative with this reflexive projection of herself thinking of Lucille, thinking of Ruth and Sylvie as eternally not there. For "there" is a place (Boston, or any other place one could name) that the pair no longer inhabit, save as imaginary location that registers their departure or absence. Robinson's compelling novel thus portrays family relations, between women, as "thronged" by the memory of loss, as well as embodying an imaginary presence that is always transient, and always in the future (the counter to the dead past of patriarchy) precisely as that which has been left behind.

The arc that can be traced between media versions of the great American nuclear family runs from its comic idealizations in *Ozzie and Harriet*, *Leave it to Beaver*, and *Happy Days* which populated the US airwaves during the Cold War era, to its deconstruction in recent films as different as *American Beauty* (1999) and *A History of Violence* (2005). Characteristically throughout this period contemporary fiction has consistently critiqued the American middle-class family in its most familiar setting – the suburbs: we have observed this in a number of recent novels we have already considered – Joyce Carol Oates's *American Appetites* and Francine Prose's *Primitive People* in particular – but one can look across the four decades following World War II to the stories of John Cheever, Grace Paley, and Raymond Carver, or novels ranging from Salinger's *Catcher in the Rye* (1951) to Thomas Berger's *Neighbors* (1980) as examples of works that unmask family life. Surely one of the most satirically barbed and wrenchingly horrific portraits of the suburban American family in recent annals is A. M. Homes's *Music for Torching* (1999). Homes is the author of *The Safety of Objects* (1990) and *Things You Should Know* (2002), collections containing several stories about the dystopia of suburbia; *The Mistress's Daughter* (2007), which depicts Homes's search for a reunion with her birth mother; *The End of Alice* (1996), a novel about an obsessive relation between an imprisoned pedophile and his 19-year-old female pen pal; and *This Book Will Save Your Life* (2006), about a man who is attempting to reignite his existence amidst the apocalyptic setting of contemporary Los Angeles. The first chapter of *Music for Torching* depicts a suburban couple, Elaine and Paul, "accidentally on purpose" setting their house on fire as a physical manifestation of their failing marriage; the novel ends with the shooting of their son, Sammy, by a classmate at school. These destructive acts serve as bookends for a novel that achieved a contingent notoriety after the fact of its publication, occurring "three weeks before the Columbine shooting," Homes explains in an interview, something that came "from nowhere, there were no warnings. But just as one can see if you look back through *Music For Torching*, there are plenty of warnings" (Adams, n.p.). "Plenty of warnings" might be a subtitle for this surreal allegory that uncovers the violence and rapacious desire lurking beneath American domesticity.

The problems that beset Paul and Elaine, their children, Daniel and Sammy, and their neighbors are familiar and destructive: in a setting where all material comforts and objects of desire are accessible and bountiful, boredom is rampant; the need for security and routine is in continuous conflict with the need for difference, for a perverse sublimity that would pierce through the layer of conformity and the habitual social schedule of dinner parties and barbecue. Between themselves, Paul and Elaine view the fire they have started that damages (but does not destroy) their house as "a declaration of their awareness, the great and formal announcement: This is not who we are, we are not like you, we have failed, we are failing, we are failures" (53). Unbridled consumerism is the fuel for the social system portrayed in *Music for Torching*, and addictions of every variety – from coffee, to recreational drugs, to sex – abound as the means to satisfy desires for something other than the good life in the suburbs has to offer its inhabitants, trapped in a kind of paradoxical hell where the punishment is to be protected, comfortable, and relatively free to act out in every way possible.

Amidst such banality, little is truly surprising, but the slightest variation within the framework of a vestigial normality seems ludicrously overdetermined. In one instance, Paul takes the family into the bathroom, shuts the door, and turns off the light, then demonstrates that by crunching down suddenly on "Wint-O-Green" life savers one can produce sparks: "Paul passes out the rest of the roll, and they all crunch down, and their mouths light up like little sparklers, a spray of glittering phosphorescence. It's Paul's moment to feel like a father, it's the first thing they've done as a family in a long time, and it's perfect; no heat, no flame, no risk of injury" (93). In fact, the entropic veneer of normalcy in *Music for Torching* is anything but: as the lid is lifted off suburbia amidst the disintegration of Paul and Elaine's marriage, Elaine undertakes a brief affair with the neighborhood "Martha Stewart," Pat, a closet lesbian into strap-ons and leather; the child of a neighboring family is institutionalized for a behavioral disorder that causes him to bite off and eat the fingers of his victims; Paul shaves his head and engages in rough sex with a younger woman who convinces him to get a tattoo on his groin. As the adults in the novel pursue their various courses of action, the children are left to their own devices, resulting in overexposure to the adult world of sexuality and violence, the latter evident in Paul and Elaine's frequent tempestuous encounters as well as the gun collections and paintball hobbies of their neighbors. The result, both entirely unexpected and entirely predictable given that there have been "plenty of warnings" that have been ignored in the pursuit of pleasurable difference, is the outbreak of violence at the local school, which results in the end of Elaine and Paul's marriage and their son's life. Homes's portrait of the contemporary suburban family is a satirical moral fable about what has gone wrong in America, yet it does not offer a putative normalcy as the cure for the disease, for it is precisely such "normalcy" that serves as the background music for the novel's aberrations. That the novel *was* published three weeks before Columbine is one of those eerie coincidences that seem, in the aftermath, to be part of a catastrophic fatality that has become all too ordinary in the order of things.

In an interview, Cris Mazza, the prolific author of nine novels and four short story collections, commented on the role of memory in

Waterbaby (2007), in which the protagonist undertakes a journey to recover her family's past:

> there absolutely must be some near-universal need to preserve, some need to "keep" certain fleeting things – whether they be real memories or daydreams and fantasies – that causes some people to write, some people to keep blogs or take photographs or make scrapbooks, some people to research family trees, etc. It's also, in all these vocations, a need to build identity, or to locate identity ... So what is it about the world, about society that makes people feel a lack of or longing for identity? To either keep a public blog of all their daily activities, thoughts, desires, etc., or pour themselves into researching distant and obscure relatives? To scan, organize and preserve hundred-year-old family photographs, or watercolor the house where they raised their children. But this question brings me right back around to this: that the truth of what really happened in any past isn't as important as the ways, and the reasons, and the methods of recreating (even reliving) memory. (Blackstone, n.p.)

Many of Mazza's hybrid experiments might be described as "scrapbooks" or pastiches of discursive material organized in such a way as to reveal emerging patterns of loss, longing, and affinity: in *Your Name Here ________* (1995), a woman attempts to resurrect her identity in the face of a devastating trauma; in the road stories of *Revelation Countdown* (1993), dislocated characters seek out the connection between agency and place; in *Many Ways to Get It, Many Ways to Say it* (2005), through the device of parallel stories set in different time periods, Mazza explores the themes of sexuality, corporeality, and power that recur throughout her fiction. In *Waterbaby*, the journey to the past and the discovery of ancestry occur via multiple narrative routes: genealogies and lists of family members, photographs and family website blogs, emails and historic records – all combine with the narrator's projection of a series of imagined scenarios that align the past with the present and show the eerie parallels between the lives of those who live hundreds of years apart. Alone, retired in her forties after a career as a successful broker, and alienated from a brother whom she feels has betrayed her, Tamara Burgess returns to the ancestral home in an isolated town on the coast of Maine looking for the truth behind the story of a child rescued from drowning by her great-great-grandfather, a lighthouse keeper, in 1875. As Mazza indicates in the interview, the undeterminable historical veracity of the story is far less important than constructions Tam places upon it, and her discovery of why the story seems so important and what it has to do with her in the present moment. By pursuing the story of the "waterbaby," Mazza's narrator reconstructs her family as a fictional assemblage into which she is bound to weave her own story as historical repetition and representing.

Waterbaby abounds with reenactments and repetitions: like the girl saved from drowning in 1875, both Tam and her brother, Gary, are "waterbabies," or champion swimmers from a young age; like her great-great-aunt Mary Catherine, whose beloved twin brother has died in childhood, Tam has lost a brother to whom she was once "twinned." Once in Maine, Tam rescues a newborn infant from a toilet in a laundromat (another "waterbaby") and then reunites the child with its wayward mother, all the while attempting to reconnect with her own mother. Researching the local story of a woman who, in 1931, mysteriously disappeared on a walk to the lighthouse her ancestors kept and whose ghost apparently haunts the landscape, Tam meets a distant cousin, Nat, whom she takes as a lover and with whom she engages in sexual reenactments of imagined encounters between the disappeared woman and her consort. Tam posits that the vanished woman (and her ghost) might be Mary Catherine, long-thought dead but returned to the scene of the family home and the place she last saw the cousin who has been sent abroad by a family fearing an "incestuous" relationship; alternatively, Tam imagines that the woman might be "Seaborn," the unnamed child saved from drowning, who returns to the site of her rescue and her death.

Tam is assisted in developing these intertwining ancestral stories by her sister, Martha, who is constructing a fact-based family history that serves as a counterweight to Tam's intuitive, imaginary genealogy. The history that Tam and Martha's confabulation reveals is one of overdetermined intimacy and alienation: cousins are fatally separated because they are "too close"; twins are separated by death, leading to family splits repeated in future generations, most notably when Tam cuts herself off from her brother after he conspires to separate her from her lover as a young woman enamored of her morally corrupt swimming coach. Tam is afflicted with epilepsy passed onto her from her father; Gary suffers from bipolar disorder (which has been shown to be genetic in origin) and from historical trauma as a 9/11 rescue worker. As the various strands of the family history come together, the question recurs as to what makes up identity: genes? personality, somehow passed on from generation to generation? historical experience? A complex compilation of records, narratives, and messages, *Waterbaby* suggests that the answers to these questions lie not in any factuality, but in the process of piecing together a life story through the stories of those who came before. The family, in this sense, is multigenerational and deeply historical: a long sequencing of identities moving through differing temporalities and landscapes that leaves only vestigial traces of a past requiring continual reconstruction in the present. Tam's embracing of this extended family leads to a reunion with her brother, but only by means of an imagined "remembering" of all that has been lost, ruined, forgotten. *Waterbaby* suggests in its title that it is a novel about being born, but more exactly it is a novel about the dynamic we are all born into: families that we determine as much as they determine us.

The Reach of Community

Just as contemporary novels reflect changes in the social and imaginary entity called "family," so, too, they register transformations in the larger collectivities of community and nation. Benedict Anderson has famously described the nation as "an imagined political community – and imagined as both inherently limited and sovereign" (*Imagined Communities*, 6). Linking "community" and "nation" in this way suggests how collectivities of various sizes and constitutions operate independently from their conceptualization as geographic or demographic bodies: they operate as their constituencies imagine them to be, according to the assumptions that the individuals making up these bodies assimilate as the primary elements of their identification with "community" and "nation." Increasingly, the mobility of individuals within the boundaries – imaginary or real – of the collective bodies of community and nation has transformed those assumptions. The nation called "the United States of America" has been since its founding in an ongoing crisis about its status *as* a nation that imagines itself a country of immigrants, open to the world, and at the same time a form of sovereignty that must maintain, protect, and close its permeable borders: this deep and, perhaps, irresolvable contradiction underlies the ongoing heated debates about immigration in an era of globalization.

Communities have always been more temporary and amorphous bodies than have nations, though thinking of the nation as an imagined community causes us, in turn, to consider the ways in which communities of all kinds are based on the limitations and need for sovereignty that Anderson says are characteristic of nations. Neighborhoods, small towns, a reading group, a peace march, a hospital ward, a group of survivors, the workplace, a blogging collective – all are specific examples of communities that occupy varying locations and temporalities; their "lives" depend on the ways in which the individuals who identify with these mobilities imagine them as bodies that they voluntarily or forcibly join as members sharing a common purpose. The complexities of identity, discussed in the next section, apply to the imagined constructs of community and nation as assemblages of identities: like identity, the collectivities of community or nation are constantly being *re*imagined as hybrid and heterogeneous entities in conflict with the desire, or need, for singularity and sovereignty. In the next section I will consider how questions of nation, migration, and assimilation emerge in contemporary novels that portray identities on the move and in between national spaces; in this section, I will discuss the ways in which post-1980 novels portray the reach of community precisely in terms of its limitations and its constitution as a mobile, heterogeneous "sovereignty" paradoxically bound over to time and place.

Born in 1935, Anne Proulx did not begin writing fiction until middle age, but with the publication of her second novel, *The Shipping News* (1993), which won both the National Book Award and the Pulitzer Prize, she has emerged as one of the major novelists since the late 1970s. The evocation of "place" and the language of place are the constants of her work, including several collections of short stories and the novels *Postcards* (1992), an epistolary novel that depicts the lives of a rural family in post-World War II America; *Accordion Crimes* (1996), which traces the adventures of a musical instrument and its owners as it is passed from hand to hand over a century and from its creation in Sicily to its destruction beneath the wheels of a truck in Florida; and *That Old Ace in the Hole* (2002), which portrays a collection of eccentric locals living in the Texas Panhandle and the attempts of Bob Dollar, the novel's protagonist, to swindle them. *The Shipping News* is avowedly a novel of place: set in a small, isolated fishing village on the Newfoundland coast, it is the story of a community plagued by its own history that struggles for survival within the confines of its location. But it is also a community of exfoliating stories that expand outward to embrace newcomers, such as the novel's protagonist, Quoyle, who comes to the village with his two daughters to live in the ancestral home – an abandoned house tied down by steel cables on a rocky headland lest it be blown away in a storm – following the collapse of his marriage and the death of his promiscuous wife, Petal Bear. As the sound of his name implies, Quoyle is "coiled" within himself, knotted up (each chapter of the novel begins with a passage from *Ashley's Book of Knots*, a sailor's manual) in a disastrous past and seeking a new life in a place that offers both the possibilities of atavism and rebirth. The community of Killick-Claw is equally caught between a rich, storied past full of tales of survivalist courage, treachery, and absurdity, and an attenuated future in which young people leave for more exciting climes and multinational corporations threaten the extinction of the local fishing industry.

A reporter by trade, Quoyle finds work in Killick-Claw with the local newspaper, *The Gammy Bird*; since there is not much real news to report, many of the stories in the paper are fabricated, including those to which Quoyle is initially assigned – automobile accidents, which he is to "report" along with the listing of ship itineraries in the region. As the novel unfolds, Quoyle becomes increasingly "knotted into" the lives and fates of the locals: Jack Buggit, the newspaper's editor, whose preference is for fishing over editing, and who apparently drowns, but is spectacularly resuscitated at his own wake near the novel's conclusion; Nutbeam, the English-born world events reporter for *The Gammy Bird* who is building a boat in order to sail away from Killick-Claw to southern climes; Billy Pretty, the local events reporter who serves as ancestral historian for Quoyle and the community; Tert Card, the managing editor of the newspaper who serves as Quoyle's nemesis; Wavey Prowse, who plays the role of mourning widow of the sailor lost at sea (her husband has actually run away with another woman) and who eventually becomes Quoyle's troubled romantic interest; Nolan, Quoyle's distant kinsman who lives in an isolated cove miles from town and who Quoyle discovers has been "haunting" his house and terrorizing his daughters; and perhaps above all, Quoyle's aunt, Agnis Hamm, a ship's upholsterer who has brought Quoyle to Killick-Claw for recovery, and who is in lifetime recovery herself from the sexual abuse she suffered as a child at the hands of her brother and Quoyle's father, Guy.

The community that Quoyle enters is an assemblage of eccentrics who are in the process of both escaping from and encountering the demons in their own lives: just as Quoyle, descended from sailors, attempts to overcome his fear of water as, now, the inhabitant of a coastal town, so Jack Buggit is compelled to confront his fear of the family curse – death by drowning, which entails preventing his son from being a fisherman – by undergoing a Lazarus-like drowning and resurrection himself; Wavey Prowse recognizes the self-destructiveness of her attachment to the invented past of a good husband; and Agnis Hamm confronts the memories of her abusive childhood as she engages in caring for Quoyle's daughters. In this realm of isolation and idiosyncrasy, "a rare place," as he views it, "[t]he glare of ice erasing dimension, distance, subjecting senses to mirage and illusion" (209), Quoyle believes that he can see the contours of his existence with an unusual intensity: "If life was an arc of light that began in darkness, ended in darkness, the first part of his life had happened in ordinary glare. Here it was as though he had found a polarized lens that deepened and intensified all seen through it" (241). The "polarized lens" is that of the community itself, replete with its oddballs, expatriates, sailors, and nomads in a place populated historically by wanderers in search of anchorage: "Vikings, the Basques, the French, English, Spanish, Portuguese. Drawn by the cod, from the days when massed fish slowed ships on the drift for the passage to the Spice Isles, expecting cities of gold. ... The only cities were of ice, bergs with cores of beryl, blue gems within white gems, that some said gave off an odor of almonds" (33). The novel's community, in other terms, is an assemblage of intensities and singularities within which the capacity for inassimilable difference is maintained. And while Quoyle eventually locates himself within the hybrid community of Killick-Claw, we are left with a sense that ties that bind individuals to place are complicated knots – perhaps overcomplicated – yet fragile and easily undone by circumstances. Ultimately, the imagined community of the *Shipping News* is only possible as long as it retains its faculty for estrangement from the world of "the ordinary glare."

The two world wars of the twentieth century frame Louise Erdrich's *The Master Butchers Singing Club* (2003), a novel that portrays the intertwined lives of the settlers of Argus, a small town located on the

North Dakota plains. The occurrence of another war conducted by the US government against the aboriginal inhabitants of the Great Plains, the Ojibwe Indians, resides in the memory of a survivor of a massacre, Step-and-a-Half, a semi-itinerant junk dealer who traverses the landscape as its historical unconscious. Argus and its environs, including the nearby Ojibwe Indian reservation, serve as the setting for many of Erdrich's 11 novels, including *Love Medicine* (1984), *The Beet Queen* (1986), *Tracks* (1988), *The Bingo Palace* (1994), *The Last Report on the Miracles at Little No Horse* (2001), *Four Souls* (2004), and *The Painted Drum* (2005). Writing as a "mixed-blood" descendant of Native American and German immigrants, Erdrich forges in these novels an epic, semi-mythical/semi-historical landscape (often compared to William Faulkner's Yoknapatawpha in this regard) populated with distinct characters clustered together for survival and bearing tales of violence and desire. The Argus of *The Master Butchers Singing Club* is a place of buried secrets, deadly accidents, and near-escapes: a family that dies of starvation, locked up in a cellar as the result of a practical joke; a newborn abandoned by its mother and saved by Step-and-a-half; a child buried alive in a homemade underground fortress; two brothers, fighting on different sides in World War II, one killed in his first day of battle by a landmine, the second wounded for life at the war's end by an unmoored shipping cable while engaged in a "safe" job after years of flying dangerous missions. In this landscape saturated with the history of violence, Erdrich portrays identities and a community dependent upon the strength of hidden connections and the spontaneous extension of care for its continuance.

At the center of the interrelated stories that make up *The Master Butcher's Singing Club* are those of the Waldvogel family and Delphine Watzka. Trained as a butcher and traumatized by wartime memories, Fidelis Waldvogel has immigrated to Argus after World War I in order to start a new life; his wife and first child, Eva and Franz, soon follow, and Franz, especially talented at making sausages, proceeds to establish a successful business while Eva bears him three more children, Markus, and the twins Emil and Erich. Several years hence, Delphine, an acrobatic performer, returns to Argus with her partner Cyprian Lazarre in order to look in on her alcoholic father, Roy, and ends up staying for good as she becomes entangled in a complex set of relationships with, first, Eva, and then, after Eva dies of cancer, Markus, as a surrogate mother, and Fidelis, as a second wife. The plot of the novel weaves the lives and memories of these principals with those of a colorful array of characters – the town sheriff, Hocks; Clarisse, Delphine's best friend and the town mortician; Tante Maria, Fidelis's sister, who has followed him to Argus as a domineering presence in the lives of his family – and as the generations age and change between wars (all of Fidelis's sons end up in military service during World War II), secrets are revealed that uncover the common history that relates all of them together in a community.

That history, as both Roy and Step-and-a-Half delineate it at different moments in the novel, emerges from what has occurred on the land itself – the unthinkable violence that has been inflicted on its original inhabitants – as well as the consubstantiation of genealogy and the experience of displacement and relocation that affects all of Argus's citizens. Soon after he comes to town, Fidelis persuades the men of the town to form a choir modeled on a choir of "master butchers" that he had known in Germany; at the end of the novel, Step-and-a-Half, who as a scavenger knows what unites the present community in terms of what has been lost, displaced, or cast aside, muses on the commonality of all the living and the dead in terms of raised chorus:

> Wild keening of women. Men exercising their voices. Up and down the scales. La-la-la. Foghorns of chords. *Adeline est morte. Elle est more et enterée.* Ina'he'kuwo' Ina'he'kuwo. *Ich weiss nicht was soll es bedeuten.* The air scoured the fields, then hit the telephone wires and trees. It entered and was funneled through the streets and around the sides of buildings in Argus. … Foolish ballads, strict anthems, German sailor's songs and the paddling songs of voyageurs, patriotic American songs. Other times, Cree lullabies, sweet lodge summons, lost ghost dance songs, counting rhymes, and hymns to the snow. Our songs travel the earth. We sing to one another. Not a single note is ever lost and no song is original. (387–8)

This evocative passage – like the notion of death-dealing butchers who sing to the heavens – assimilates the contradiction of death-in-life that Erdrich suggests lies at the heart of historical experience and the formation of community. But this recognition of a common mortality, rather than leading to fatalism, offers to Delphine an opening onto the future in which she ultimately finds "[c]ontentment … Her house at the end of the world. Horizon to all sides. You could see the soft, ancient line of it by stepping out the door. From the west, later and later every night, flame reflected up into the bursting of clouds. Skeins of fire and the vast black fields" (302). *The Master Butchers Singing Club* offers a vision of an impermanent community rooted in locality, an entangling of singular individuals whose paths fatefully cross in specific times and places, yet who, in that impermanence, share a common relation to the land and the destinies acted out upon it.

The community of the displaced and the disinherited is the subject of Gloria Naylor's *Bailey's Cafe* (1992). One of the leading African American novelists of the post-World War II era, Naylor has depicted the lives of urban black women in *The Women of Brewster Place* (1982; followed by *The Men of Brewster Place* in 1998), satirized upward mobility in *Linden Hills* (1988), and portrayed a multigenerational African American family in *Mama Day* (1988); Naylor has also written a fictionalized memoir, *1996* (2005), recounting her experiences with government surveillance. Naylor has a gift for developing striking characters and representing their interiorities by combining stream of consciousness with indirect discourse and oral storytelling. In *Bailey's Cafe*, we are taken directly into the dreams and memories of several men and women who have drifted from various locales to a rundown neighborhood where the two principal establishments are the restaurant of the novel's title and Eve's "boardinghouse," which serves as a brothel and, at times, as a place of refuse for abandoned and abused women. Overseeing the cross-braided stories related through the novel's several principal characters, each speaking through the language of a unique, idiosyncratic consciousness, is the owner of the diner, who has washed ashore in this derelict neighborhood with memories of horrific violence as a soldier during World War II. He forthrightly invites the reader to listen to the music of these narratives: "I'm at this grill for the same reason they keep coming. And if you're expecting to get the answers in a few notes, you're mistaken. … There's a whole set to be played here if you want to stick around and listen to the music" (4). The narrator and master of ceremonies in this novel was not born with the name of Bailey, which is the name he assumed in taking over the enterprise that had always been known as Bailey's Cafe; nominally dislocated himself, he introduces the intertwined stories we are about to read as a jazz set played in his café, which is variously depicted throughout the novel as a way station for the lost and weary, a limbo for souls in transition, or a hell for those who fates are sealed.

The individual stories of the novel include those of Sadie, suffering from a lifetime of alcoholism, yet with a mania for cleanliness that has sustained her as an itinerant house cleaner until she finds a permanent place as a housekeeper at Eve's; Mary, a stunningly beautiful woman who, despairing of her beauty as the only thing that men see in her, has mutilated her face; Esther, who has been terribly abused in the cellar of her home and who will only service men at Esther's in a darkened, cellar-like room; Jessie Bell, a heroin user who has risen from the slums to marry into a rich family only to fall back into poverty and prostitution because of her addiction; Miriam, an Ethiopian woman whose pregnancy signifies the possibility of rebirth for the neighborhood; and "Miss Maple," a transvestite with a brilliant past who serves as the bouncer at Eve's. What binds this narrative "set" together is the capacity of the individual tellers to endure gender discrimination, social castigation, racism, and abuse, yet Bailey's Cafe is not a novel of communal redemption or mere survival for a group of people thrown together by circumstances. Eve, for example, deliberately conducts Jessie Bell through cycles of addiction and withdrawal in order to ensure her dependency; given an opportunity to start a new life with a man who cares for her, Sadie, knowing all too well that her alcoholism will eventually destroy the relationship, decides to remain poor and alone; and the promise of Miriam's child, who is viewed as a possible Messiah by the regulars in Bailey's Cafe, disappears when Miriam accidentally drowns herself and her son is sent to an adoptive home. Each of these examples suggests that the stories to be told in *Bailey's Cafe* occur in the midst of life viewed as an ironic cycle of hope, disappointment, and acceptance. As a jazz set, a cluster of songs and plaints, the novel is a work continuously in progress – there are no happy or tragic endings. Indeed, as Bailey suggests near the novel's closing, there are no endings at all: "[a]ll these folks are in transition: they come midway in their stories and go on" (219). The community of outcasts in Naylor's novel are united by their capacity to give voice to their experiences of hard lives and social marginalization: the normal strategies of storytelling and the conventions of beginnings, middles, and endings are not sufficient to convey the ways in which, for Naylor, this and all communities, and the identities within it, are fundamentally "folks ... in transition."

If *Bailey's Cafe* can be considered as portraying an ironic and worldly view of a community poised between tragedy and hope,

Thomas Berger's *The Feud* (1983) can be viewed by comparison as a blistering depiction of the community as hellish dystopia. Over a span of five decades and in 24 novels – from his first, *Crazy in Berlin* (1958), to his most recent, *Adventures of the Artificial Woman* (2004) – Berger has used comedy and parody to depict the absurdities and cruelties of contemporary existence. In *Little Big Man* (1964), which remains his most well-known novel, westward expansion and the plight of Native Americans is rendered in the picaresque story told by Jack Cobb, who is on the verge of death and has seen it all at the age of 121 years; in *Neighbors* (1980), which might be considered a warm-up for *The Feud*, the combined boredom and lunacy of the American suburb are explored when new people move in next door; in *Changing the Past* (1989), a man is given the opportunity to live out alternative past lives as another identity in Berger's send-up of contemporary self-fashioning. *The Feud* takes place in what superficially appears to be a version of white-picket-fence, small-town America fantasized during the height of the Cold War and the Reagan years as a homogeneous place of close family and community ties, neat houses, a strong work ethic, and complete satisfaction with the commodities and lifestyles afforded to the (white) middle class. The novel depicts two neighboring small towns, Hornbeck and Millville, whose citizens engage in a series of increasingly violent confrontations that originate in Bud Bullard's Millville hardware store when Dolf Beeler, a citizen of Hornbeck, refuses to discard an unlit cigar following the injunction that no smoking be allowed around the hazardous materials of paint and varnish. Owing to the aggressive intrusiveness of Bud's kinsman, Reverton, who happens to be in the store at the time and who falsely poses throughout the novel as a "railroad detective," threats are exchanged as Reverton waves a gun (a starter's pistol loaded with blanks) in Dolf's face. When the hardware store burns down that very evening, the feud between the Bullards and the Beelers, which expands into a feud between the two communities and rival sheriffs, commences in earnest. The result is civic mayhem involving multiple assaults, crimes, and deaths, all directly or indirectly attributable to the original, seemingly harmless exchange between Dolf Beeler and Bud's son, Junior, who is minding the counter at the time. Amidst the narrative of rival clans and townships is a parodic Romeo and Juliet story of a Beeler son romancing a Bullard daughter, but the romance fizzles out when Tony Beeler perceives that 14-year-old Eva Bullard is more interested in satisfying her hunger for doughnuts than her desire for sex, and everywhere in the novel, "American appetites" are on display in the carnival of violence that the novel portrays.

Indeed, appetite, in the broadest sense – for violence, food, and sex – appears to be the engine of the social order in *The Feud*, and what lies behind its organization into communities of rivalry. The towns and inhabitants of Hornbeck and Millville are more remarkable for their similarities than their differences in a world where everyone knows everyone else, where kinship relations extend across town limits, and where racial segregation (Millville is where the "black neighborhood" is located) and racial prejudice are accepted as the norm. As Dolf says to Reverton in the initial confrontation: "Look here, officer, I'm a foreman down at the plant, right here in Millville. I live right over in Hornbeck. Everybody knows me over there. … And anyone down work can vouch for me come Monday. I'm a second cousin to the mayor over there, you know, Hornbeck? Horace Humple? You might know him" (6). Yet these homogeneous, mirrored communities operate according to a logic of violent reciprocity that converts similarities into arbitrary differences over which blood is spilt; as one citizen of Hornbeck relates, referring to the local sheriff: "You know, he can't do nothing to yuh if you're over the town line. The only way he could do that would be if him and the Millville police had what you call a reciprosky agreement, whereby each force could chase somebody into the other territory in actual pursuit, you know?" (133). In fact, the two communities do have an unstated "reciprosky" agreement, one that enables them to achieve self-identity by inflicting violence on the other. The social conditions Berger portrays in *The Feud* founded upon a mirroring, violent reciprocity have been described by the anthropological theorist René Girard as at the foundations of sacrificial Western culture and religion (see *Violence and the Sacred*, 143–68), but in a more limited historical framework, the novel surely has reference to the Cold War rivalry between the United States and Russia which led to the mirroring "mutally assured destruction" policies of the arms race. *The Feud* thus stands not only as a small-town allegorization of national superpower politics, but also as an indictment of violence in America, which serves as a catalyst in the novel's sardonic portrayal of "community building" as collectives of concern and response form around each new assault or transgression. For Berger, the "imagined community" is analogous to the nation as a collective that knows itself, and its difference from the other, by virtue of an enemy who is wholly familiar.

Evan Dara has published but two novels to date, *The Lost Scrapbook* (1995) and *The Easy Chain* (2008), both written under the reclusive author's pseudonym, and both, as Tom Le Clair has noted, heirs to the fiction of William Gaddis. Reviewing *The Lost Scrapbook*, LeClair writes that "Dara is a consummate ventriloquist of our time's voices and a remarkable ringmaster of our culture's circus acts. These two kinds of live performer are a little dated and so are scrapbooks, but Dara is not deterred from imitating them. The pleasure of oral communication and bound-together lives are qualities, he suggests, we're now missing" ("Voices from an American Nightmare," X11). As its title indicates, *The Lost Scrapbook* is a palimpsest, an assemblage of multiple voices that come together as a community of speech by virtue of being recorded and transcribed within the confines of Dara's encyclopedic novel. *The Lost Scrapbook* is an echo chamber in which voices merge and diverge; conversations between two parties turn into the transcribed outcries of many at a town-hall meeting; monologues become a gathering of verbal fragments originating from multiple characters; as readers, we are often cast into the middle of ongoing discussions as if we were eavesdropping on a party line. The topics of conversation are scattered and digressive: a student responding to questioners during a vocational aptitude test; discussions about Baroque music, Chomskian linguistics, Wiley Coyote, hitchhiking, relativity theory, workout strategies, store coupons, smoking; transcripts of radio shows, legal briefs, a television variety show. The effect is initially chaotic, yet as we listen a pattern begins to emerge: all of these are the voices of a community of the dispossessed, registering the effects of a local catastrophe – a democracy of voices protesting an environmental disaster that occurs as an utter failure of democracy in contemporary America.

In *The Lost Scrapbook*, a chemical plant, located in the Missouri town of Isaura, which produces photographic materials and that employs, according to the company's president, "nearly one-fifth of the labor force of the Isaura region ... the city's largest taxpayer by far, responsible for some 36% of Isaura's total real-estate levy" (372), has been dumping chemicals and contaminating the ground water for decades. This leads to a long-delayed government investigation, federal indictments and, eventually, the permanent removal of hundreds of residents from their houses within the most dangerous zone of contamination. The complicity of governmental agencies at every level in the corporation's ability to conceal the contamination until it is too late to save the community is all too apparent in the typical "how could this happen here?" reportage that takes place following the indictments. But the reader does not find out directly about the environmental crimes of the Ozark Corporation until the last third of Dara's long novel, most forcefully when a town-hall meeting about citizens' concerns regarding the potential for contamination explodes into a barrage of voices protesting or defending the corporation's misdeeds. Up to that point, we are witness to conversations and interior monologues that seem to provide only widely scattered hints about the disaster that lies at the heart of the novel and leads to the destruction of a community. Looking back to earlier parts of the novel where it seems a disconnected array of characters are talking about everything under the sun, we come to recognize the connections between dispersed scenes such as one depicting the famous linguist and progressive political theorist Noam Chomsky being turned away at the last minute from a network interview because he might say something "too radical," and another describing a woman after lovemaking whose thoughts wander into a reflection on American advertising: a "*world of lies, of distortions and inessentialities*" that compels one to "*learn to feel inadequate, and to be ashamed of what you are; accept the power of others to form, to shape, to determine your preferences, your thoughts, your hidden enclaves; internalize the master myth, specifically in order to feel excluded from it; realize that you are nothing – a cipher, a target, a marketing opportunity*" (232; original emphasis). Chomsky, a well-known adversary of the military-industrial complex whose voice has been silenced by the media, is thus related to a woman in post-coital reverie, reflecting on the extent to which corporate capitalism overrides the voice and the identity of the consumer.

Collectively, all of the novel's voices implicitly or explicitly register a protest against the devastation of the community entailed by the infiltration of corporate America into every aspect of life. The great contradiction of *The Lost Scrapbook* is that they do so separately, already dispersed, a cacophony ever fading into silence. In the novel's conclusion, after an extensive catalogue of names of American towns, an elegiac narrator describes an imaginary community of the future as "our willed determinism and sought-after structure, the nostalgic dynamism that strumpets fractal consciousness, that totals the holo-movement, that goes beyond the Encompassing, beyond the reaches of memory and even beyond those exercises in extended empathy … this definitive reclamation, this grand extreme regathering into silence" (476). This virtual community of disasporic voices "reclaimed" by the novel we are reading is bound to fall into quietude, as the projection of voice is inevitably merely an interruption of silence. Yet there is registered, within the pages of the book and amidst the represented sounds of human voices in conversation, something that resists and survives deadly (in)corporations, if only it can be imagined how all of the voices are speaking together. *The Lost Scrapbook* thus recovers community as the work of reading fiction.

From There to Here: Migration and Nation

The contradictions inherent in the concept of the nation as an "imaginary community" are no more apparent than in recent American novels that seek to represent the experience of immigration in an era when the mobility of identity and globalization would seem to throw a monkey wrench into notions of limitation and sovereignty. Perhaps it is this very contradiction that helps to fuel xenophobic fears about impermeable borders and "illegal aliens." To be sure, national identity has always been a contested issue in a nation of immigrants, but one that has become increasingly pressured by evolving economic and political developments since the late 1970s. What is the United States if it can no longer define itself in opposition to its darkly mirrored twin in the Cold War binary of superpower vs. superpower? What does it mean to be an "American" in the age of global capitalism, multinational corporations, and an ever more visibly multicultural society? What is the relationship between migration, or the mobility of identities across the landscape, immigration, or the movement of identities into the "imagined community," and nation, or the contemporary sovereign/permeable, limited/boundless space in which such movements occur? There are a multitude of important post-1980 American novels that take up these questions in fictions of immigration and nation, including, in addition to the works I consider below, novels by Ha Jin, Bharati Mukerjee, Julia Alvarez, Francisco Goldman, and Juniot Diaz. Here, I can only take up only a handful of novels as compelling examples that portray the relation between nation and identity at a time when they are conceivable only as transitional states.

When it was published in 1995, Chang-Rae Lee's first novel, *Native Speaker*, met with widespread acclaim as a story about Korean-Americans struggling to become "Americans" while maintaining their own identities. Set in the boroughs of New York City, *Native Speaker* is at once a political thriller, a love story, and a tale of immigration. Its protagonist, Henry Park, was born in Korea but brought to the United States as a young child by his parents; his father, an engineer with a master's degree in his own country, becomes the sole owner and operator of a lucrative neighborhood grocery in New York, and spends his life making money and learning enough English so that his business can succeed and his son become an educated American citizen. Henry finds his way into a certain line of work – corporate spying – and marries an attractive, bright, socially committed Caucasian woman, Leila, from whom he has become emotionally detached following the accidental death of their 7-year-old son: his secrecy about his job and his apparent coldness towards his wife nearly destroys their marriage. The novel focuses on the events surrounding Henry's investigation of John Kwang, a rich and charismatic Korean American businessman who is running for mayor with a progressive campaign that promises to mend the rifts between warring ethnic factions in the city, particularly those between Asians and African Americans. Henry's infiltration of the Kwang organization as a campaign worker leads to Kwang's downfall, and even though Kwang himself is largely responsible for his own demise, Henry's guilt over his treachery leads him to quit his occupation, reunite with his wife, and join her in the work of teaching immigrant children English pronunciation.

A novel about the politics of ethnicity, racial difference, and racial assimilation, *Native Speaker*'s true subject, as its title indicates, is language, and the ways in which spoken language reveals or conceals identity. Henry's job as spy causes him to take on multiple identities – to tell stories and speak in voices not entirely his own – just as he feels that the English language, which he has mastered, is a kind of mask that he assumes when he speaks. Listening to John Kwang speak, Henry reflects that:

> I couldn't help but think there was a mysterious dubbing going on, the very idea I wouldn't give quarter to when I would speak to strangers,

> the checkout girl, the mechanic, the professor, their faces dully awaiting my real speech, my truer talk and voice. When I was young I'd look in the mirror and address it, as if daring the boy there; I would say something dead and normal, like, "Pleased to make your acquaintance," and I could barely convince myself that it was I who was talking. (179–80)

Henry's "sub-rosa vocation" (47) seems apt; the notion of one's speech both betraying and masking identity is portrayed throughout *Native Speaker* as determining the condition of the immigrant or hyphenated American who has left one homeland of speech and community for another that he or she never fully inhabits. Henry sees his father as believing that his "chosen nation … operated on a determined set of procedures, certain rules of engagement. These were the inalienable rights of the immigrant" (47); these rules extend beyond speech to patterns of acculturation that inevitably involve a kind of procedural masking of the self: "You were never unkind in your dealings, but then you were not generous. Your family was your life, though you rarely saw them. You kept close handsome sums of cash in small denominations. You were steadily cornering the market in self-pride" (47). Henry's involvement with Kwang and the betrayal of "one of his own" leads to a deepened recognition of the doubling and distancing of the self required by his father's immigrant contract with America, and his own complex identity as a Korean American. At the novel's end, he accepts his fate as a hyphenated citizen who "like my kind possess another dimension. We will learn every lesson of accent and idiom, we will dismantle every last pretense and practice you hold, noble as well as ruinous. You can keep nothing safe from our eyes and ears. This is your own history" (320).

Henry's reflections in the novel's denouement suggests that his liminal "kind" – those who become so well-schooled in the language that they appear as "native speakers" – serve to imitatively unmask the history and cultural assumptions of those who possess it from birth; here, Henry represents himself as a linguistic espionage agent, spying out the secrets and destroying the pretences of the assimilative culture. At the same time, Henry joins with his wife in a comic final scene disguised as "the Speech Monster" who cowers when non-English speaking children to whom Leila is teaching the phrase of the day ("gently down the stream") are able to repeat it, however inaccurately:

> The kids are mostly just foreign language speakers, anyway, and she thinks it is better with their high number and kind to give them some laughs ... It doesn't matter what they understand. She wants them to know that there is nothing to fear, she wants to offer up a pale white woman horsing around with the language to show them that it's fine to mess it all up. (349)

A duplicitous character throughout *Native Speaker*, Henry is thus doubled at the novel's end: both a solemn, perfect imitator of the native language that is never entirely his own, the secretive subject of knowledge; and, in his role as "Speech Monster," an agent for "messing it all up," transforming it into a patois that reflects the diversity of the "numbers and kinds" of new immigrants these children represent. These future speakers, *Native Speaker* suggests in the proliferation of voices with which it concludes, hold the perceived "threat" converted into the promise of a language that is at once alien and native, possessed by none, and by all.

The subtlety and detail that she brings to the stories of *The Interpreter of Maladies* (1999) and *Unaccustomed Earth* (2008) are fully present from the opening words of Jhumpa Lahiri's novel of Bengali immigration to America, *The Namesake* (2003):

> On a sticky August evening two weeks before her due date, Ashima Ganguli stands in a kitchen of a Central Square apartment, combining Rice Krispies and Planters peanuts and chopped red onion in a bowl. She adds salt, lemon juice, thin slices of green chili pepper, wishing there were mustard seed oil to pour into the mix. Ashima had been consuming this concoction throughout her pregnancy, a humble approximation of a snack sold for pennies on Calcutta sidewalks and in railway platforms throughout India, spilling from newspaper cones. (1)

The novel concludes with another scene of Ashima preparing food in which, as here, the ingredients she can find in a foreign country don't quite add up to the real thing, just as she never feels completely at home within a nation and a culture that will be hers for most of her adult life. Born in India, Ashima has come to the United States with her Bengalese husband, Ashoke Ganguli, with whom she is united in a traditional arranged marriage and who is studying engineering at MIT. She is pregnant with her first child, a son to be named "Gogol" whose life as a first-generation Bengali American is the focus of Lahiri's novel about naming, identity, and transition. How Gogol got his name in commemoration of the famous nineteenth-century Russian novelist and short-story writer, how his naming haunts and affects his life, and why he alternately rejects and accepts his given name are matters that thread the cloth of his existence as he comes to understand how identity is contingent upon circumstance. Like his mother, always displaced in America and uncomfortable with what it has to offer, Gogol feels dispossessed by virtue of his naming even though he appears to be fully assimilated into the typical (and, at times in *The Namesake*, stereotypical) lifestyle of a late-century American urban professional.

For Gogol has gotten his name by accident: his father, rescued from a train wreck in India because he is spotted by searchers who see him waving a torn page from a book containing his favorite story (Gogol's "The Overcoat"), decides to name his son after the author when a hospital administrator demands a name on the birth certificate. Following Bengali tradition, Ashima and Ashoke had been waiting for Ashima's grandmother to name the child, but the letter containing the name has not arrived by the time Gogol must come home from the hospital, so chance has led to the imposition of a name indicative of his lifelong sense of being misnamed, misplaced, neither at home in the America where he grows up nor the India he visits on vacations with his parents. The slippage between naming and identity that dogs his life is a constant source of irritation and uncomfortable reflection for Gogol: when he enters school, his parents want him to be officially know by his "good name," "Nikhal," a version of the Russian author's first name; but Gogol can't identify with the name as a child, and so retains the "pet name" listed on his birth certificate (which also becomes his "good name" outside the family), though when he turns 18, he decides to assume "Nikhal" as his legal adult name. Such complications of naming lead him to consider at one point that "[the] writer he is named after – Gogol isn't his first name. His first name is Nikolai. Not only does Gogol Ganguli have a pet name turned good name, but a last name turned first name. And so it occurs to him that no one he knows in the world … shares his name. Not even his namesake" (78). The situation becomes even more involuted when we are informed that "[t]hough Gogol doesn't know it yet, even Nikolai Gogol renamed himself simplifying his surname at the age of twenty-two form Gogol-Yanofsky to Gogol upon publication in the *Literary Gazette*. (He had also published under the name Yanov, and once signed his work "OOOO" in honor of the four *o*'s in his full name)" (97). Names in *The Namesake* are accidental, truncated, migratory, and repetitive: like Ashima's makeshift Indian snack recipe, they don't quite add up; indeed, as the play on four 0s, or four zeros, might suggest, no matter how much they are multiplied they do not equal the sum of identity.

As Gogol succeeds as a citizen of the republic – he becomes a Yale-educated architect and goes to work for a small firm in New York – he struggles through a series of relationships: a liaison with a fellow student at Yale; a temporary affair with a married woman; a near-miss with the daughter of a wealthy, cultured Anglo family who turn out, despite their liberal façade, to have classist and racist prejudices incipient in Gogol himself, as the death of his father causes him to realize. He comes to marry Moushumi, a distant childhood relative who is also first-generation Bengali American, but their marriage collapses owing to the growing distance between them as Gogol's ever-present sense of dislocation clashes with Moushumi's cosmopolitanism; their fate is sealed with Moushumi's accidental revelation of a months-long affair with another man. While Moushumi is at home in the world, Gogol is at home in no world; like his mother, he is a perpetual foreigner: as Ashima regards it, "being a foreigner ... is a sort of lifelong pregnancy – a perpetual wait, a constant burden, a continuous feeling out of sorts. ... a parenthesis in what had once been ordinary life, only to discover that the previous life has vanished, replaced by something more complicated and demanding" (49–50). After her husband's death, Ashima determines that she will spend the rest of her days spending six months of the year in India staying with relatives, and six months of the year in America staying with her adult children. Her son's life as portrayed in *The Namesake*, like his name, is equally "complicated and demanding" – the life of native-born American who perceives himself from both here and elsewhere, if in name only. Lahiri's novel thus delineates the condition of the "foreigner," perpetually in between.

When Lucy Josephine Potter, the protagonist of Jamaica Kincaid's *Lucy* (1990), asks her mother why she named her as she did, her mother replies, "'I named you after Satan himself. Lucy, short for Lucifer. What a botheration you were from the moment you were conceived'" (152). Like much of Kincaid's writing, including the novels *Annie John* (1985), *Autobiography of My Mother* (1995), and

Mr. Potter (2002), and the story collection *At the Bottom of the River* (1984), Lucy contains marked autobiographical elements: Jamaica Kincaid's birth name, for example, is Elaine Potter Richardson; she changed her name following her migration from the West Indies island of Antigua to the United States at the age of 17. Like Kincaid, Lucy has come to America to escape her past and to take on the role of governess to the children of an upper-class family:

> The household where I lived was made up of a husband, a wife, and the four girl children. The husband and wife looked alike and their four children looked just like them. In photographs of themselves, which they placed all over the house, their six yellow-haired heads of various sizes were bunched together as if they were a bouquet of flowers tied together by an unseen string. (12)

As Lucy's naming suggests, she has fallen from "paradise" into this white, affluent, homogeneous realm where she hopes to escape and erase a past that has turned her into an angry, resentful young woman; ironically, what Mariah and Lewis, the husband and wife lookalikes, would regard as the paradise of Lucy's native home when seen from cruise ships and resort enclaves is, for her, an island prison of limited alternatives where the colonial past lives on in the touristic present.

Lucy is angry because she has felt betrayed by her mother since the age of 9: until that time, she had been the only child in her family, but when her mother has three male children in rapid succession, Lucy feels cast aside in the patriarchal environment she inhabits, especially by her mother:

> My father did not know me at all; I did not expect him to imagine a life for me filled with excitement and triumph. But my mother knew me well, as well as she knew herself: I, at the time, even thought of us as identical; and whenever I saw her eyes fill up with tears at the thought of how proud she would be at some deed her sons had accomplished, I felt a sword go through my heart, for there was no accompanying scenario in which she saw me, her only identical offspring, in a remotely similar situation. (130)

Coming to America, Lucy hopes to put behind her this betrayal of her future, and complete the separation from her mother who Lucy tells a relative "'should not have married my father … should not have had children … should not have thrown away her intelligence … should not have paid so little attention to mine. … I am not like her at all'" (123). Yet what Lucy experiences in the inverse "paradise" to which she immigrates is alienation and estrangement in a culture that regards her as exotic and different, but in ways not dissimilar from those she had hoped to escape in a home where the daughter was demeaned by being ignored: "I used to think a change in venue would banish forever from my life the things I most despised. But that was not to be so. As each day unfolded before me, I could see the sameness in everything; I could see the present take a shape – the shape of my past" (90). Like Ashima and Gogol in *The Namesake*, Lucy does not fit in anywhere. Though she and Mariah develop a complex mother/daughter, master/servant relationship, and though Lucy eventually leaves this family of similitude in order to strike out on her own, supporting herself as a photographer's assistant which allows her to pursue her interests in writing and photography, she never views herself as having transcended her bonds to past and homeland: "I was now living the life I had always wanted to live. I was living apart from my family in a place where no one knew much about me; almost no one knew even my name … the feeling of happiness, the feeling of longing fulfilled that I thought would come with this situation was nowhere to be found inside me" (158).

The novel's tense, intimate story of a daughter's separation from her mother, and a declaration of independence that leads to an equivocal freedom as a perpetual alien with a past that can neither be accepted nor cast off in the new life, can be seen as an allegory of immigration. Leaving the mother country and the patriarchal past of the colonial order, Lucy experiences a reinscription of that past in the country that initially represents to her the openness of the future. Kincaid's novel reveals a complex mosaic of sameness and differences operating in the movement from there to here: the daughter's identification with the mother and the homeland, and her need to establish herself as different; Lucy's difference as a "resident alien," and the leveling of her subjectivity as unknown, without a name; the gender hierarchies of the culture she leaves, repeated, with a difference, in the class and gender hierarchies of the culture she enters. Considering what the future holds for her, Lucy states that "my life stretched out ahead of me like a book of blank pages" (163). Her decision to fill those blank pages with writing – the novel's final autobiographical gesture – thus impressing upon the white blankness the black marks of inscription, offers a way of mediating the experience of migration by writing it down, an act that both represents and unleashes the past in the flood of emotion that overwhelms her: "I wept and wept so much that the tears fell on the page and caused all the words to become one great blur" (164). Lucy's struggle for self-definition as a woman in a strange land ends on this ambiguous note, with the blurring of the writing (down) of her transitory identity, as if this is all of it that remains.

The prolific T. Coraghessan Boyle (also known as T. C. Boyle) has published fiction on a wide range of subjects: the explorer Mungo Park in *Water Music* (1982); the inventor of cornflakes and health-food advocate, Dr. John Harvey Kellogg, in *The Road to Wellville* (1993); environmentalism in *A Friend of the Earth* (2000) and *Drop City* (2003); the group of students and colleagues surrounding the famous "sexologist" Alfred C. Kinsey in *The Inner Circle* (2004); and identity theft in *Talk, Talk* (2006). One of Boyle's most compelling novels is *The Tortilla Curtain*, a dark allegory about the affluent suburbs of southern California and the influx of "illegals" across the border that separates California from Mexico, many of them seeking employment in the service industries that support the lifestyles of well-heeled "Angelenos." The novel orchestrates a social topography in its intersecting narratives of migrants and suburbanites: perched on cliffs overlooking Topanga Canyon are the Mossbachers, Delaney and Kyra, affluent white professionals living in the sequestered subdivision of Arroyo Blanco; down below, in the depths of the canyon, Cándido Rincon and his pregnant wife, América, having come north from Baja in search of better life, hide out from immigration authorities and scavenge for food and shelter in a desperate attempt to survive. Complete with apocalyptic scenes of fire and flood, *The Tortilla Curtain* draws upon the mythology of Los Angeles as paradise lost in portraying the geographical proximity and social distance of these two couples whose lives collide when Delaney, "a liberal humanist with an unblemished driving record and a freshly waxed Japanese car with personalized plates" (3), accidentally hits Cándido with his car; the injury is painful but not serious, so the two men, each for his own reasons, agree not to inform the police, and Delaney gives Cándido $20 in guilt money, but this is only the first of several points at which their paths will cross. Suburban paranoia, the combined dependency upon and marginalization of the migrant "other," the ruin of nature and nature's revenge, the violence of racism – all emerge in Boyle's novel as elements of a social order that seems ever on the verge of collapse from its own weight. For Boyle, as for Kincaid, coming to America means encountering the irreconcilable contradiction of entrapment within freedom.

As its title indicates, *The Tortilla Curtain* is about borders, walls, and gaps of several kinds: the border that runs between a land once united under Spanish colonizers, and which now divides the nations of Mexico and the United States; the wall that the citizens of Arroyo Blanco wish to put around the subdivision in order to keep out coyotes and itinerants; the walls of the canyon itself, which collapse in a devastating mudslide after torrential rains have poured upon bare hills where the vegetation has been burned away by brush fires ignited by humans; the unbreachable social and cultural gaps that exist between people occupying proximate space. Broadly speaking, the Mossbachers inhabit a cultural of disavowal, where one willfully ignores the displaced and impoverished human beings literally sitting on one's doorstep, while being fashionably concerned about the planet. Thus within the space of a few minutes, Delaney, a nature writer concerned about the disappearance of certain animal species from Topanga Canyon, conscientiously chooses paper over plastic in the checkout line at the grocery store, considers writing about the endangered horned toad, and engages in a vexed conversation with a neighbor, Jack, about walling in Arroyo Grande:

> "Look Delaney," Jack went on ... "The illegals in San Diego County contributed seventy million in tax revenues and at the same time they used up two hundred and forty million in services – welfare, emergency care, schooling and the like. And you want to pay for that? ... You want another crazy Mexican throwing himself under your wheels, hoping for an insurance payoff? Or worse, you want one of *them* behind the wheel bearing down on you, no insurance, no brakes, no nothing?" (102)

While Delaney does not entirely share Jack's racist sentiments or fears, the juxtaposition of a convenient environmentalism, an affluent lifestyle, and a supermarket conversation about physically walling out the third world are all part of a cultural situation that relies on continuous compartmentalization – a kind of mental bordering-off of those matters that are well beyond the narrow comfort zone of the citizens of Arroyo Grande. Yet, as *The Tortilla Curtain* reveals in its dramatic climax, the borders, mental and physical, between citizens and "illegals," and between man and nature, do not work. Through a series of contingent circumstances, Cándido, América, their newborn child, and Delaney are swept away in a torrent during a downpour that floods the formerly dry gullies of the canyon; in its final moment, the novel portrays Cándido and América, washed up on a perch of land, their child lost in the flood, but reaching down into the torrent attempting to grasp the white hand of the struggling Delaney. The allegorical import of this redemptive gesture seems clear, even if it rings hollow: there is something more fundamental than national, economic, and racial boundaries that brings us into contact and joins us together in the survival and retrieval of the "human." But only in the face of a natural or manmade catastrophe, only confronting our common mortality, Boyle's novel proposes, does the universality of our condition become operative. By then, as the loss of the next generation embodied in the drowned child suggests, it may be too late.

At first glance, it may seem odd to conclude a consideration of family, community, migration, and nation in post-1980 American fiction with a discussion of Michael Chabon's serio-comic noir thriller and alternative history, *The Yiddish Policeman's Union* (2007). Chabon's first novel, *The Wonder Boys*, merges academic and popular culture in a story about writer's block and creative apprenticeship; his second, *The Amazing Adventures of Kavalier & Clay* (2000), concerns the partnership between an illustrator and a writer during the "golden age" of comic books and comic strips in the 1940s. *The Yiddish Policeman's Union* is clearly Chabon's most ambitious work, taking him several years to write and involving the discarding of entire drafts of a novel that is over 400 pages long in print. As a fictionalized alternative history, it bears some similarities to Philip Roth's *The Plot Against America* (2004), which envisions Franklin Roosevelt losing the 1940 presidential election to Charles Lindbergh and the consequences that ensue in the imagined turn of America toward fascism and anti-Semitism, as well as the popular novels of Harry Turtledove, which project scenarios such as that depicting the South as having won the American Civil War, or the Spanish Armada succeeding in the invasion of England near the end of the sixteenth century. As a noir detective thriller, *The Yiddish Policeman's Union* is peppered with street lingo (much of it variations on Yiddish), down-and-out characters, seedy hotels, cross-hatched plots, and eerie coincidences that come "out of the past." Merging these genres, Chabon has written in *The Yiddish Policeman's Union* a narrative of dispossession that offers a fragmented mirroring of the most intransigent conflict of our time in the Middle East – one that presses most forcefully on what constitutes a community, a nation, and a people.

The Yiddish Policeman's Union is set in the Federal District of Sitka, Alaska, a temporary Jewish republic with a population of 3.2 million that has been set up by the United States for European Jews being persecuted by Nazis during World War II, but in the contemporary present of the novel is about to "revert" back to the control of the United States, which will result in a new diaspora from the provisional homeland. Much is different in this alternate scenario: after a brief war in 1948, the state of Israel has ceased to exist, and Palestine is portrayed as a nightmarish landscape of warring factions; two million Jews have perished in the Holocaust at the hands of the Nazis, but millions more have escaped to the Alaskan safe haven; World War II has lasted until 1946, when Berlin is destroyed by nuclear weapons; the Federal Republic of Sitka, where Yiddish and English intermix, is a sprawling metropolis in which tensions between the Jews and the native Tlingit Indians often run high. Against this backdrop, homicide detective Meyer Landsman is called upon to investigate the execution-style murder of a seemingly harmless drug addict and chess player who lives in the same sordid residential hotel as Meyer. Meyer's pursuit of the investigation leads to the unraveling of a labyrinthine plot that involves a political conspiracy to establish a new messiah, his kidnapping and imprisonment by a remote sect of religious fanatics, the blowing-up of the Dome of the Rock in Jerusalem, chess-club politics, the unsolved murder of Meyer's sister, his penetration of a Hassidic enclave, his reunion with his estranged wife Bina Gelbfish, who becomes his supervisor at the onset of the investigation, and the commencement of the journey toward an unknown future undertaken by the departing Jewish population of Sitka. In effect, the novel portrays an assemblage of transitory national and racial groups, sects, and communities that contend with each other for cultural preservation and ascendancy in a symbolic, dystopian setting where the solution to the local crime pursued by detective-protagonist provides clues to the larger puzzle of what makes a nation.

One of the most significant secondary characters in *The Yiddish Policeman's Union* is Itzik Zimbalist, the rabbinical "boundary maven" for an ultraconservative community of Jews living on Verbov Island in Sitka Bay; the island's name derives from that of a village in the

Ukraine. It turns out that Zimbalist is the father of the murdered man, who has been tagged as a candidate for the messiah, but his professional role in this community into which Meyer is "starshot, teleported, spun clear through the wormhole to the planet of the Jews" (101) is to designate and protect the shifting boundaries of the "eruv," or community, especially as they apply to the restriction on carrying objects across thresholds on the Sabbath. Chabon portrays Zimbalist as a trickster, politically powerful because he can designate who is inside and who is outside, what each can possess, where each can go: in short, he controls mobility and identity within this segregated enclave. Consistent with his occupation under Jewish law as one who mixes or assembles separated households in the work of drawing the boundaries of the amalgamated "eruv" (which means "mixture" in Hebrew), Zimbalist is a hybrid figure who possesses a prodigious collection of wire and string for making boundaries, and whose place of business is "a stone building with a zinc roof and big doors on rollers, at the wide end of a cobbled platz" (107). Chabon elaborates on the immediate neighborhood:

> Half a dozen crooked lanes tumble into [the platz], following paths first laid down by long-vanished Ukrainian goats or aurochs, past housefronts that are faithful copies of lost Ukrainian originals. A Disney shtetl, bright and clean as a freshly forged birth certificate. An artful jumble of mud-brown and mustard-yellow houses, wood and plaster with thatched roofs. Across from Zimbalist's shop ... stands the house of Heskel Shpilman, tenth in the dynastic line from the original rebbe of Verbov ... three neat white cubes of spotless stucco, with mansard roofs of blue slate tile and tall windows ... Even before they turned to money laundering, smuggling, and graft, Verbover rebbes distinguished themselves from the competition by the splendor of their waistcoats, the French silver on their Sabbath table, the soft Italian boots on their feet. (106–7)

Meyer has entered a segregated realm of laws, genealogies, and boundaries, yet one where the borders are constructed ad hoc, a simulacrum of the original homeland ("A Disney shtetl") where the boundary-makers themselves are cultural amalgamations well down the chain in the dynastic line.

Verbov Island is, in many ways, the world conceived as an assemblage of nations and borders in miniature, historically dependent on the laws of exclusion and inclusion, and on political and geographical boundaries over which wars are fought and entire populations are cast out into the wilderness. Yet *The Yiddish Policeman's Union*'s comic, dystopic mirroring of the increasingly mobile, migrant collectives of nation or state reveals their inherent contradictions, established upon fundamentalist conceptions of law and order in a world of makeshift boundaries aligned with the arbitrations of power, and populated by subjects whose singularity is belied by their cultural hybridity. Most significantly, the language of the novel speaks to these circumstances: according to the reviewer for *The Jewish Reader*, Chabon "manages to make his English-language book read, at times, like an overly literal translation from a Yiddish original, to winning comic effect (Lambert, n.p.). The language of the novel is pointedly an amalgamation of translations and mistranslations, original languages and creolized languages, a pastiche of Yiddish and English, street slang and high metaphor. Commenting on the writing of *The Yiddish Policeman's Union*, Chabon has said that "'I felt like I had to invent a whole new language, a dialect,'" and such invention is evident in the examples cited by his interlocutor: "For the book, Mr. Chabon dug into New York's underworld slang, filling in at spots with his own linguistic creations. A latke is a beat cop and a sholem is a gun – a bit of word play, as "sholem" in Yiddish means "peace," and a "piece" in English is slang for a gun" (Cohen, n.p.). The linguistic impasto of the novel is consonant with its comic, yet deeply serious send-up of identity conceived in terms of nation, race, religious belief, and destiny. *The Yiddish Policeman's Union* thus questions all of the lines drawn in the sand that have entailed such catastrophic consequences for our, or any, time; in its own lingo, it places the emphasis on the first term of the imaginary community, and an ambivalent future of wandering that awaits those beyond its boundaries.

Epilogue

As a genre that, from the beginning, has always combined and incorporated other genres in producing new versions of itself, the novel is perennially oriented toward the future, even as it assimilates the past. During the period covered by this book, we have undergone a digital revolution which, arguably, is equivalent in scope and impact to the print revolution and culture that had a primary role in the rise of the novel in the first instance. While it is risky to make predictions about the future of the novel, at least one aspect of that future is "now" if we consider the ways in which the contemporary American novel has begun to incorporate digital and visual media into its making. I have already referred to Shelley Jackson's *Patchwork Girl* (1995), a work that comes to the reader/viewer on a CD-ROM and urges upon her an interactive, personal journey through the novel. Because the entire text novel is hyperlinked, one can jump from one link to another at will, virtually constructing out of bits and pieces of text (the novel refers both in title and thematically to Mary Shelley's *Frankenstein*) a novel of one's own. The rhizomic nature of hypertext novels thus generates a different kind of reader as well as a different kind of novel – one that is already evolving on the Internet with the appearance of collaborative, multi-authored, "open source" fictions that can virtually go on forever and that anyone with access to a broadband connection can write/read. Indeed, it is clear that many of the new forms of social communication that the digital revolution has fomented – texting, blogging, twittering, Second Life, massively multiplayer online role-playing games – are rapidly leading to the development of a new fictional genres that go under many names.

Yet novels, conceived as singular totalities within covers (paper or digital) and bearing the names of one or more authors, will continue to be written and read, even as they incorporate the digital and the visual, not to mention – as the novel has always done – the products of vernacular and popular culture. One recent example is Mark Z. Danielewski's *House of Leaves* (2000), a novel that originally circulated as a dispersed group of stories and messages circulated on the Internet that features at its center a manuscript on a mysterious film "documenting" a haunted house with an expanding interior. Danielewski experiments with different typographical fonts for different speakers, nearly blank pages with single words or haiku-like poems printed in small type on various parts of the page, and voluminous footnotes give the sense that this is a collaborative work which has passed through many hands. Danielewski's second novel, *Only Revolutions* (2006), extends his experimentation with typography and visual space in a road novel printed vertically in one direction on the recto pages, and in another on the verso pages, causing one to read bi-directionally and to flip the novel (whenever one wishes) to read the text on a given page. While these techniques may superficially appear to be but typographical gimmicks, in Danielewski's novels they are employed in complex narratives that generate substantial reflections on the process of reading narrative as such.

To the these novelistic innovations can be added the phenomenon of the graphic novel, and while I have said that this form of contemporary narrative lies outside the scope of this book, certainly such work as Art Spiegelman's *Maus: A Survivor's Tale* (1986; 1992), originally published as a magazine, then published in two bound volumes, then as a CD-ROM, stands as an example of how text and graphics can be combined to generate narratives as complex and compelling as any linear novel: *Maus* won a Pulitzer Prize special citation in 1992. Once more, as with hypertext or Danielewski's typographical experimentations, the reader of *Maus*, a narrative of Holocaust survival, must develop new strategies for reading in moving between image and text, panel and panel. The importance and success of *Maus* has led to the serious examination of the graphic novel as a literary genre, and is one of a succession of graphic novels by contemporary American writers such as Jerome Charyn's and François Boucq's *The Magician's Wife* (1987), an hallucinatory noir thriller; Howard Cruse's *Stuck Rubber Baby* (1996), set during the Civil Rights movement in the South; and

Will Eisner's *To the Heart of the Storm* (1991), a young soldier's story of growing up amidst poverty and anti-Semitism.

While these examples provide indications of the future of the contemporary novel – or at least some of that future – the proliferation of styles, techniques, and generic mixtures manifested in the novels examined in this book provide convincing evidence that novel has many futures. Certainly it will continue to be an amalgamated genre in which realism sits alongside postmodern pastiche such as one finds in Jonathan Lethem's compelling *Motherless Brooklyn* (1999), a "gangster novel" and *Bildungsroman* whose protagonist suffers from Tourette's syndrome; or where traditional character development and storytelling occur within multiple scenarios constituting a hybrid reality, as in *Mosquito* (2000), Gayl Jones's picaresque novel about the wanderings of Sojourner Jane Nadine Johnson, an African American truck driver. Because the contemporary American novel is fundamentally an ongoing literary experiment that reflects the heterogeneity and diversity of the society and culture in which it is produced, what is most critical to its future is a marketplace – readers, authors, publishers – open to enormous changes of the last minute, to once more paraphrase Grace Paley. To be sure, there are justifiable concerns about the lifespan of the book and the narrowing of creative outlets, and there is, of course, no such thing as a sure future. But the sheer continuity of the contemporary American since the late 1970s provides convincing evidence that if we persist in reading, eclectically but carefully, openly but shrewdly, with the sense that the language counts and the story matters, then the chances are good that there is much more to come.

Notes

1 See Tanner, *City of Words*, for the most capacious discussion to date of contemporary American fiction from 1950 to 1970, as this body of work negotiates between individual freedom and social constraint.
2 O'Connor coins the phrase "Christ-haunted landscape" in her essay, "The Catholic Novelist in the South," to refer to the tendency of Southern fiction to portray grotesque religious figures. The widely circulated term "technocratic capitalism" in Postman's hands refers to an economic development that has its origins in the eighteenth century and continues to evolve as "global capitalism," with the emergence of new technologies which offer at ever-higher rates of velocity access to the dispersal of information and the satisfaction of consumer desires. It is clear that O'Connor conservatively saw these changes coming in the South as an encroachment of secularism and the profanation of the human, but her response is to communicate these concerns via satire rather than the diatribes characteristic of some of her protagonists. Bacon and Schaub provide important accounts of how O'Connor's writing, and contemporary fiction writ large, is informed by Cold War politics.
3 The postmodernist and avant-garde language experiments of the contemporary novel are, in many ways, parallel to the emergence of the "L=A=N=G=U=A=G=E" poets in the 1970s, including Charles Bernstein, Bob Perlman, Ron Silliman, Lyn Hejinian, and Leslie Scalapino, who stress the work of language, its role in the formation of the social order, and the involvement of the reader in the generation of poetic significance.
4 The term was adumbrated in and gained widespread critical popularity as the result of Robert Scholes's landmark discussions of contemporary fiction, *The Fabulators* and *Fabulation and Metafiction*.

5 See McHale for a seminal discussion of how, capaciously defined, "postmodern fiction" privileges ontology (the study of being and how things come to be) above epistemology (the study of what we know and how we know it), which is more the domain of modernist fiction. Gass's sense of fiction as an addition to reality, rather than a viewing of it, is clearly ontological.

6 In the twinned essays "The Literature of Exhaustion" and "The Literature of Replenishment," Barth discusses what it means to be a writer "in an age of 'final solutions – at least *felt* ultimacies in everything from weaponry to theology" (*Friday Book*, 67), when all the great themes and narrative strategies have been exhausted, yet with the recognition that this has been the case and that the novel, viewed as "self-transcendent parody" (*Friday Book*, 205), has always maintained the capacity to break its own generic boundaries and thus, in Gass's sense, serve as an additive to discursive reality.

7 Here, Barth forecasts what Andreas Huyssen in *After the Great Divide* will suggest is the watershed between modernism and postmodernism, the capacity of the latter to merge "high" art and popular art that is symptomatic of postmodernism's capacity to transmute hierarchy into an equalized surface of cultural interactions.

8 For in-depth discussions of connections between deconstruction and contemporary American fiction, see Caramello, Clayton, Klinkowitz, O'Donnell, *Passionate Doubts*, and Saltzman. The best discussion of the "language" of contemporary American fiction is that of Chénetier.

9 The key work that initiated many of these questions is White's *Metahistory*, which has had profound influences on the formation of postcolonialism and the understanding of the relationship between the historic and the fictive that informs so much contemporary American writing.

10 Morrison's *Beloved* (1987), to be discussed in a subsequent chapter, addresses the history of slavery more directly in its use of the Margaret Garner case, the story of a fugitive from slavery put on trial for killing one of her children rather than allowing the child to be brought back into bondage. The characteristics listed here are often attributed to genre of "magical realism" which merge fantasy and realism and whose origins lie in the work of the Latin American "Boom" writers such as Julio Cortázar, Gabriel García Márquez, Carlos Fuentes, and Mario Vargas Llosa, with strains further back to the writing of Jorge Luis Borges and William Faulkner. Interestingly, the subjects of Morrison's master's thesis at Cornell University were Faulkner and Virginia Woolf.

11 My commentary on *Going Native* condenses a previously-published discussion, "Speed, Metaphor, and the Postmodern Road Novel."

12 The phrase "subject in process" ("sujet en procès") is used in the sense that the French feminist theorist, Julia Kristeva, develops in *Revolution in Poetic Language* (1984) and *Powers of Horror* (1982), where the self is portrayed as a linguistic process or speech act, always on the verge of becoming, always involving a negotiation between mind and body that entirely overturns the Cartesian "split" of "I think, therefore I am." The "revolution" Kristeva describes is clearly linked to the advent of modernist writing and the portrayals of identity to be found in the poetic avant-garde of Mallarmé, Baudelaire, and Lautréamont, and the fictional experimentalism of Joyce, Céline, Proust, and Barnes.

13 It would be incorrect to assume from this description, however, that when it comes to the question of identity, only white, male writers are interested in postmodern experimentation or that the portrayal of ethnicity relies solely or primarily on existential models. During the same period mentioned, we can consider the examples of Ishmael Reed in *Mumbo Jumbo* (1972), Maxine Hong Kingston in *The Woman Warrior* (1976), or Clarence Major's *Reflex and Bone Structure* (1975) as employing a number of postmodern techniques in the portrayal of identity, and identity itself as fragmented, highly self-reflexive, a miscellany of intensities. While something of an oversimplification, what can be said with some certainty, however, is that many American writers of color in the 1960s and 1970s were most concerned with establishing the presence and visibility of African American, Asian American, and Native American identities, just as many women writers were concerned with portraying strong, empowered female characters, and felt that realistic modes of narrative containing psychologically complex protagonists was the most effective way to do so.

14 Forming itself in the 1960s and 1970s, the arrival of a new pluralistic American canon is most clearly marked in subsequent decades with the publication of the first edition of the *Heath Anthology of American Literature* (1989), the *Columbia Literary History of the United States* (1988), and the *Columbia History of the American Novel* (1991), which seek to advance multicultural and hemispheric approaches to the study of American literature. Additionally, key anthologies such as *Aiiieeeee!: An Anthology of Asian American Writers* (1974), *This Bridge Called My Back: Writings by Radical Women of Color* (1981), and *Breaking the Ice: An Anthology of Contemporary African American Fiction* (1990) have contributed significantly to the opening up of the canon in contemporary American literature.

15 The increase of novels such as those by Liss, Holman, Carr, Kurzweil, and Boyle in the United States and the attendant fascination with the "Victorian" or "Enlightenment" eras screened through the lens of

modernist/postmodernist irony and aesthetics is matched in the United Kingdom by, to mention a few examples, Iain Pears's *An Instance of the Fingerpost* (1998), a Rashoman-like narrative set in seventeenth-century Oxford; Charles Palliser's *The Quincunx* (1990), an intricate, Dickensian novel of mystery and inheritance set in mid-nineteenth-century London; Sarah Waters's *Fingersmith*, a story of class/gender conflict and friendship between women in the English countryside and London of the nineteenth century; several novels of Peter Ackroyd, including *Hawksmoor* (1985), *Chatterton* (1987), and *The Clerkenwell Tales* (2004); or Lawrence Norfolk's *Lemprière's Dictionary* (1993), a multifaceted portrayal of European life and culture in the eighteenth century whose central figure is the actual historical author of a famous dictionary of mythology. To this short list of contemporary metahistorical novels coming from the United Kingdom should be added David Mitchell's brilliant *Cloud Atlas* (2004), comprising six complexly interlinked narratives that move between the South Sea islands of the mid-nineteenth century to a far distant, post-apocalyptic future.

16 The decision of Oxford University Press in 1988 to publish a projected 40 volumes of works by nineteenth-century African American women writers from the Schomburg Library in Harlem under the direction of the renowned scholar Henry Louis Gates, Jr., is but one sign among many of the vigorous interest among scholars and writers in the recovery of the African American past, including its literary past. The Schomburg Center for Research in Black Culture is the chief repository of African American materials in the United States; it began in 1926 when Arthur Schomburg, a collector of African and African American art and literature, donated a large portion of his collection to the then-designated "Division of Negro Literature, History and Prints" at the 135th St. branch of the New York Public Library.

17 My assessment is informed by the work of "trauma theory" in literary studies, founded upon Shoshana Felman and Dori Laub's *Testimony: Crises of Witnessing in Literature, Psychoanalysis and History*, and Cathy Caruth's *Unclaimed Experience: Trauma, Narrative, and History.* In thinking about history as something more than "just the facts," yet still bearing a delayed and transmuted referentiality to "what really happened," Caruth writes that "[t]hrough the notion of trauma ... we can understand that a rethinking of reference is aimed not at eliminating history but at resituating it in our understanding, that is, at permitting *history* to arise where *immediate understanding* may not" (11). It is this concept of history that stands behind the traumatic historical narratives considered here.

References

Note: This is a list of works discussed or noted in detail; authors of works briefly mentioned or listed are included in the Index.

Acker, Kathy. *Empire of the Senseless.* New York: Grove Weidenfeld, 1988.

Adams, Jill. "An Interview with A. M. Homes." *Barcelona Review*, 58–9 (August 2007). http://www.barcelonareview.com/59/e_int.htm.

Allison, Dorothy. *Bastard Out of Carolina.* New York: Plume, 1993 [orig. 1992].

Alter, Robert. *Partial Magic: The Novel as Self-Conscious Genre.* Cambridge, MA: Harvard University Press, 1975.

Anderson, Benedict. *Imagined Communities: Reflections on the Origin and Spread of Nationalism.* New York: Verso, 1991.

Anderson, Laurie. *Home of the Brave.* Los Angeles: Warner Brothers, 1986.

Antrim, Donald. *The Verificationist.* New York: Alfred A. Knopf, 2000.

Auster, Paul. *City of Glass*, in *The New York Trilogy.* New York: Penguin, 1987.

Bacon, Jon Lance. *Flannery O'Connor and Cold War Culture.* New York: Cambridge University Press, 1994.

Baker, Nicholson. *The Mezzanine.* New York: Vintage, 1990 [orig. 1988].

Bakhtin, Mikhail. *Rabelais and His World.* Trans. Hélène Iswolsky. Bloomington: Indiana University Press, 1984.

Bakhtin, M. M. *The Dialogic Imagination: Four Essays.* Ed. Michael Holquist; trans. Caryl Emerson and Michael Holquist. Austin: University of Texas Press, 1981.

Baldwin, James. "Everybody's Protest Novel." *Partisan Review*, 16:6 (1949): 578–85.

Banks, Russell. *The Sweet Hereafter.* New York: HarperCollins, 1991.

Barth, John. *The Friday Book: Essays and Other Non-Fiction*. New York: Putnam's, 1984.
Bartlett, Neil. "Caracole" (review). *Review of Contemporary Fiction*, 16:3 (1996): 61–8.
Baudrillard, Jean. *Selected Writings*. 2nd edn. Ed. and intro. Mark Poster. Palo Alto, CA: Stanford University Press, 2001.
Bellow, Saul. *Herzog*. Greenwich, CT: Fawcett-Crest, 1964.
Berger, Thomas. *The Feud*. Boston: Little, Brown, 1989 [orig. 1983].
Bernheimer, Kate. *The Complete Tales of Ketzia Gold*. Normal, IL: FC2, 2002.
Blackstone, Charles. "An Interview with Cris Mazza." *Bookslut* (November, 2007). http://www.bookslut.com/features/2007_11_011944.php.
Boyd, Brian. *Vladimir Nabokov: The Russian Years*. Princeton, NJ: Princeton University Press, 1993.
Boyle, T. C. *The Tortilla Curtain*. New York: Viking Penguin, 1995.
Burns, Carole. "Off the Page: Joanna Scott." *Washington Post.com* (March 11, 2004). http://www.washingtonpost.com/wp-dyn/articles/A33583-2004Mar5.html.
Butler, Judith. *Gender Trouble: Feminism and the Subversion of Identity*. 2nd edn. New York: Routledge, 1999 [orig. 1990].
Caramello, Charles. *Silverless Mirrors: Book, Self, and Postmodern American Fiction*. Tallahassee: University Presses of Florida, 1983.
Caruth, Cathy. *Unclaimed Experience: Trauma, Narrative, and History*. Baltimore: Johns Hopkins University Press, 1996.
Castillo, Ana. *The Mixquiahuala Letters*. New York: Anchor Books, 1992 [orig. 1986].
Chabon, Michael. *The Yiddish Policeman's Union*. New York: HarperCollins, 2007.
Chénetier, Marc. *Beyond Suspicion: New American Fiction Since 1960*. Trans. Elizabeth A. Houlding. Philadelphia: University of Pennsylvania Press, 1996.
Clayton, Jay. *The Pleasures of Babel: Contemporary American Literature and Theory*. New York: Oxford University Press, 1993.
Cliff, Michelle. "History as Fiction, Fiction as History." *Ploughshares*, 20:2–3 (1994): 196–202.
Cliff, Michelle. *No Telephone to Heaven*. New York: Penguin, 1987.
Cohen, Patricia. "The Frozen Chosen." *New York Times* Web Edition, April 29, 2007. http://www.nytimes.com/2007/04/29/books/29pcoh.html.
Cooper, Dennis. *Try*. New York: Grove Press, 1994.
Coover, Robert. *A Night at the Movies or, You Must Remember This*. New York: Simon & Schuster, 1987.
Daitch, Susan. *The Colorist*. New York: Vintage, 1990 [orig. 1989].

Danielewski, Mark Z. *House of Leaves*. New York: Pantheon, 2000.
Danielewski, Mark Z. *Only Revolutions*. New York: Pantheon, 2006.
Danticat, Edwidge. *The Farming of Bones*. New York: Penguin, 1998.
Dara, Evan. *The Lost Scrapbook*. New York: Aurora, 1995.
de la Durantaye, Leland. "The Pattern of Cruelty and the Cruelty of Pattern in Vladimir Nabokov." *Cambridge Quarterly*, 35:4 (2006): 301–26.
Deleuze, Gilles and Félix Guattari, *A Thousand Plateaus: Capitalism and Schizophrenia*. Trans. Brian Massumi. Minneapolis: University of Minnesota Press, 1987.
DeLillo, Don. *Underworld*. New York: Scribner, 1997.
DeLillo, Don. *White Noise*. New York: Viking Penguin, 1985.
Dempsey, David. "The Dusty Answer of Modern War" (review of Norman Mailer, *The Naked and the Dead*). *New York Times*, May 9, 1948: BR6.
Doctorow, E. L. *The Waterworks*. New York: Penguin, 1994.
Ducornet, Rikki. *The Jade Cabinet*. Normal, IL: Dalkey Archive, 1993.
Elkin, Stanley. *The Franchiser*. Boston: David R. Godine, 1976.
Enck, John J. "John Hawkes: An Interview." *Wisconsin Studies in Contemporary Literature*, 6:2 (1965): 141–55.
Erdrich, Louise. *The Master Butchers Singing Club*. New York: Harper Collins, 2003.
Eugenides, Jeffrey. *Middlesex*. New York: Farrar, Straus & Giroux, 2002.
Everett, Percival. *Erasure*. New York: Hyperion, 2001.
Felman, Shoshana and Dori Laub. *Testimony: Crises of Witnessing in Literature, Psychoanalysis, and History*. New York: Routledge, 1992.
Foer, Jonathan Safran. *Extremely Loud and Incredibly Close*. New York: Houghton Mifflin, 2005.
Forster, E. M. *Aspects of the Novel*. New York: Harcourt, Brace & World: 1956.
Franzen, Jonathan. *The Corrections*. New York: Farrar, Straus & Giroux, 2001.
Fukuyama, Francis. "The End of History." *National Interest*, Summer, 1989.
Gaddis, William. *Carpenter's Gothic*. New York: Viking, 1985.
Gass, William H. *Fiction and the Figures of Life*. Boston: David R. Godine, 1970.
Gass, William H. *The Tunnel*. New York: Knopf, 1995.
Gates, Henry Louis Jr. "Writing 'Race' and the Difference it Makes." *Critical Inquiry*, 12:1 (1985): 1–20.
Gibson, William. *Neuromancer*. New York: Ace Books, 1984.
Girard, René. *Violence and the Sacred*. Trans. Patrick Gregory. Baltimore: Johns Hopkins University Press, 1977.
Glissant, Edouard. *Caribbean Discourse: Selected Essays*. Trans. and intro. J. Michael Dash. Charlottesville: University Press of Virginia, 1989.

Goldstein, Richard. "The Most Dangerous Writer in America." *Village Voice* Web edition, February 29, 2000. http://www.villagevoice.com/2000–02–29/news/the-most-dangerous-writer-in-america/1.

Green, Jeremy. *Late Postmodernism: American Fiction at the Millennium.* New York: Palgrave Macmillan, 2005.

Greene, Gayle. *Changing the Story: Feminist Fiction and Tradition.* Bloomington: Indiana University Press, 1991.

Haraway, Donna. *Simians, Cyborgs, and Women: The Reinvention of Nature.* New York: Routledge, 1991.

Hassan, Ihab. *The Dismemberment of Orpheus: Toward a Postmodern Literature.* New York: Oxford University Press, 1971.

Hawkes, John. *The Cannibal.* New York: New Directions, 1949.

Hawkes, John. "Flannery O'Connor's Devil." *Sewanee Review*, 70 (1962): 395–407.

Hayles, N. Katherine. *How We Became Posthuman: Virtual Bodies in Cybernetics, Literature, and Informatics.* Chicago: University of Chicago Press, 1999.

Homes, A. M. *Music for Torching.* New York: HarperCollins, 1999.

Howard, Maureen. *Natural History.* New York: W. W. Norton, 1992.

Howe, Fanny. *Indivisible.* Los Angeles, CA: Semiotext(e), 2000.

Hume, Kathryn. *American Dream, American Nightmare: Fiction Since 1960.* Champaign-Urbana: University of Illinois Press, 2000.

Hutcheon, Linda. *A Poetics of Postmodernism: History, Theory, Fiction.* New York: Routledge, 1988.

Huyssen, Andreas. *After the Great Divide: Modernism, Mass Culture, Postmodernism.* Bloomington: Indiana University Press, 1986.

Jackson, Shelley. *Half Life.* New York: HarperCollins, 2006.

Jackson, Shelley. *Patchwork Girl.* Watertown MA: Eastgate Systems, 1995.

Jameson, Fredric. *Postmodernism, or, the Cultural Logic of Late Capitalism.* Durham, NC: Duke University Press, 1991.

Jameson, Fredric. *The Prison-House of Language: A Critical Account of Structuralism and Russian Formalism.* Princeton, NJ: Princeton University Press, 1974.

Jason, Phillip K. "How Dare She?: Susan Fromberg Schaeffer's *Buffalo Afternoon* and the Issue of Authenticity." *Critique*, 34:3 (1993): 183–92.

Johnson, Charles. *Being and Race: Black Writing Since 1970.* Bloomington: Indiana University Press, 1988.

Johnson, Charles. *Middle Passage.* New York: Penguin, 1990.

Johnson, Denis. "Interview" with Bret Anthony Johnston. National Book Foundation website: http://www.nationalbook.org/nba2007_f_johnson_interv.html.

Johnson, Denis. *Tree of Smoke.* New York: Farrar, Straus & Giroux, 2007.

Jones, Edward P. *The Known World.* New York: HarperCollins, 2003.
Kahler, Erich. *The Inward Turn of Narrative.* Princeton: Princeton University Press, 1974.
Karl, Frederick. *American Fictions 1940/1980: A Comprehensive History and Critical Evaluation.* New York: Harper & Row, 1983.
Kerouac, Jack. *On the Road.* New York: Penguin, 1957.
Kincaid, Jamaica. *Lucy.* New York: Farrar, Straus & Giroux, 1990.
Kingston, Maxine Hong. *Tripmaster Monkey: His Fake Book.* New York: Viking, 1989.
Kirn, Walter. "Everything is Included" (review of *Extremely Loud & Incredibly Close*). *New York Times*, April 3, 2005.
Klinkowitz, Jerome. *Literary Disruptions: the Making of a Post-Contemporary American Fiction.* Urbana: University of Illinois Press, 1975.
Kristeva, Julia. *Powers of Horror: An Essay on Abjection.* Trans. Leon S. Roudiez. New York: Columbia University Press, 1982.
Kristeva, Julia. *Revolution in Poetic Language.* Trans. Leon S. Roudiez and Margaret Waller. New York: Columbia University Press, 1984.
Lahiri, Jhumpa. *The Namesake.* Boston: Houghton Mifflin, 2003.
Lambert, Joseph. "Review" of *The Yiddish Policeman's Union. The Jewish Reader*, May 2007. http://yiddishbookcenter.org/story.php?n=10382.
Leavitt, David. *The Lost Language of Cranes.* New York: Bloomsbury, 2005 [orig. 1986].
LeClair, Tom. *The Art of Excess: Mastery in Contemporary American Fiction.* Urbana: University of Illinois Press, 1989.
LeClair, Tom. "Voices from an American Nightmare" (review of *The Lost Scrapbook*). *Washington Post Book World*, June 9, 1996: X11.
LeClair, Tom and Larry McCaffrey, eds. *Anything Can Happen: Interviews with Contemporary American Novelists.* Urbana: University of Illinois Press, 1983.
Lee, Chang-Rae. *Native Speaker.* New York: Riverhead Books, 1995.
Lyotard, Jean François. *The Postmodern Condition: A Report on Knowledge.* Minneapolis: University of Minnesota Press, 1984.
Mailer, Norman. *The Naked and the Dead.* 50th anniversary edition. New York: Picador, 1998.
Marcus, Ben. *Notable American Women.* New York: Vintage, 2002.
Markson, David. *Wittgenstein's Mistress.* Normal, IL: Dalkey Archives, 1988.
Martin, Valerie. "The Means of Evil" (review of *The Known World*). *Guardian*, July 31, 2004.
Maso, Carole. *The American Woman in the Chinese Hat.* Normal, IL: Dalkey Archives, 1994. Rpt. New York: Penguin, 1995.
Mason, Bobbie Ann. *In Country.* New York: Harper & Row, 1985.
Mazza, Cris. *Waterbaby.* Brooklyn, NY: Soft Skull Press, 2007.

McCaffrey, Larry, ed. *Storming the Reality Studio: A Casebook of Cyberpunk and Postmodern Science Fiction.* Durham, NC: Duke University Press, 1991.

McCarthy, Cormac. *The Road.* New York: Random House, 2006.

McElroy, Joseph. *Women and Men.* New York: Random House, 1987.

McHale, Brian. *Postmodernist Fiction.* New York: Methuen, 1987.

McKeon, Michael. *The Origins of the English Novel 1600–1740.* Baltimore: Johns Hopkins University Press, 1987.

Millhauser, Steven. *Martin Dressler: The Tale of an American Dreamer.* New York: Random House, 1996.

Moody, Rick. "Surveyors of the Enlightenment" [Review of Thomas Pynchon, *Mason & Dixon*]. *Atlantic Monthly*, July, 1997. http://www.theatlantic.com/issues/97jul/pynchon.htm.

Moore, Steven. "An Interview with Carole Maso." *Review of Contemporary Fiction* 14:2 (1994): 186–91,"cited in Grant Stirling, "Exhausting Heteronarrative: *The American Woman in the Chinese Hat.*" *Modern Fiction Studies* 44:4 (1998): 935–58.

Morrison, Toni. *Beloved.* New York: Knopf, 1987.

Morrison, Toni. *Playing in the Dark: Whiteness and the Literary Imagination.* New York: Vintage, 1993.

Morrison, Toni. *Song of Solomon.* New York: Vintage, 1977.

Nabokov, Vladimir. *The Annotated Lolita.* Ed., intro., and notes by Alfred Appel, Jr. New York: Vintage, 1991.

Nabokov, Vladimir. *Pale Fire.* New York: Vintage, 1989 [orig. 1962].

Naylor, Gloria. *Bailey's Cafe.* New York: Vintage, 1993 [orig. 1992].

Oates, Joyce Carol. *American Appetites.* New York: Dutton, 1989.

Obama, Barack. "*A More Perfect Union.*" Speech delivered in Philadelphia, March 18, 2008.

O'Brien, Tim. *The Things They Carried.* New York: Houghton Mifflin, 1990.

O'Connor, Flannery. "The Catholic Novelist in the South," in *Collected Works*, ed. Sally Fitzgerald. New York: Library of America, 1988: 801–6.

O'Connor, Flannery. *The Habit of Being: Letters of Flannery O'Connor.* Ed. Sally Fitzgerald. New York: Farrar, Straus & Giroux: 1979.

O'Connor, Flannery. *Wise Blood.* New York: Farrar, Straus & Giroux: 1952.

O'Donnell, Patrick. *Passionate Doubts: Designs of Interpretation in Contemporary American Fiction.* Iowa City: University of Iowa Press, 1986.

O'Donnell, Patrick. "Speed, Metaphor, and the Postmodern Road Novel: Stephen Wright and Others." *Mississippi Review* web edition, 2:5 (May, 1996): http://www.mississippireview.com/1996/odonnell.html.

Olson, Toby. *The Blond Box.* Normal, IL: FC2, 2003.

O'Nan, Stewart. *The Names of the Dead.* New York: Penguin, 1996.

Palahniuk, Chuck. *Choke*. New York: Random House, 2001.
Phillips, Jayne Anne. *Shelter*. New York: Random House, 1994.
Piercy, Marge. *He, She and It*. New York: Random House, 1991.
Postman, Neil. *Technolopoly: The Surrender of Culture to Technology*. New York: Knopf, 1992.
Powers, Richard. *Three Farmers on their Way to a Dance*. Rpt. New York: McGraw-Hill, 1987 [orig. 1985].
Price, Richard. *Lush Life*. New York: Farrar, Straus & Giroux, 2008.
Prose, Francine. *Primitive People*. New York: Harper Collins, 1992.
Proulx, Annie. *The Shipping News*. New York: Scribner, 2003 [orig. 1993].
Pynchon, Thomas. *Gravity's Rainbow*. New York: Viking, 1973.
Pynchon, Thomas. *Mason & Dixon*. New York: Holt, 1997.
Rebein, Robert. *Hicks, Tribes, and Dirty Realists: American Fiction after Postmodernism*. Lexington: University of Kentucky Press, 2001.
Robinson, Marilynne. *Houskeeping*. New York: Farrar, Straus & Giroux, 1980.
Roth, Philip. *The Human Stain*. New York: Vintage, 2000.
Roth, Philip. *Reading Myself and Others*. New York: Farrar, Straus & Giroux, 1975.
Salinger, J. D. *The Catcher in the Rye*. New York: Little, Brown, 1951.
Saltzman, Arthur M. *Designs of Darkness in Contemporary American Fiction*. Philadelphia: University of Pennsylvania Press, 1990.
Schaeffer, Susan Fromberg. *Buffalo Afternoon*. W. W. Norton, 1989.
Schaub, Thomas Hill. *American Fiction in the Cold War*. Madison: University of Wisconsin Press, 1991.
Scholes, Robert. *Fabulation and Metafiction*. Urbana: University of Illinois Press, 1979.
Scholes, Robert. *The Fabulators*. New York: Oxford University Press, 1966.
Scott, Joanna. *The Manikin*. New York: Picador, 1996.
Scott, Joanna. "Maureen Howard." *Bomb* web edition, 63 (Spring, 1998). http://www.bombsite.com/issues/63/articles/2144.
Shaviro, Steven. "Geek Love is All You Need" (review of Shelley Jackson, *Half Life*), *electronic book review*, May 14, 2007. http://www.electronicbookreview.com/thread/fictionspresent/conjoined.
Showalter, Elaine. *A Jury of Her Peers: American Women Writers from Anne Bradstreet to Annie Proulx*. New York: Knopf, 2009.
Siegel, Ben. "Introduction: Erasing and Embracing the Past: America and its Jewish Writers – Women and Men," in *Daughters of Valor: Contemporary Jewish American Women Writers*, ed. Jay L. Halio and Ben Siegel. Newark: University of Delaware Press, 1997.
Silko, Leslie. *Almanac of the Dead*. New York: Simon & Schuster, 1991.

Simmon, Scott. "*Gravity's Rainbow* Described." *Critique*, 16 (1974): 54–67.
Sontag, Susan. *The Volcano Lover: A Romance*. New York: Farrar Straus & Giroux, 1992.
Sova, Dawn B. *Literature Suppressed on Social Grounds (Banned Books)*. New York: Facts on File, 1998.
Spiegelman, Art. *Maus: A Survivor's Tale*. New York: Penguin, 1996 [orig 1986, 1992].
Tanner, Tony. *City of Words: American Fiction 1950–1970*. New York: Harper & Row, 1971.
Theroux, Alexander. *Darconville's Cat*. New York: Doubleday, 1981.
Tillman, Lynne. *American Genius: A Comedy*. New York: Soft Skull Press, 2006.
Tomasula, Steve. *The Book of Portraiture*. Normal, IL: FC 2, 2006.
Vizenor, Gerald. *The Heirs of Columbus*. Middletown, CT: Wesleyan University Press, 1991.
Vollmann, William T. *Europe Central*. New York: Viking Penguin, 2005.
Wallace, David Foster. *Infinite Jest*. Boston: Little, Brown, 1996.
Watt, Ian. *The Rise of the Novel: Studies in Defoe, Richardson, and Fielding*. Berkeley: University of California Press, 1957.
White, Edmund. *Caracole*. New York: Vintage, 1985.
White, Hayden. *Metahistory: The Historical Imagination in Nineteenth-Century Europe*. Baltimore: Johns Hopkins University Press, 1973.
Whitehead, Colson. *The Intuitionist*. New York: Random House, 1999.
Wideman, John Edgar. *Philadelphia Fire*. New York: Mariner Books, 2005 [orig. 1990].
Winter, Jessica. "American Ingenious: The Sly Brilliance of Experimental Novelist Lynne Tillman." *Slate*, Oct 12, 2006. http://www.slate.com/id/2151371.
Wolcott, James. "Gass Attack" (review of *The Tunnel*). *New Criterion On Line* (February, 1995). http://newcriterion.com:81/archive/13/feb95/gass.htm.
Wong, Sau Ling Cynthia. "Chinese American Literature," in *An Interethnic Companion to Asian American Literature*, ed. King-Kok Cheung. New York: Cambridge University Press, 1996: 39–61.
Wright, Stephen. *Going Native*. New York: Dell, 1994.
Yardley, Jonathan. "J. D. Salinger's Holden Caulfield, Aging Gracelessly." *Washington Post*, October 19, 2004, C01.

Index